The Gates of Hell

Anne Roche
The Gates of Hell

The Struggle for the Catholic Church

McClelland and Stewart Limited

© Anne Roche 1975

ALL RIGHTS RESERVED

0-7710-7685-1

The Canadian Publishers
McClelland and Stewart Limited
25 Hollinger Road, Toronto

Grateful acknowledgement is made to the United States Catholic Conference for permission to quote from their edition of the *Credo of the People of God*; and to Father Paul Crane, S.J. to quote from the *Christian Order*, February 1974.

To my father, John Roche

Contents

1. The Gates of Hell 11
2. The Letter and the Spirit of Vatican II 38
3. The Word Made Flesh 59
4. A Garden Enclosed 80
5. New Lives for Old 94
6. Shepherds and Crooks 107
7. The Cream of Antigonish 141
8. Murder in the Cathedral Part One 163
9. Murder in the Cathedral Part Two 178
10. A Note on Faith 205
11. Notes for a Guerrilla Catholic 213

Notes 233
Appendix A
The Credo of the People of God 239
Appendix B
Excerpt from Christian Order 249

The Gates of Hell

CHAPTER 1

THE GATES OF HELL

There are but two alternatives, the way to Rome and the way to Atheism: Anglicanism is the halfway house on the one side, and Liberalism is the halfway house on the other.

JOHN HENRY NEWMAN

Fifteen years ago when one Catholic met another, each assumed that the other would share a basic agreement on principle and respond in the same way to any question to which the Church had addressed herself magisterially—contraception, divorce, religious education, sexual morality—whether or not the Catholic was at that time actually obeying the Church on these matters. That is not true anymore. "Liberal" and "conservative" Catholics, labelled and defined in a way inconceivable then, are no longer in any sort of basic agreement. The liberal now holds that if he is disobeying the Church on contraception, for instance, it is the Church that is in the wrong in its ruling; therefore, his disobedience merits no punishment.

Fifteen years ago, Catholics who accepted the Church's authority but could not obey it, and those who found that they had stopped believing what the Church taught, quietly, without benefit of clergy, excommunicated themselves. They absented themselves from the sacraments and expected nothing from the ministering Church. In doing this, they often caused themselves great suffering, especially the women who had been, and remained, devotional Catholics, but who by some circumstance such as an invalid marriage found themselves outside the Church. The separated but believing Catholic was often reconciled to the Church on his deathbed when the end of his life put the only possible period to his disobedience. Neither the Catholic, nor his Church, considered this procedure hypocritical. Both would have considered it infinitely more dishonourable to have gone on receiving the sacrament which is the visible symbol of each soul's communion with the Church on earth, in heaven, and in purgatory (that is, with the Communion of Saints), while one's heart and mind were voluntarily out of communion, outside the law. The most unlearned Catholic was capable of that stoical and delicate Catholic honour, of that sophisticated understanding of the law of the Church that would not ask what it would not give.

Yet today, the liberal intellectuals who consider themselves the élite of the post-Conciliar Church do not seem to feel any tension between their conduct and their honour. They break the Church's laws confidently, defend their disobedience, counsel others to it, and continue to approach the Sacrament of Union. The divorced and remarried liberal Catholic layman, the married priest who refuses to discontinue his ministry, the university professor who is consciously teaching heresy, all no longer feel that their actions are a barrier to their reception of grace through the Church. They do not see any dishonour in having their cake and eating it.

Rosemary Ruether, one of the most prominent radical Catholic theologians in America, remarked on this phenomenon:

> Even the practices that once would have marked a "Roman Catholic" from one who had "left the Church" have largely collapsed. Many of those who are most intimately concerned with developing new thought forms and community groupings may never see the inside of a

parish church from one year to the next, have abandoned practices like confession some years ago, many practise birth control, and either be or be associated with married priests, and nevertheless with good conscience identify themselves as Roman Catholics. The most one can say is that a Roman Catholic is one who grew up in or joined the Roman Catholic Church, mostly in its pre-Vatican II dress, and who now, despite enormous changes that have taken place in their own consciousness, continues to find identification with this historic tradition of Western Christianity and its future meaningful, or at least, something that is so much a part of their biographies that they need to make it meaningful even if they are not quite sure anymore what it means.[1]

What development during a short space of years could have produced such a remarkable statement from a practising theologian who not only refuses to leave a Church whose current teaching she largely rejects, but who also has been allowed to continue unrebuked by the authority of that same Church? The easiest way to account for the collapse of Catholic orthodoxy is to blame (or credit) the Second Vatican Council, which, in the popular mind, was an event that changed all the most cherished and most hotly defended tenets of Catholicism. Since even many Catholics hold this view of the Council's work, it is not surprising that outsiders should believe it too. Novelist Brian Moore charged that by "changing all the ground rules" Pope John XXIII and the Council had brought about the end of Catholicism. Recently, a Jehovah's Witness proselytising at my door countered my usual remark that I am a Catholic satisfied with my dispensation with the question: "But how do you feel about the Catholic Church changing all its laws?" This view that the doctrines of the Church were either retired or contradicted by the Council has become a settled part of popular wisdom.

Yet it is completely untrue. The Council left Catholic doctrine untouched, even went to great lengths to reiterate it. The several catechisms of the Second Vatican Council issued by bishops anxious to defend that Council's integrity contain nothing new and omit nothing traditional. Anything considered essential by the Council of Trent, which began the Counter-Reformation in the sixteenth century, may be found in these catechisms.

Nevertheless, the Second Vatican Council was the unwitting vehicle of a second Protestant reformation. Again, from within the ranks of the Church's theologians, there is an assault on papal authority, on the Church's claim to interpret the Scriptures authoritatively and teach infallibly, and on Catholic laws governing human behaviour, especially in marriage. The new reformers had little effect on the written documents produced by the Council. However, they scored a dazzling propaganda success. They created an aura of excited change about the Council. They took control of the practical aftermath, the putting into operation of the Council's decisions. Therefore, although for example the Council intended the reform of the liturgy to be gradual, cautious, and firmly coherent with tradition, the liturgists who carried out the reform produced instead a liturgical revolution that threw the Church at once into unutterable chaos. Likewise, the *Document on Religious Liberty* was used against its own moderate intentions to justify a runaway "pluralism" whose one basis was contempt for traditional Catholic belief. There are thus *two* Second Vatican Councils to be considered—the one that under the guidance of the Holy Ghost actually took place, and which any reader who cares to devote himself to a perusal of its documents can identify; and the second Council of the popular imagination, the creation of the reformers' propaganda, the one that was supposed to have changed everything Catholic, and which sent forth "the spirit of Vatican II." I shall be considering this double image of the Council in a later chapter. It suffices for the moment to note the presence in the Church since the Council of a vigorous, protestant dissenting group of influential professionals, theologians lay and clerical, teachers and religious superiors, nuns and priests.

In the early days of this revolution, immediately after the Council, Catholics who called this new challenge to the authority of the Church a "reformation" and accused Catholic liberals of protestantizing the Church were sneered at as bigots, trapped in a Counter-Reformation mentality. Now, however, confidently entrenched, liberal reformers accept the charge as high praise. In the article quoted above, which is remarkable for its cheerful acceptance of the most serious conservative charges against liberal Catholicism, Ruether states:

> I would not feel any difficulty in speaking of one aspect of Vatican II *aggiornamento* as a protestantisation of the Roman Catholic Church. It seems to me that any modern Roman Catholic theologian has absorbed and indeed taken for granted the achievements of Protestantism, especially its theological and biblical critical developments. Catholic reform thus started in the Vatican Council with people who were already disciples of Protestant crisis theology. Catholic theology today in its increasing approximation to the curriculum of the Protestant seminary and often in its movement actually to amalgamate with such seminaries shows its need to absorb the work of Protestantism.

Likewise, Hans Küng, who became during the Council one of the most famous radical Catholic theologians, praised the liturgical reform as "a huge step forwards in meeting those special concerns of Protestants."

However, one must be careful about using the term "protestant" to describe the new post-Conciliar reformation. Catholics use it for convenience to describe a state of being in open oppostion to what the Church stands for and to her call to obedience. In actual fact, when the Catholic becomes clear about what the new reformers are teaching, he finds to his astonishment that he is joined in his opposition to it by the most conservative of the followers of the Protestant reformers of the sixteenth century. He finds that he is closer in world view to Missouri Synod Lutherans or Christian Reform Calvinists than to cradle Catholics turned liberal.

The contemporary reformation is different in kind from the reform of Luther and Calvin. They attacked the Roman Church principally for what they considered her corruption of the purity of Christian doctrine. They wanted to rip away accretions and return to the primitive simplicity of the early Church. Nevertheless, for all their rejection of the interpretative authority of the Roman Church, for all their insistence that each Christian guided by the Holy Ghost could discover the Word of God in Scripture, they were as rigidly orthodox as the Roman Church itself. Rejection of Protestant orthodoxy got the heretic burned to a crisp as surely as if the Holy Inquisition had nabbed him, as, for example, was the case with the unfortunate anti-Trinitarian Michael Servetus, who, escaping to Protestant Geneva from Catholic France, was on Calvin's insistence arrested, condemned, and burned at the stake. The sixteenth-century reformers would have been equally horrified by the new reformers' talk of "pluralism" and "situational ethics." It is not doctrinal purity that exercises post-Conciliar reformers. Although, especially in the field of liturgy, they often cite the practice of the early Church as they imagine it to have been, they do so not to restore some overlaid treasure but to excuse their getting rid of a present Catholic practice they dislike.

Moreover, when the new reformers charge the Church with corruption (with being a "whore" as Philip Berrigan delicately put it), they do not mean the same sort of corruption that disfigured the pre-Tridentine Catholic Church. Luther reproached the Church for genuine abuses: the sale of indulgences and relics, the ignorance and moral laxity of many of the clergy, the chaotic state of the liturgy. The magnificent Council of Trent (1545-1563) corrected these abuses, and its reforms held until the Second Vatican Council. The tragedy was that Trent had not taken place a century earlier. Luther's charges, and Trent's reforms, are not the ones the new reformers have in mind. Generally very much to the contrary. They reject not only Catholic discipline concerning the clergy, but also much of Christianity's sexual morality. They approve of divorce and pre-marital sex. They break vows of priestly celibacy.

For the new reformers, the Church is a whore because she is, and has been ever since Constantine, they say, on the side of "repressive" regimes. They want her not to opt out of politics but to commit herself with all her formidable strength against these repressive governments and social systems. The truth in this charge is that, being on the side of order, the Church historically tends to side with any government that keeps it, the more so since she expects little from earthly governments anyway and will settle for their defence of certain principles she considers crucial. Luther and Calvin had no quarrel with that position; they were both enthusiastically on the side of very coercive civil governments. It is not "Protestant" to be against the regime any more than it is "Catholic" to support it. Nor are the post-Vatican II reformers against *every* repressive government. They are deeply influenced by the contemporary leftist, Marxist climate that prevails among Western intellectuals. They want the Church to throw its weight against the present governments of Spain, Chile, Portugal, the white states in Africa, but not against those of China, Russia, Albania, Zambia, Uganda, or Peru.

The new reformers have different motives from Luther's and Calvin's. The orthodox Catholic has gradually come to recognize this and to realize that "Protestantism" is too sweeping and imprecise a term for what he means to define, which is that attitude towards the world that is diametrically opposed to that which he holds, and which is held also by orthodox Protestants, by orthodox Jews, Hindus, and Moslems. He realizes that the new reformers are trying to bring about a change not in doctrine but in world view. The Catholic finds that what he calls "liberal Protestantism" is what orthodox Protestants call "secularism," "secular humanism," or simply "liberalism."

Yet, according to Cardinal Newman, the great nineteenth-century convert to Catholicism, Catholics are not essentially wrong in using the term "Protestantism" for the disorder in the Church. Newman, after half a lifetime's effort to make Anglicanism, his branch of reformed religion, satisfy his heart and mind, decided that there was no successful middle way, and fled from his beloved "halfway house" to Rome. He saw in Anglicanism, as in all the reformed churches, a basic tendency to rebellion that opened them up to the process of disintegration. He called this tendency "the spirit of lawlessness which came in with the Reformation." In the 1830s, when Newman was still ardently defending Anglicanism's claim to true Catholicism, the lawless spirit was manifesting itself within his Church in a party of intellectuals whose political and religious program was called liberalism. Newman recognized, through all the "enlightened views, largeness of mind, liberality of sentiment" of his Oxford contemporaries who expounded it, that liberalism was the "offspring" of the Reformation's spirit of lawlessness. In this spirit, in the name of religious freedom, liberals urged the right, indeed the duty, of the individual conscience to question and repudiate dogma. Therefore, Newman defined liberalism as "the anti-dogmatic principle and its developments."[2] In the sixteenth century, the spirit of lawlessness had shattered Protestantism into numerous sects, each proclaiming its unique orthodoxy. In the nineteenth century, it would, embodied in liberalism, impel Protestant belief towards atheism.

To proceed according to liberal logic, said Newman, is eventually to proceed out of Christianity. For the Christian is a man whose world view is determined by certain givens, the truths revealed in the Bible. He considers these truths above both his understanding and his speculation. He thus accepts the subordination of the *known* to the *Knower*, of the *creature* to the *Creator*. But the liberal, according to Newman, makes the basic "mistake of subjecting to human judgement those revealed doctrines which are in their nature beyond and independent of it, and of claiming to determine on intrinsic grounds the truth and value of propositions which rest for their reception simply on the external authority of the Divine Word." Therefore, the liberal is on principle "insubordinate." (The Devil, said Dr. Johnson, was the first Whig, i.e., liberal.) The liberal's view of the world and actions within it will be "free"—though it is "false liberty"—from any direction but his own.

Protestantism, with its claim to private judgement, ought to be more fertile soil for the growth of liberalism than Catholicism, which accepts revealed truths as authoritatively interpreted by the teaching Church, the Magisterium—which is why, as Newman wrote, it is as "inconsistent" for a Catholic to call himself a liberal as for a Protestant to call himself an anti-liberal.

In his brilliant *Note* on liberalism which is still, over a century later, the most concise and accurate description of that philosophy, Newman enunciated the propositions, the anti-dogmatic dogmas, which comprise the liberal creed: theological doctrines are merely opinions; it is dishonest to believe what cannot be proven; revealed doctrines must give way to scientific conclusions; Christianity is necessarily modified by the times; there is a right of private judgement such that no authority on earth is competent to interfere with the liberty of individuals in reasoning or judging for themselves; there is a right of conscience such that everyone may lawfully advance a claim to profess and teach anything that seems right to him no matter how destructive it is to religion or society. From these religious principles, certain political principles naturally evolve: there is no such thing as a national or state conscience; the state has no duty to maintain religious truth—it need concern itself only with the legality, not the morality, of its acts; it is lawful to rebel against legitimate governments; the people are the legitimate source of power; the state can produce virtuous behaviour in its citizens by state-controlled universal education, since vice and religious subservience have the same parent, ignorance.

Since neither the individual nor the state is bound to fixed principles, and since either may react to new information by changing laws, change itself is established as the first principle of liberalism. Change is always for the better, and to hold on, in the face of seductive new suggestions, to some traditional teaching or value is to be not only non-progressive, but destructively reactionary. Newman, watching in alarm as the cleverest, most energetic young men at Oxford embraced the liberal creed and forced it upon the Anglican Church, described then the exact sentiments of the conservative Catholic faced with the same situation now:

> I felt affection for my own Church, but not tenderness; I felt dismay at her prospects, anger and scorn at her do-

nothing perplexity. I thought that if liberalism once got a footing within her, it was sure of the victory in the event.

It is particularly interesting to read Newman today on the incubation of liberalism in the Anglican Church because of its similarity to the Catholic post-Conciliar situation, and because we are able to judge the accuracy of his prophecies. For he was right about the fate of the Anglican Church. One by one it has yielded up Christian bastions to the secular liberalism Newman preached against. In 1974, no one thought it extraordinary that the retiring Archbishop of Canterbury should be praised in the press for his leadership in liberal causes and the "reform" of the divorce, homosexuality, and abortion laws. The Bishop of Woolwich created barely a ripple with his recent proposals to legalize rape and incest. Probably even Newman's gift of prophecy would not have stretched to cover an Archbishop of Canterbury voting for abortion on demand; nevertheless, that is what happened in 1967 when the bench of Anglican bishops, sitting in the House of Lords, would not join the opposition to the Labour Party's bill to liberalize the abortion law. The bishops, prattling about religious freedom, fussed about providing "safeguards" to the Act. (Only liberals, who don't believe in original sin, ever expect safeguards to work.) The eight lords in opposition consisted of seven Catholics (their leader, Lord Longford, was a convert) and one Protestant peer with a Catholic wife. Once again, it was the unreformed Roman Church, seemingly impervious to the liberal *zeitgeist*, that jealously guarded traditional Christian morality. Amid the tumults within and without, the Church kept her members from choosing the simple and dangerous solution. As another great convert, G.K. Chesterton, said, "The Catholic Church is the only thing that can save a man from the degrading slavery of being a child of his age."

For Newman and his friends, there was the intransigent Church of Rome to fall back upon. The Catholic Church seemed able to prevent liberalism from getting a serious hold within her gates. Rome dealt ruthlessly with the moderate liberalism of Lacordaire and Montalambert in the 1830s and with the more serious threat of Modernism at the turn of the century. Yet now, in the decade since the Second Vatican Council, the Catholic Church is not so much besieged as occupied by a confident liberalism at every level of authority. We can turn again to Newman for an explanation as to why the attack has been so successful this time around. He described how liberalism, from its incubation in a political party, spread to become "the deep, plausible scepticism . . . of the educated lay world." Early liberals, so praiseworthily anxious to separate Church and State, did not thereby bring about a state with *no* religion. They brought about a state that was certainly non-Christian, but whose new persuasive orthodoxy was secular liberalism. And they forced upon this state the duty and the power to compel its children to be educated in that religion.

It would be difficult today to find a university student, Catholic or non-Catholic, who does not subscribe to all the anti-dogmatic dogmas, who does not believe that the truths of revelation must give way to the conclusions of science, who is not positive that the rights of conscience and judgement are sacrosanct, surpassing revelation. It would be incredible to find one who denies that the people are the legitimate source of power or thinks that the decision of the majority ought sometimes to be resisted. This settled liberalism permeates Catholic schooling. My son, in a Catholic elementary school, encounters this advice from one of his textbooks: "The adult who is truly a 'grown-up' abides by the decision of the majority." Which seems to leave St. Thomas More and St. John Fisher out of the maturity stakes. The World Council of Churches supports revolution. The leaders of major Christian bodies deny miracles. When an orthodox Catholic argues today about disputed Christian values, he is invariably accused of being "dogmatic." But what if that which he is defending *is dogma*?

The Catholics, lay and clerical, who are making the second Reformation have had a liberal education. Ironically, where Catholicism was suspect and persecuted, the real "separateness" of its world view was most successfully maintained in its schools, but where Catholics began "to open themselves to the world" (as liberals always put it), to accommodate themselves to the aspirations of the secular state, to take its money and try to match the offerings of state schools, the inevitable happened. Catholic students have imbibed the spirit of lawlessness and have been directed into anti-dogmatism. "The deep, plausible scepticism" of the secular world is as pervasive in Catholic educational institutions and seminaries as at Berkeley, even though most of the priests who teach at them bound themselves by the oath against Modernism and anti-dogmatism. Yet they teach today what the Church condemned in 1907 and 1910. They deny the possiblity of revealed dogma, they "demythologise" the Scriptures, they reject the teaching authority of the Church. For an oath against these errors is void in a Church whose leaders are afraid to enforce it. Therefore, the sworn enemies of the Catholic world view do not leave the Church, though millions of other discouraged Catholics do, and latter-day Newmans find no refuge in it.

Fifty years after her condemnation of secular liberal humanism, the Roman Catholic Church has it all to do again. And the Second Vatican Council, which should have helped her in that struggle, actually served to give respectability for the first time to the anti-dogmatic principle that is the soul of liberalism. It permitted a concerted assault on the Catholic world view that is all the more difficult to resist because it seems to come from the teaching Church.

There are now, as a result of the unaccountable collapse of authority, two irreconcilably opposed world views—the liberal and the conservative, or the anti-dogmatic and dogmatic—within the Catholic Church. (It is a tribute to the extraordinary effectiveness of liberal propaganda that the words "dogmatist" and "dogmatic" have become pejoratives.) The conservative is a dogmatist. He asserts with Newman: "Dogma has been the fundamental principle of my religion; I know no other religion; I cannot enter into the idea of any other sort of religion; religion, as a mere sentiment, is to me a dream and a mockery." The conservative makes "the tacit acknowledgement that all that is finally important in human existence is behind us; that the crucial explorations have been undertaken and that it is given to men to know what are the great truths that emerged from them. Whatever is to come cannot outweigh the importance to man of what has gone before."[3]

The liberal is committed to nothing that has gone before. The conservative is committed to certain "great truths," those he believes were revealed by God and transmitted by the Church. Obviously, there must be a great gulf set between those two positions. And, hateful though it is, the ordinary Catholic has to take sides. The two views cannot be reconciled, though one may presumably undergo a conversion to either. What has happened in practice since the Council is that Catholics wait uneasily until it is decided for them—by their heart or mind or subconscious or the Holy Ghost or whatever. For example, conservatives for the most part let the changes in worship proceed, not being convinced that they involved essential principles. But when a really crucial issue, like the Church's reiteration of her traditional teaching on the transmission of human life arose through the publication in 1968 of the encyclical *Humanae Vitae*, the Catholic's inner voice instantly sorted him out. For *Humanae Vitae* was the perfect test case. The liberal accepted the claims of science, of a changing society, of ecumenism. The conservative accepted the Church's claim to teach what she had always taught, what she says is unchangeably true. All liberals reject *Humanae Vitae*; all conservatives accept it.

The split in the Church is now so deep that, for the first time since the sixteenth-century Reformation, Catholics turn to non-Catholics for the comfort of like-mindedness. A conservative Catholic feels more sympathy with the world view of ardent Moslem leader Colonel Quaddifi than with that of Marxist-oriented theologian Gregory Baum. Liberal Catholics feel closer to situational ethics prophet Joseph Fletcher than to some tough old Cardinal like O'Boyle or Ottaviani, or to any member of Catholics United for the Faith. Conservatives would as soon consort with Chairman Mao as with the World Council of Churches. A sort of back-handed ecumenism brings together Catholics United for the Faith, Missouri Synod Lutherans, and Council for the Faith Anglicans. They have discovered that they have more in common with each other than they do with their liberal co-religionists. On the other hand, liberal Catholics find solace in close ties with the United Church, whose only official orthodoxy is its devotion to grape juice instead of wine for Holy Communion. Gregory Baum, for example, usually preaches in United Churches in Toronto—a fact for which one can only be grateful to the United Church.

Given the protests of conservative Catholics against the "protestantizing" of the Church, this new-found friendship with conservative Protestants seems contradictory. Certainly, they are no closer on theological questions than before, they are as disparate in style and temperament, but they have found that what they *do* share is a world view and what they both hate and combat is the anti-dogmatic principle, the unquestioning acceptance of change, the essential rightness of "pluralism," and the possibility of situational ethics. Therefore, though conservative Catholics and conservative Protestants equally dislike the watering down of principle that generally passes for ecumenism, a most hopeful prospect for real ecumenical cooperation has opened up. The recent collaboration of Catholics and Protestants on the abortion issue has taken place in a spirit of charity and mutual trust and dependence that has been one of the great experiences in this Catholic layman's life.

Ecumenical understanding seems to be impossible only between liberal and conservative Catholics. They are divided on almost everything that seems important to them, and they have long ago stopped listening to each other. Each group attends its own catechetical and religious gatherings and reads and writes for its own newspapers. The only bridge between them is provided by the abortion issue, many liberals still holding to traditional Catholic teaching in this matter. This bridge will fall away from the liberal end very soon—Ruether, Baum, Drinan, the National Association of the Laity, and a gaggle of Jesuits and progressive nuns have already crossed to the other side. Likewise, the abortion issue has brought back to the conservative world view many who had abandoned it.

The liberal-conservative split cuts through every level of participation in the Church. Of course, active liberals and conservatives—that is, liberals energetic enough and conservatives furious enough to bestir themselves to action or protest—make up only a tiny part of the huge body of the Catholic faithful. There are two prevalent liberal attitudes towards these hundreds of millions of believers. The first is that most of the laity are ignorant, bigoted, hypocritical, immature, a dead weight on the Church, requiring from her only her magic rites at certain moments in their lives. Ironically, liberals otherwise so keen on "community" and on the charm and purity of the unlettered, animistic Asian and African peoples, feel great contempt for the ordinary Catholic community and its practices. After an adult education lecture in my town on the Council's "New People of God" theology, the priest distributed a questionnaire which asked rhetorically: "Do we have too many people in the Church? Shouldn't we be stressing quality instead of quantity?" This is typical of the liberal élitism that is so much worse than the old Church's egalitarian approach to proselytising, whereby the Faith was offered to the poorest, stupidest, most outcast people.[4]

The second liberal idea about the Catholic masses is akin to the one liberals hold about themselves—that the masses are moderate and irenic, wanting only to get on with saying their prayers quietly and bringing about the implementation of Vatican II, which work is being hindered by reactionary conservatives. Nothing could be farther from the truth. The mass of the Catholic laity is conservative to a degree and is not so much apathetic as mute and shy. Change makes it very surly, but it has no machinery for complaining effectively. Often I have been at a Mass where some liturgical horror has been perpetrated, and since I am known for disliking the new liturgy, quite a few people will say to me after Mass: "Wasn't that terrible?"

"Tell the priest that," I say.

"Oh, no, I couldn't do that."

"Then stay with me while I tell him," I reply.

No, they can't do that either. In their loyal Catholic world, you don't bawl out priests. But whenever liberals make the mistake of putting one of their proposals to a vote by a large number of Catholics, they are always defeated, as has been shown lately by the "Communion in the hand" issue in the United States. It is totally wrong to assume that because an innovating priest gets no feedback from his congregation, it is because it approves of anything he is doing.

This great mass of Catholics will inherit whatever sort of Church is left after the activists on both sides fight it out. If the liberal world view triumphs, most of them will quietly leave the Church, because, as Newman said, "liberalism is too cold a principle for the masses." These silent Catholics cannot and will not do much to influence the outcome of the struggle. They will to a man be on the side of the priest who will baptize their infants and against the new liturgist who refuses, but their mute orthodoxy will not work to the advantage of the priest who needs its support. I believe, because I grew up among them, that the very holiest Catholics are to be found in the silent, sometimes illiterate majority. My grandmother could barely read; I wish my faith and love of God were as strong as hers.

Like every civil war, the one in which Catholics are engaged since the Second Vatican Council is tragic and bitter and hardest on civilians. The Gospel words about Christ coming to bring a sword, to set brother against brother, become painfully immediate when you are brought up sharply by the shock of finding that a close friend is teaching his children that *Humanae Vitae* is "sick," when you see Laura Sabia in Mass every Sunday and hear her plugging abortion and abusing the Church on her talk-show any weekday, when you hear a young keen priest denying the Resurrection.

The Church is the Mystical Body of Christ and the members of that Body are warring together. The whole Body will be diminished by this struggle. But it is difficult to suggest how the battle might be brought to an end. Liberals will not return to dogmatism and authority, and conservatives will not join them in their progressive faithlessness. Liberals will go on watering down doctrine and precept in the interests of ecumenism, and conservatives will go on engaging in polemics in the defence of the whole structure of belief. In the meantime, authority at all levels seems paralysed, unable to bring itself even to try to enforce its undeniably orthodox pronouncements. No one expects, perhaps not even conservatives hope for, a calling down of anathemas.

One of the most trying things about liberals is that they profess to believe that the tumult in the Church, the decline in attendance, the defection of thousands of priests and nuns, the confusion in catechetics, are all signs of strength, of new vitality. These are growing pains, they say, essential to the Church's coming maturity. This is of course an act of faith, and there is no point in adducing evidence against it. They will be saying it still when the last Catholic church is boarded up. However, a great number of Catholics, from the Pope downwards, agree that the Church is in a bad way. "One does not need to be a prophet to realize that without a dramatic reversal of the present trend there will be no future for the Church in English-speaking countries," warned the British Cardinal Heenan. As gloomy a prognostication came from the Pope Paul VI himself, speaking in September 1974 to a group of pilgrims: "To one who looks at things superfically, it seems that the Church is fated to die, to be replaced by an easier, experimental, rational and scientific conception of the world—without dogmas, without hierarchies, without limits to the possible enjoyment of life." He admitted that the Church's troubles came from inside dissidents, "afflicting, weakening and enervating" her. (It didn't cheer up the faithful much to have the story appear everywhere under a picture of the Pope wearing, like a desperate politician, an Indian feather headdress.)

A despairing recognition of the cause of the Church's plight will not help rescue her from it. Nor will the Pope's declaration, true though it is, that "Faith is the prime necessity for overcoming today's difficulties" go far to offset the influence of the Church's powerful dissident professionals. The Church, through Vatican II, is still committed to all the Catholic dogmas. If the Pope and the bishops still believe that the Church is the repository of truth, it is their particular duty to defend her. The hierarchy as a group has stopped doing that. Individual bishops are valiant, but most seem to have succumbed to a sense of inevitable doom. It is today easier and more healthful for a bishop to scold the United States for using too much gas than for him to suspend some heretical or loose-living priest, or to have a showdown with his catechism committee.

It is especially lucky for the new reformers that the hierarchy of the Church should at this particular moment decline to exercise its authority, because what they are offering is not the stuff new churches are made of. What they are proclaiming "with good conscience" seems new and startling because of its novel Catholic surroundings, but it is in fact liberal Protestantism of the most shopworn variety, old hat in the 1920s when Bishop Barnes of Birmingham preached it, and titillating only to bored Catholic clerics when Honest to God Robinson made a media splash with it fifteen years ago. It has nothing to offer to Protestantism that the mainline Protestant churches have not already swallowed (and died of), or that the stricter evangelical Protestant bodies have not scornfully rejected. It has had to face no test that might lend it seriousness and respectability, no challenge from Church authorities that might make it recant or leave. Meanwhile, it is poisoning the Catholic Church, and keeping alive the liberal Protestantism that was withering until it came on the scene.

What, other than a vague Catholic patriotism, keeps them in the Church, these new reformers with their proud list of practices their Church still calls sins, who are "not quite sure anymore what it means" to be Catholic? Ruether puts an accurate finger on the reason why. They have so far been fortunate in a hierarchy that lacks both the will and the guts to throw them out:

> There is simply no need to create a new church in order to have a different point of view from the bishop or the Pope. One has only to create a discussion group, a new school or a publication or simply talk with friends. Moreover there is a strong disposition toward insisting on occupying the historical territory of Roman Catholicism and carrying on this conversation in and with it . . . pluralism of the most rampant sort has come. The episcopal leadership can ignore it, resist it or wall itself off from it, but it has become powerless to expel it.

The prospects are not strong that the hierarchy will soon act to restore the teaching of orthodoxy to the faithful. Liberal priests with the use of the Church's excellent power structure and communications system do not feel the need to give it up. They are listened to with far more respect by the secular world because they are speaking from within the Roman Catholic Church. Nothing that Gregory Baum, for instance, says would indicate that he shares any of the beliefs of the Catholic Church, but it is difficult to imagine him leaving it. Who would then think his Marxist, liberal Protestant views worth repeating? But when they emanate from a Catholic university, a fact that is always mentioned in news reports, they are unfailingly interesting.

Catholic reformers like Ruether confidently discount any possiblity of their being forced outside "the historical territory of Roman Catholicism" into new religious groupings, both because "the new consciousness released by the Council cannot be expelled, so that a smaller but unchanged Roman sect can continue business as usual," and because "the relation of religious ideology to political power that caused every ideological change to be expressed in separate churches no longer exists in the same way." Ruether may be being overconfident. There is at least a possiblity, backed by historical precedent, that the Roman Catholic hierarchy may decide that "the new consciousness" is anti-Catholic and anti-Christian and exert itself to expel it, in which case the bishops could count on the ardent counter-reformation support of a very large part of the laity. Also, it seems perfectly possible that the growing Marxist wing of the Catholic Church in South American countries, and in Spain and Portugal, might ally itself with left-wing governments and break away from Rome.

Prelates like da Silva in Chile, Helder Camara in Brazil, and Tarancon in Spain can easily be envisaged as heads of such left-wing national Catholic churches. In which case, Rome would certainly be driven into counter-reformation definitions and expulsions.

The Catholic has to contemplate the possibility that the institutional Church, orthodox and Roman, may disappear in many countries, as it disappeared before in England and the

Scandinavian countries, and as it has today in China, the Ukraine, and Albania. The only possible optimism is long term—a reliance on the promise of Christ that He would be with His Church until the world itself went up in smoke, that though she might lose all the battles, yet in the end the Gates of Hell would not prevail against her. This is the famous Petrine Promise on which the Roman Catholic Church has historically based her claim to authority. It is found in the sixteenth chapter of the Gospel of St. Matthew:

> He saith unto them, But whom say ye that I am? And Simon Peter answered and said, Thou art the Christ, the son of the living God. And Jesus answered and said to him, Blessed art thou, Simon Bar-Jona: for flesh and blood hath not revealed it unto thee, but my Father which is in heaven. And I say also unto thee, That thou art Peter, and upon this rock I will build my Church; and the gates of hell shall not prevail against it. And I will give unto thee the keys of the kingdom of heaven; and whatsoever thou shalt bind on earth shall be bound in heaven; and whatsoever thou shalt loose on earth shall be loosed in heaven.

Before the sixteenth-century Reformation, all Catholic Christians believed both parts of this promise, the primacy of Peter and his successors and the indefectibility and invincibility of the Church. After the Reformation, only Roman Catholics accepted the authority of the occupant of the Chair of Peter. For the Roman Catholic believed absolutely that the Church of the Promise, the Church that would have always with it Christ's invisible Presence, was to be recognized by the external sign of that Presence, the other half of the Promise—the man with the keys of the kingdom, Peter and each of his successors, the Bishop of Rome, the Sovereign Pontiff, our Holy Father the Pope.

And for Counter-Reformation Catholics, the promise became their talisman against despair when the Faith they professed was being driven underground all over Europe. In the desperate confusion, when a pious layman might suddenly hear his priest revile the Holy Eucharist or forbid him to pray for the souls of his dead, the promise provided a simple rule of thumb—"Where Peter is, there is the Church." It worked as well, too, for the learned and sophisticated. When Sir Thomas More in the Tower was reproached for his pride in that he would not bow his judgement to subscribe to an oath which all his peers and all but one bishop had signed, the promise kept him untroubled. As it did the one lonely bishop, John Fisher.

All Roman Catholics still implicitly believe that this promise refers to them, and that the Church must finally triumph over all her enemies. Even lapsed Catholics believe it, which is why they so rarely convert to another church. Even the most enthusiastically destructive radical Catholic believes it. That is why Dan Berrigan and Garry Wills and Rosemary Ruether stay inside, though they say that it is because of Catholic patriotism, a wish to remain with their own people (most of whom they despise). The endless repetition of the promise since the Counter-Reformation, the indelible imprinting of it on the mind of every Catholic child by every Catholic school, explains why the men and women who are making the second reformation find it so hard (they say "unnecessary") to leave the Church. They are happily confident that the Church will survive anything they can do to it.

And, of course, for conservatives now, as in the sixteenth century, the promise is their only hope. They repeat it again and again, an incantation against the powers of darkness. I have seen it hundreds of times in the columns of conservative newspapers since the tumult began. It will appear at the end of an otherwise gloomy article as the only consolation the writer can offer. When, several years ago, I wrote the pessimistic article that was the genesis of this book, I was deluged by letters from conservative Catholics, agreeing with everything except my fear that the Church would succumb to pressure and void some vital doctrine, like that of the real Presence. Impossible, said my correspondents. Didn't I remember that Jesus said that the gates of hell would not prevail?

No Catholic so illiterate but knew these words and believed them. No priest so ignorant but could expound them.

And I believe them, too. I try to correct for the false sense of safety they can give. I remember that in the times when the gates of hell have swung open against the Church, her lovers had to fight bitterly to save her. Liberals scoff at the "Counter-Reformation mentality" that marked the pre-Vatican II Church. Catholics can come down from the barricades now, they say. We will open ourselves to the world. We will bring all differences to the Church's broad bosom. We will be one, not integrist, not dogmatic, not in a universal Church with one Creed, but one in amicable disunity.

Whether or not this "spirit of Vatican II" irenicism will wipe out religious differences, it is very successfully wiping out the Catholic Church. Recently in the Catholic press a conservative prelate expressed his opinion that by the end of this century organized Catholicism would have disappeared in the United States. I would not be surprised to find before I die no Church open for me to attend. That has already happened to many Catholics in France and French Canada. It is beginning in English Canada. The priest has just been removed from the Newfoundland parish my father was born in. A priest accompanied the first settlers to that village. The Catholics are still there; the priest is gone. It is not likely that a priest will return there in my father's lifetime. Or in mine.

I think that there is a very good chance that mine may be the last generation of baptized Catholics to practise Catholicism in the West for a long time. The new catechism is robbing the Church of a generation of Catholic young. Catholic children are not being taught what the Mass still calls "the Catholic faith which comes to us from the Apostles." Catholic children have not heard the Promise. Catholic adults are having their faith in it undermined.

In my parish in a heavily Catholic, working-class industrial Ontario town, a young Holy Cross Father at an adult education Scripture seminar quite matter-of-factly denied the Petrine Promise. In the light that modern psychology sheds on the Gospels, he said, we now realize that the Promise cannot have happened as the Gospel tells it, for at that time Peter's spiritual development cannot have reached the point where he could have been able to recognize that Jesus was indeed the Messiah, "the son of the living God." This passage was instead "a Pentecostal utterance." That is, after Pentecost, filled with the Holy Spirit, the disciples realized that Christ must have been the Son of God, whereupon they proclaimed it.[5]

The priest left it like this, but some of the audience went home to reflect upon his remarks. Matthew's account makes it clear that Peter's primacy rested on, was a reward for, his sudden recognition of the identity of Christ. The name "Peter" translates as "Rock"; Christ is making a play on words. The firm foundation of the Church, the power of the keys, the security against the gates of hell, hang on Peter's profession of faith. Ergo, if Peter's profession *was* "a Pentecostal utterance," the rest of the passage, to put it frankly, was invented by the Apostles to justify what they felt was their mission.

Of course, Protestants are familiar with this sort of reasoning, but most of us, thus unceremoniously introduced to these Bultmann-style apologetics, were shaken. When this priest's lecture was praised in a Catholic paper with a large readership, some of us signed a letter to the editor pointing out what was said. We also wrote a bishop. No denial. No defence or retraction. No one even said, "Tut! Tut!" These adult education classes were almost immediately resubsidized by all the parishes in the deanery; the priest went on teaching Catholic adolescents, indeed was given the job of preparing a catechetical program for adolescents for the whole of Canada.

The Catholic church is really up against it when her own priests are trying to destroy in Catholics any reason for being Catholic, for belonging to an institutional church with such rigorous moral standards. These liberal clerics seem to envisage that the destruction of the bad old confident missionizing Church will bring about the flowering of an unstructured loving People of God, chained to no orthodoxy, no patriotism, no superstitions, given to no heroics. A combination of Oxfam, the Humanist Society, and a Pentecostalist prayer group.

I asked another priest at this same lecture series to give me a good reason why, if a Catholic must no longer believe that his Church is the true Church instituted by Jesus Christ, he should bother to go on belonging to it when the laws of other churches are so much easier to obey. Why, for instance, should I struggle to be faithful to the difficult laws governing Catholic marriage, when if I joined the United Church of Canada, I could, with a good conscience gained from obeying my Synod, practise any form of birth control, even abortion, or get a divorce and remarry with my Church's blessing? He made a joke of it: "Oh, I wouldn't run off and join the United Church." But why not? He has not thought out why not.

This beautiful untramelled People of God will not come to pass. Instead, if the Church allows her teachers to proceed in this Modernist way, most of her members will leave. This process is already well under way. And if the Catholic Church perishes as an institutionalized presence in society, there is no hope for the Protestant Churches. Christians will belong to no fold, with no shepherd.

Throughout this book, when I speak of the Church, I am speaking of that part of it which, as Vatican II puts it, "is constituted and organized in the world as a society, subsists in the Catholic Church which is governed by the successor of Peter and by the Bishops in communion with him." I believe, with the Council, that this "entity with visible delineation" possesses the fullness of truth, "although many elements of sanctification and of truth are found outside of its visible structure." I believe that "they are fully incorporated in the society of the Church who, possessing the Spirit of Christ, accept her entire system and all the means of salvation given to her, and are united with her as part of her visible bodily structure and through her with Christ, who rules her through the Supreme Pontiff and the Bishops." I believe, again with the Council, "that the Church . . . is necessary for salvation," and that therefore, "whosoever, knowing that the Catholic Church was made necessary by Christ, would refuse to enter it or to remain in it, could not be saved."

It would be strange indeed if I did not believe this, instructed as I was from infancy by Catholics of such deep faith and love. I do not thereby intend any disparagement of other Christian churches or non-Catholic religions. Though I belong to that part of the Church defined above, I also accept that any man who "acknowledges the Creator," and tries to serve Him belongs to the Church, that God is not "far distant from those who in shadows and images" seek Him, and that those also belong who do not know God yet serve Him "through the dictates of conscience."

Believing that the church to which one belongs is the true Church is not an exercise of bigotry but of human nature. I think, I *know*, that the Catholic Church has the fullness of truth; Anglicans, Jews, and Moslems think the same about their dispensations. Surely one would not adhere to a religion or an ideology if one did not believe it to be the best. There is no need for Catholics to feel squeamish about teaching their children what they were taught about the Church and what the Second Vatican Council so recently reiterated.

A belief that one's religion or ideology is the best is always accompanied by the temptation to bigotry and uncharity, and Catholics must pray that they do not succumb to it. But it is not charity, it is not permissible ecumenism, to allow the Catholic faith to be eroded. If, as Newman said, "we allow men to speak against the Church, its ordinances, or its teaching without remonstrating with them, we are deficient in jealous custody of the Revealed Truths which Christ has left us." The great Cardinal, who came to the Catholic Church because he found that it had the fullness of truth, had some advice on how the defence of orthodoxy might be carried on. Catholics can only be "successful in the fight, quitting themselves like men, conquering and ruling the fury of the world, and maintaining the Church in purity and power, when they condense their feelings by a severe discipline, and are loving in the midst of firmness, strictness and holiness."

Eventually, the Church must decide who is going to occupy "the historical territory of Roman Catholicism," those who "with good conscience" have abandoned Catholic practices, who are not sure what Catholicism means, or those who are "Catholic" as the Second Vatican Council defined them, who "accept [the Church's] entire system and all the means of salvation given to her," and are united with the Pope and bishops. It may take a long time. We are enduring again that "temporary suspense of the function of the Ecclesia docens [the teaching Church]" which nearly destroyed the Church after the great Council of Nicaea in 325 A.D., when "the Body of Bishops failed in their confession of the faith. They spoke variously, one against another; . . . there was weakness, fear of consequences, misguidance, delusion, hallucination, endless, hopeless, extending itself into nearly every corner of the Catholic Church."[6] Then it was the laity, faithful and obstinate, who were "the ecclesiastical strength of Athanasius, Hilary, Eusebius of Vercellae, and other great solitary confessors, who would have failed without them."

Now, in the face of the liberal establishment and the paralysed hierarchy, the laity have another chance to show that they are true to their baptism. We will perforce be less elegant in defence of orthodoxy than skilled theologians are in their assault on it. We do not, however, intend to be frightened off by orders, like the recent one from Bishop Rausch, to stay out of the dialogue between the bishops and the Biblical Association. The Bishop warned "third parties," i.e., conservative worried laity, not to criticize the scholars' findings, even when they sound to the layman to be exactly opposite to what a bishop once taught him at Confirmation. When the dust clears, we fully intend to be occupying the historical ground of Roman Catholicism, accepting her entire system, receiving her Sacraments, obeying her bishops.

If there ever was a time for Counter-Reformation mentality it is now. Now, at the acknowledged end of Christian civilization with our society crumbling about us, with totalitarian and materialist alternatives offering themselves attractively, with many of the other Christian bodies giving up the struggle on divorce, purity, abortion, euthanasia, with the Catholic Church torn from within, now is the time for the Catholic to admit that Catholic Christianity is an extreme and total position, worth living and dying for, worth passing on to his children, worth defending against his priests. Who would want to be a moderate Catholic? Erasmus was a moderate in the immoderation of the first Reformation. Who now prays to Erasmus? It was immoderate Catholics who saved the Church then, as after Nicaea, and a grateful Church canonized them.

In a revolution, as this is, the moderate goes first to the wall, and his cause perishes with him.

You immoderate saints, Peter and Paul, Augustine and Athanasius, Francis of Assisi, Catherine of Siena, Ignatius of Loyola, Teresa of Avila, Thérèse of Lisieux, Edmund Campion, John Fisher, Thomas More, *orate pro nobis*.

CHAPTER 2

THE LETTER AND THE SPIRIT OF VATICAN II

yet to institute any thinge in such wise, to Goddes displeasure, as at the makinge might not lawfully be performed, the Spirit of God that governeth His Churche, never hath it suffered, nor never after shall, his whole Catholicke Churche lawfully gathered together in generall counsell (as Christ hath made playne promises in Scripture).

THOMAS MORE

In 1961, when the preparations for the Second Vatican Council were under way, a young United Church minister said to me, with a certain amount of satisfaction: "The Council is really going to stand your Church on its head."

"How do you mean?" I asked him. Like most Catholics, I was still quite uninterested in the Council. In those years, excitement about it was keenest in non-Catholic circles. Catholics couldn't quite see why Pope John had called it, but we didn't foresee any trouble about adding it to the Catholic experience.

"Well," he said, "at last we'll see some changes with you Romans."

"What sort of changes?"

"You'll have to throw out those Marian dogmas. And Papal Infallibility. And you'll have to join the twentieth century and get rid of all that birth-control jazz."

"You're wrong," I told him. "I hope you Protestants aren't expecting the Church to make that sort of change, because if you are you're going to be disappointed. The Church can't change any dogmas or traditional teaching. She won't either. That's not what Pope John means by ecumenism and *aggiornamento*. *Aggiornamento* only means 'a bringing up to date,' not a major change."

"Ah, well," he said, "we'll see. I think you're living in the past."

The Council came and went. And I was proven right. It left Catholic doctrine intact. There was no retreat from faith. But he was right, too. The Council did stand the Church on its head. And a sad sight it has been. Poor old Holy Mother Church with her skirts tumbled about her ears, her underwear revealed, some of it monogrammed silk, some of it darned rags, her corsets burst, all her treasures fallen out of her pockets, her mind confused, her muffled voice pleading, "Dearly beloved sons, it behooves you to treat your mother with respect and do what she tells you." And her favourite sons stand around murmuring that poor old Mother is really past it and the sooner we put her quietly away the better.

Pope John promised us a new Pentecost. Whether that is what we got and are enjoying now, in the second decade since the opening of Vatican II, is a matter of endless and rancorous debate among Catholics. Certainly, the Council produced some of the external effects of the first Pentecost—thunderous noises, a pretty boisterous wind, bishops running out into the streets sounding as if they were full of new wine. There are differences, though, from that first visit of the Holy Ghost. For one thing, Peter, Spirit-filled, made 3,000 converts that day. The Vatican II bishops have unfortunately sometimes produced the opposite effect. The new wine seems to have caused a massive hangover and a lot of headaches.

Nobody is happy about the outcome, neither the liberals who hoped for a brave new world, nor the conservatives who did not want their clock put forward. And both groups keep asking, "What went wrong?"

In 1959, the recently elected Pope John XXIII issued a call for what was to be the Second Vatican Council. The First Vatican Council had been cut off unfinished in 1870 by the invasion of the Papal States in the Franco-Prussian War, though not before it proclaimed the dogma of Papal Infallibility. Vatican II was opened by Pope John on October 11, 1962, and closed by Pope Paul VI on December 7, 1965, after four sessions. It involved about 2,300 bishops and produced sixteen documents. There was a general, euphoric sense that the Church was beginning a new era in which there was to be no distinction between her concerns and the concerns of the world. No longer would the Church look inward upon narrowly Roman Catholic interests. The Council was to be *ecumenical* in fact as well as in spirit; observer-delegates were invited from other Christian churches. It was to be *pastoral* rather than *dogmatic* in character. It meant to offer wise and persuasive direction to the modern world in matters of importance to both religious and secular man—the implications of technology, the distribution of wealth, the rights and duties of conscience, the relation of Church and State. It meant to conduct its business in the open, and though decorum prevented it from allowing the intrusion of television cameras, it provided for extensive press coverage.

There was tremendous interest in the Council throughout the non-Catholic world. The media quickly found favourite sources of leaks from the closed sessions and made stars of certain bishops and theologians. During the early years of the Council the Catholic was continually being surprised by the way his Protestant friends would fall on him demanding inside news and insights from the Council, and embarrassed by having little to add to the titillations of the world press, since nothing was said about the Council's proceedings in the sermon at Sunday Mass, which, since few Catholics read the Catholic press, is the only point of contact between laity and officialdom. Besides, Protestants brought to our Roman doings a feverish, suspicious sort of interest Catholics didn't have.

Protestants brought up to hate and fear the Scarlet Woman drunk with the blood of the saints, wanted from us intrigue and magic, mysterious rites and fierce condemnations, dogmas they could disagree with, and images they could abhor.

The Roman Catholic Church that went into Vatican II, the twenty-first General Council in its history, was on the surface increasingly successful, with a central papal authority of great strength, and a centralized administration able to reach quickly into every corner of the world. It was administered by an efficient, specially trained, and dedicated clerical bureaucracy. Since the beginning of the twentieth century, when it had successfully squashed the Modernist heresy, it had maintained a tight control over what was taught by every Catholic college, seminary, parish priest, and parochial school teacher. It dealt easily with troublesome theologians, controlled the Catholic press, and had access to a good deal of space in secular media. The Church was rich, populous, and growing. When it was rated second only to General Motors in efficiency, people were surprised only that it had not ranked first. Priests were obedient, chaste, and hardworking; the laity had the Sacraments regularly administered to them; their children were taught in Catholic schools. Though there had been dark chapters in his papacy—the silence of the Church about the Nazi persecution of the Jews, the expulsion of Catholic missionaries from China—Pius XII left a confident Church, seemingly secure spiritually and materially.

That is how most outsiders saw the Church, the "Church of Power." That, too, is the way Catholic liberals remember the pre-Conciliar Church to have been, a powerful and worldly corporation, with the executives in the Roman Curia calling the shots and the laity in the parishes kept satisfied by weekly visits to "ecclesiastical filling stations." Somehow, during the Council, liberals forgot what it was that had kept them attached to the Church, its transcendental side, the side that mattered to the 99 per cent of Catholics who were not clerics: the mystical experience of the Mass, the solace of Confession, and of the countless forms of Catholic piety. For most Catholics were comfortable in the Church. They accepted its explanation of the human condition and either obeyed its laws, going to

Confession when they broke them, or lapsed if they could no longer give their assent.

The revolt brewing in the Church did not come from the laity. Pope John's opening up of the windows, as he is said to have called it, unleashed a *clerical* revolution. Nowadays it is fashionable to say, when dealing with the chaos since Vatican II, that it is a result of decades of oppression, that the Church was bound to erupt sooner or later and that Vatican II provided a blow-hole. This view of the clamped-down Church falling into Pope John's liberating hands, and the gamble he took that the Council might destroy rather than liberate the Church, is best expressed by Malachi Martin in his apocalyptic book, *Three Popes and a Cardinal*:

> Roncalli knew that his own Church was a tightly sealed container of bottled liberties, enslaved wills, drumming and shaking with end products of grave dissatisfaction, disillusionment and hopelessness, a kind of desperation, and a desire to be free. To unseal that container, to let all loose and rampant, to give rights to those whose rights had been non-existent for centuries, to let the perpetually silent speak their mind, to ask the professional receivers to be givers, to acknowledge deficiencies, faults, errors and heartlessness in high places, to consort with those who had been previously damned as erroneous, vice-ridden, inimical, ungodly: this, in practical terms, was to smile invitingly at chaos, to cry "Holy! Holy! Holy!" and let loose the dogs of confusion.

This viewpoint suggests that all the priests and theologians who took the required oath against Modernism did it with a gun at their heads. However, swear to it they did—and they kept it too, most of them, until the Council, because teaching unorthodoxy was certain to get them "silenced," that is, removed from the agreeable teaching posts they held.

At any rate, there were enough dissatisfied clerics to ensure a confrontation at the Council. Ironically, Pope John, credited by Martin and others with planning the Council as a daring and desperate gamble, was entirely unaware of the danger. He expected it to last only a few months, and revealed during his opening address that his idea of ecumenism was simply that the Protestant and non-Christian guests at the Council should return to the bosom of Holy Mother Church. Yet, he had collected all the scattered dissidents—bishops who wanted to regain some of the rightful powers they had lost after the First Vatican Council; theologians and biblical scholars, revolting against control and censorship, often smarting from reproof and "silencing"; ecumenists of all degrees, from ardent converts from Anglicanism yearning to have their brothers join them, to radical Protestant-leaning enthusiasts like Küng; liturgical reformers panting to try out their ideas—they all took the road to Rome, with their own axes for grinding, determined to cast off Roman shackles.

The Council debates were conducted in Latin. (Cardinal Cushing's offer to pay for a simultaneous translation system was refused, whereupon he said that since he did not understand Latin, he might as well go home, and did.) This insistence on the use of Latin as the Church's proper means of communication proved to be the last gesture of support for a universal tongue in a universal Church, since the first text presented, the schema on the liturgy, was to move the Church to end the use of Latin.

Many newspapers carried a picture of the splendid opening of the Council in St. Peter's. The spectacle was hard to resist. Thousands of prelates in scarlet and white and gold, the Pope carried high on the *sedia gestatoria*, the burnished twisted altar columns, the glorious solemn High Mass, the pomp and circumstance of the Roman Church at its most gorgeous and baroque. Ten years later, on the anniversary, many Catholic papers reprinted it wistfully. Seen from the perspective of the barren new liturgy, it looked even more splendid. That was, for many observers, the best moment of the Council.

It was perhaps the last edifying moment for observers, too, for General Councils quickly turn into ecclesiastical dogfights. In the past, Councils have seen fist-fights, armed interventions, arrests, lock-ins and lock-outs, schisms, and anathemas. Vatican I in 1870 left two generations of bitterness as Lord Acton and his liberal friends came home to brood over the brutality of the tactics used to get Papal Infallibility defined and to look forward to getting their revenge. The recent Council was no exception.

Most of the bishops went to the Council committed to no particular program of reform but warmly disposed towards what one of their number called a "moderate progressive" line. The Church's most conservative priests, the cardinals who headed the Curial Congregations, the offices of government of the universal Church, were pointedly not enchanted by Pope John's vision of the Council. They had a very good idea of the challenges it was likely to present to papal authority and traditional Catholic teaching, and the battle lines were drawn up long before the Council met. Members of the Curia dominated most of the preparatory commissions which drew up the texts for discussion by the Council. As might have been expected, most of these first drafts were formal, hard-line expositions of traditional Catholic teaching, and, also as might have been expected, any bishop who wanted them changed was going to have a fight on his hands.

The arch-conservative of all, Cardinal Ottaviani, Secretary of the Congregation of the Holy Office, that body whose very name called up dread visions of inquisitions and anathemas, put the position for intransigence very well in an interview in 1962:

> My personal position is that of a man who has, from the nature of his office, the duty to keep the deposit of faith intact and who, at the same time, must leave full freedom to the progress which is necessary to better clarify, understand and expose Catholic teaching. Let us never forget: not all that is new is true and good merely because it is new. There are some opinions in theology today which are, if not false, at least debatable. In this situation, it is a completely positive action to defend the basic data of Holy Scripture and of Tradition, to avoid permitting some truths of faith to be obscured, under pretext of progress and adaptation.[1]

Ottaviani was for the liberals the villain of villains, this old blind priest with his heels dug in, but he was nonetheless right. He and his supporters put a brake on enthusiasm and forced the Council fathers to examine and justify every sentence to which they intended to commit the Church. Liberals accused them of destroying Pope John's magnificent vision, of subverting Pope Paul by playing on his fears, and of blocking legislated reforms. To read Henri Fesquet of *Le Monde*, or the pseudonymous "Xavier Rynne" on the four sessions, is to be caught up in a titanic struggle between the forces of darkness and the forces of light. And to them there was no doubt as to which side those old cardinals belonged, those pious men who had served the Church through long lives and were prepared to endure a little obloquy to go on serving her in the way they knew.

Time and again, just when the "forces of light" were about to triumph, those dogged old men would stand up and object and manoeuvre and reiterate the traditional positions, and after the elaborate Latin name-calling, and the amendments, and the appeals to the Pope, and the final vote, the promulgated result would be the moderate, compromise but uncompromised, documents of Vatican II. To all those tough holy old career officers—Tisserant, Ruffini, Ottaviani, Browne, Staffa, Carli, Siri, Parente, and the wily Secretary General of the Council, Felici—the universal Church owes a vote of thanks. I salute them.

The most disturbing feature of the Council was not, however, the episcopal slanging matches but the rise and eventual dominance of a new Church élite—the *periti*, the experts, the skilled theologians and Latinists who came as advisers to the bishops, but who quickly became a power to reckon with, a council within the Council. They soon formed an independent body, granting press conferences, lobbying, distributing their own schemata, holding "little councils," lecturing to groups of bishops in the evenings, and going home between sessions to write, lecture, and criticize. Eventually, they set up their own documentation service.

Who, by the time the Council had ended, had not heard of

Schillebeeckx, Häring, Rahner, Congar, John Courtney Murray? Who was not familiar with Hans Küng's triumphant grin and Gregory Baum's mild smile? The open attempts of the *periti* to manipulate the Council, and the news that issued from it, drew an outburst from Cardinal Heenan in the Third Session. "*Timeo peritos adnexa ferentes,*" he said. (The sense is "I fear the experts when they start interpreting what I said." The Cardinal was giving an early warning against "the Spirit of Vatican II," which was to become, as one conservative writer put it, "a Trojan Horse in the City of God.") It was useless, Cardinal Heenan said, to talk of a College of Bishops if the *periti*, in books, articles, and classrooms contradicted and scorned what those bishops taught. He was, in particular, attacking the *periti* who were writing that the Church's teaching on contraception was about to change, and that Catholics could, in the meantime, use their own judgement about practising birth control.

The Third Session also saw a nasty row when Secretary General Felici, reminding the *periti* of their oath of secrecy, tried to shut them up and stop them from starring at press conferences. They immediately leaked his attempt to the media, and one of their chief apologists, Henri Fesquet, raised a fine furor about how "truth" was being stifled at the Council.

The atmosphere of excited dissent created by some of the *periti* spread through their press conferences and writing to the world. The impression they created that many Church teachings were about to be changed, the sense they communicated of a coming force ignoring a trembling authority, built up during the Council years a quite different image of the Church from the pre-Conciliar one. So, when the *letter* of the Second Vatican Council, the sixteen documents promulgated, dashed their hopes, the disappointed theologians appealed to a "spirit of Vatican II," which only they could interpret to the world. *Timeo peritos adnexa ferentes*, indeed. In the last ten years Catholics have heard little else. Even the bishops have adopted the experts' tactics: when Rome *does* issue some forthright instruction that some bishops don't particularly want to obey (for instance, the recent order that the experimental practice of having children make their first Holy Communion before their first Confession must stop), there is a flurry of statements from bishops explaining that Rome did not really mean that at all.

Most Catholics have had the frustrating experience of an encounter with "the spirit of Vatican II." You will be sitting quietly in some group, probably an adult education seminar (which has become a tremendous weapon for re-education), and your young priest-lecturer will flatly state that since Vatican II the Church now teaches such and such, for example, that the Catholic Church is no longer to be thought of as the one true Church, a visible entity, teaching infallibly. This statement seems odd to you, but you are unused to contradicting priests, especially when they have studied in Rome. You go home, dig out the Council documents, find the relevant passage in the *Dogmatic Constitution on the Church*, Chapter I, paragraph 8, which seems to you to say that the Church has not changed her mind about herself[2] and that the young priest may be mistaken. You read it out next time the group meets. Does the young priest say: "I'm terribly sorry. How could I have made such a mistake? I must have been misled by my ecumenical enthusiasm. *Mea culpa*"? Wrong. What he said to me, when this happened as I have told it, was: "I question your theology," and he went on at warm length about the new People of God theology and what the passage really meant when read in the spirit of Vatican II. There was nowhere to go from there but home to bed.

When the ordinary Catholic, shaken by the post-Conciliar chaos, finally gets around to reading the Council documents (a penitential exercise, considering their style and meandering length), he is at a loss to understand what all the fuss was about. The documents reassert all the doctrines of the Church, and even those that produced such episcopal warfare, as for example the *Declaration on Religious Liberty*, seem to the layman (at any rate to the North American and European layman) to be merely a putting down on paper of what the Church has been teaching throughout his lifetime. He does not understand theologians' rows, but the documents seem to present him with no startling break from traditional teaching.

Then why, in the light of the orthodoxy of the

promulgated documents of the Council, was it followed by a virtual collapse of authority and widespread liturgical, theological, and catechetical anarchy? Why did one hear from almost every Catholic of one's acquaintance the plaint: "I don't know what to believe anymore"? Why did bishops like the American Wright and the Australian Stewart feel called upon to issue what amounted to catechisms of Vatican II, listing the traditional doctrines and disciplines and giving paragraph references to where in the Council documents they could be found? Why, more than a decade after the opening of the Council did Cardinal Wright (who as Bishop of Pittsburgh exactly typified the "moderate progressive" at the Council, citing Maritain in support of the necessity of religious liberty, and speaking against clericalism) still feel it necessary to state:

> Anyone who thinks that anything was cancelled by Vatican II Council has not the slightest idea of what he is talking about. Vatican Council II repeatedly appealed to the witness and content of previous Church Councils. How could it do other than build on the foundations of our fathers in the faith—not blast them out of existence—if it intended to develop yet further our understanding of the faith and our more full access to the Kingdom of God? Whether it kept, in every instance, the *exact words* of the Catechism of Trent is, of course, another question: it did not contradict a single *truth* of the Council of Trent or any other historic Council. It could not do so—and be *true to itself*. And yet, of course, one does hear inane phrases like . . . "all that stuff has been cancelled by Vatican II" even from surprising lips.[3]

Why, most solemnly of all, did Pope Paul make his "profession of faith," which became known as the *Credo of the People of God*? On the Feast of the Apostles Peter and Paul, June 30, 1968, "aware of the disquiet which agitates certain modern quarters with regard to the faith," and of the "kind of passion for change and novelty" with which "even Catholics" were seized, Paul VI uttered his *Credo*. On the Feast of Peter, Paul VI reaffirmed his belief in the Petrine Promise: "as once at

Caesarea Phillipi the Apostle Peter spoke on behalf of the Twelve to make a true confession, beyond human opinions, of Christ as Son of the Living God, so today his humble successor, Pastor of the Universal Church, raises his voice to give, on behalf of all the People of God, a firm witness to the divine Truth entrusted to the Church to be announced to all nations."

The *Credo* was a clear, full, and uncompromising *Catholic* Creed. It contained the peculiarly Roman Catholic doctrines of the Immaculate Conception, the Assumption, Transubstantiation, and Purgatory. It said that the Church was "a visible, hierarchical society under the successor of Peter." It even said that, yes, there are angels. And it scrupulously referred one to the places in *Lumen Gentium*, Vatican II's *Dogmatic Constitution on the Church*, where one might check that all this was still the Church's current teaching.

Pope Paul's *Credo* irritated liberals very much. "Integrist," they sniffed. "Post-Tridentine." "Irrelevant," said Gabriel Moran, catechetical guru-at-large. It comforted conservatives—those whom it reached—and though it could not end the confusion, it located the official teaching Church again for the orthodox laity.[4]

Many conservatives, though they rejoiced in the *Credo*, saw it as a locking of the stable door after the theologians had escaped. If you are a Catholic, and you think that the Mass is not a sacrifice but simply a memorial meal, that the Virgin Birth is a pious myth, that the "Infancy Narratives" and miracles are poetic rather than historical, and that there was no original sin and fall of man, and if, further, you think that the Catholic Church now teaches these things, then you got it from the *periti* and their disciples, not from the teaching Church. You've got a bad dose of "the spirit of Vatican II," and I refer you to Vatican II's actual *words*, to the two dogmatic constitutions, on the Church and on Divine Revelation, as a start towards recovery. And *you* refer that nice little nun, too, when she protests: "Oh, but I heard it in a lecture by Father Richards!"

And there, of course, is where the dissenting theologians have succeeded, with that powerful substratum of authority—the priests and nuns who are not theologians themselves, but who teach religion courses in Catholic schools and colleges. They have either been indoctrinated in the "new theology" at one of the post-Conciliar catechetical centres, like the famous (notorious) Corpus Christi in London, England, or at Divine Word, in London, Ontario, or simply picked it up from occasional lectures by Moran, Ruether, McBrien, Curran, Keyserlingk, etc., and from articles in *Commonweal, America*, and the *National Catholic Reporter*. These nuns and priest write, review, and evaluate the new catechisms, and teach them to adults and children.

> The new consciousness of the Council [wrote Rosemary Ruether] has effected a sweeping take over of all the structures of catechetics and religious formation in the Church on every level. . . . The general tone of the material. . . . is clearly ecumenical, universalistic and humanistic in a way that breaks the moulds of much of what one used to think of as religious let alone Roman Catholic. . . . The same sweeping change of consciousness can be found in any programme of religious formation in Catholic colleges, seminaries, education of women's religious orders, adult education and even parish discussion programmes. If a parish offers a discussion class, even though the pastor is likely to be a pre-Vatican II intransigent, his young parish assistant will teach the course and will probably use at least the *New Catechism* from Holland, if not even more radical material.[5]

This fifth column of men and women religious (generally not, as Ruether notes, the parish priests) has carried out the revolution that the theologians failed to get on the statute books at Vatican II. They have produced a gap in Catholicity that cannot be filled in.

"The spirit of Vatican II," rather than any concrete wrong the Council did, was what drove some Catholics to repudiate it altogether, and many others to view it with dislike. Because they so greatly disapprove of the post-Conciliar activities of the more progressive Council figures like Cardinal Suenens and the Dutch bishops, they distrust everything that the Council said. They see that the Pope's authority is weakened and they blame Vatican II's definition of collegiality. They hear the Church's teaching denied by her theologians and they blame the Council's *Declaration on Religious Liberty*. This is too simple a connection—after it therefore because of it—but there is enough truth in it to make already suspicious people intemperate.

A look at the way the *Declaration on Religious Liberty* has been used to support the revolt against Church authority can serve as one example among many of how the Council was exploited by "the spirit of Vatican II." This text was bitterly fought over at the Council, though to the layman reading it now, it seems merely a rather idealistic statement of popular wisdom in the West, with all the philosophical weaknesses of a popular position. By some ecclesiastical skulduggery, Cardinal Felici had managed at the end of the Third Session to get the vote on the text postponed to the Fourth Session, so that it might be revised. Opponents of the *schema* feared that it would promote religious indifferentism and contradict earlier Church teaching that error had no rights.

The Declaration states that:

> Religious freedom . . . means that all men are to be immune from coercion on the part of individuals or of social groups and of any human power, in such wise that no one is to be forced to act in a manner contrary to his own beliefs, whether privately or publicly, whether alone or in association with others, within due limits. [Religious freedom] has to do with immunity from coercion in civil society. Therefore it leaves untouched traditional Catholic doctrine on the moral duty of men and societies toward the true religion and toward the one Church of Christ.

The document did not discuss the *duties* of conscience, nor the nature of freedom *within* the Church.

The Americans at the Council made no bones about wanting the *Declaration* for political reasons. It would look bad, they said, if the Church, while insisting that civil governments should grant religious freedom, should herself refuse to declare it as a principle. Bishops from Communist countries wanted it, too. And Cardinal Heenan pointed out how well religious freedom had worked in the Church's favour in England. Their testimony outweighed the protests of Ottaviani, Felici, and other doubters.

The *Declaration* was passed and praised. The Church was now one with the United Nations and the Soviet Union in guaranteeing religious liberty. On looking back it is difficult to see why the Council fathers considered it so pre-eminently important, why it was worth such a long and bitter struggle, or what the Church can hope to get out of it to her advantage. For, in the light of the Church's experience over the last ten years, some considerations suggest themselves: (1) the West already has religious freedom (though Spanish Baptists and Jehovah's Witnesses everywhere might disagree); however (2) few people *really* believe that error has any rights, liberals least of all,[6] and one would probably succumb to the temptation to shut up one's opponents by force, if one had the power; therefore it follows that (3) it is probably prudent to disarm the tempter by taking away the justification for killing people or shutting them up if one *should* get the power; also (4) no number of Church documents is going to bring about religious freedom in Communist (or Moslem) countries; and (5) the *Declaration* itself gives lots of elbow room for denying religious liberty "if the just demands of public order" are threatened, and certainly Chairman Mao and Enver Hoxha are perfectly correct in saying that Catholicism threatens their public order, even the very roots of its existence[7] and finally (6) only a liberal who has been asleep for half a century would agree with the opening words of this *Declaration*: "A sense of the dignity of the human person has been impressing itself more and more deeply on the consciousness of contemporary man."

The *Declaration* may be a long-term good but it has worked to the Church's immediate internal disadvantage and, it can be argued, to Western society's civil disadvantage, as well. In society, the overemphasis on pluralism and conscience has often paralysed Catholics in the struggle against abortion and other forms of social engineering. In the Church, it has effectively tied the hands of the authorities who would not, ten years ago, have hesitated in reprimanding or firing a priest or professor who taught heresy in a Catholic seminary or university. Now, the cry of religious freedom is raised, and Vatican II is cited, even though the *Declaration* did not address itself to the problem of freedom to teach dissenting opinion within the Church. The Church itself has lost the confidence it used to feel in its conviction that it is better to suppress one man's freedom of speech than to jeopardize the faith of countless others who have a right to protection.

So now, in the words of Father John Kelly, C.S.B., president of St. Michael's College, University of Toronto, "the teaching of heresy in a Catholic University need not necessarily be sufficient justification for the firing of tenured staff." The *Catholic Register* for February 10, 1973, quotes him thus:

> You don't tell a scholar what he must or must not discover. . . . We have a choice of being an institution with a policy of free inquiry, or becoming a college which takes a predetermined line which is what happens in State controlled universities in Communist countries. . . . Things are taught at St. Michael's which are inconsistent with true Christianity. But Catholicism has a built-in place of honour. . . . You have to trust in the good sense and commitment of those at the University to allow Catholicism to survive, develop and prosper.

Even Ford Motor Company could fire an employee who constantly denigrated Ford cars and plugged the excellence of Toyota. But in 1974, at a Catholic University, armed with the "spirit" of Vatican II's *Declaration on Religious Liberty*, we are reduced to *trusting* each fallible professor to *allow* Catholic teaching to *survive*. We cannot even fire him on the practical grounds that he's knocking the product.

The other instruments of Vatican II have been manipulated in the same way—the *Constitution on the Liturgy* to destroy Catholic piety, the *Decree on Ecumenism* to serve neo-Modernism. Conservatives now have the choice of blaming the Council for its lack of foresight or of trying to take back the reins of interpretation and authority.

The vagueness of the Vatican II documents is both a strength and a weakness. The Council promulgated only two of them as "dogmatic," one on the Church, *Lumen Gentium*, and the other on Divine Revelation. The second document on the *Church in the Modern World, Gaudium et Spes*, was "pastoral." Both liberal and conservative exegetes seized on this distinction. Presumably, a "pastoral" document did not commit the Church irrevocably to anything, and it allowed each side to put in things that the other did not agree with. This provision worked to the conservative advantage, so much so that E. Schillebeeckx, O.P., perhaps the most famous of the *periti*, special adviser to the very progressive Dutch bishops at the Council, and principal author of the controversial Dutch catechism, called it "one of the most important shadows cast on the Council debates." He deplores it in his book *Vatican II: the Real Achievement*. He admits that the majority (liberal) had first raised the distinction for utilitarian reasons, and that it had proved a costly mistake:

> An attempt was made to level out the new dogmatic aspects by appealing to the Council's pastoral character. Thus the impression was created that the actual doctrine of the Church was not to be sought in this Council but in earlier ones as well and in the papal encyclicals of this century. This makes it possible to have divergent interpretations of the Council documents.

It does, indeed, and Schillebeeckx berates himself and his colleagues for letting this happen. For to his dismay, he is now confronted by the spectacle of *conservative* bishops and *periti, adnexa ferentes*. (Schillebeeckx, in the same book, gives the perfect progressive explanation of what happened during the Council, and after: "The appetite has grown in the eating.")

Any examination of the Council and its aftermath must include some reflection on the two popes of the Council and a consideration of what the myth-makers have done to them. The triumphalist liberal reporting of the Council gave us a heroic picture of the struggle between progress and reaction, with Pope John leading the army of light and Pope Paul, though hesitantly, finally ranging himself on the side of reaction. For the liberals, Catholic and secular, John XXIII became forever "Good Pope John," who had flung open his Church's windows, while Pope Paul was termed "the Pope of Buts," the "Hamlet of Milan," who had gone about shutting them again. Conservatives, on the other hand, tend to set their teeth when "Good Pope John" comes up, and they feel a warm and forgiving affection for beleaguered Pope Paul.

The picture the world has of John XXIII is that of a simple peasant, warm and earthy, impatient with ceremony and convention. This view of Pope John is true but inadequate. He *was* the son of Italian peasants, but he himself had little to do with their life, for by the time he was eleven, he was already being groomed for a career in the Church and living in a minor seminary. This move brought about an alienation from his family which caused him pain and which he did not overcome until, in old age, he and his brothers and sisters became close again. Pictures of him show "the little priest," not yet in his teens, in cassock and hat, then later the Vatican career diplomat that he was for the bulk of his priestly life, the clever, successful, and humane papal representative to Bulgaria, Turkey and Greece, Paris, and UNESCO. The process of rising to the top in the administration of the Church is much the same as in the secular world. It was no surprise when he became a Cardinal Prince of the Church in 1953, nor when he was chosen Pope in 1958. He was at the time an obvious choice, for restless cardinals, largely shut out of decision-making during Pius XII's strong personal rule, wanted a stop-gap pope, an old man who had shown no radical tendencies and could be counted on to die fairly soon. But the Holy Ghost has a very trying sense of humour, and they elected Roncalli.

Nothing could be less accurate than the view of Pope John as a man out to radicalize his Church. Liberal admirers praise his openness to the modern world, yet do not mention that it was during his pontificate that the French "worker priests" were suppressed; that Pope John, while Cardinal of Venice, had forced the Christian Democrats to close down their left-wing newspaper *Il Popolo Veneto*. Nor was he the man likely to relax traditional Catholic sexual morality, since he had even forbidden his priests to visit the Biennale art exhibition in 1954 because of the erotic pictures it contained. (When the exhibit was cleaned up later, he visited it himself, as a mark of his approval. Naturally, his visit, and not his censure, is reported in the hagiographies.)

Nor was he likely to throw out any time-hallowed Catholic pieties, since his *Journal* and his lifelong practices show that he was a man of the simplest and most unsophisticated piety. Before he became Pope, he went yearly on pilgrimage to Lourdes. He said fifteen mysteries of the rosary every day, and had a childlike devotion to Our Lady. A few days before he opened the Council, he went to pray at Loreto[8] for Mary's blessing on its proceedings. And he urged the Council to accept "with serenity" everything that the Council of Trent, the great Counter-Reformation Council the liberals hate so much, had proclaimed.

Pope John seems to have been genuinely surprised at the tempest unleashed by the Council and appalled by the direction it seemed to be taking. His apprehension darkened the last months of his life, and he humbly offered his agonizing sufferings for the Council's success. Cardinal Heenan, speaking in America after the Council, is reported to have said that Pope John went to him at the end of the First Session, begging him to use his influence to try to stop the Council from proceeding further.[9] That was impossible, of course, and undesirable. Pope John died before the Second Session and Pope Paul reaped the whirlwind.

Pope Paul's was an unenviable task. He was forced by his position to dampen the euphoria that produced unreasonable expectations. Small, frail, and shy, it was inevitable that he should suffer from comparison with his exuberant predecessor and be blamed for dimming the glory of Pope John's dream. Considered a liberal at his election, he soon found himself having to take un-liberal and authoritarian stands. For example, he ordered the bishops to include, without discussion, four "clarifications," intended as assurance that traditional Catholic teaching would remain unchanged, to the section of *Gaudium et Spes* which deals with marriage, and he reserved for himself decisions on birth control and priestly celibacy. With *Humanae Vitae*, he brought down upon himself a torrent of abuse from within his own Church.

It is plain that the polarization in the Church and the disaffection of so many Catholics cause him great suffering. Orthodox Catholics love him for his brave, lonely, and prophetic stand. He would, perhaps, be a little comforted if he knew the warmth that the inarticulate majority feels for him and has no machinery for conveying to him. For you can't write the Pope with a hope that he will see your letter.[10]

Pope Paul does not have the tough strength of Pius XII or the warm charm of John XXIII. Even his best friends disagree with many of his prudential judgements, like the replacement of Cardinal Mindzenty as Hungarian Primate, or his compromises over the liturgy. But conservative Catholics forgive him everything because of his courage over *Humanae Vitae, Mysterium Fidei*, and the *Credo of the People of God*, even though they believe he could not have acted otherwise. It is impossible to be unmoved by his suffering, his humility, and his doggedness as revealed in his speech declaring 1975 a Holy Year. Partway through the proceedings, he threw away his prepared text and spoke from his heart:

> I feel my littleness and the overwhelming disproportion between the message I announce and my ability to express it, and even to live it. At the same time, I cannot just pass over in silence the fact that I have been sent. I am not speaking of myself, my friends, I am not announcing to you some idea which I have set up on my own or borrowed from the wise. I am announcing to you the word of Christ. I am sent by Him. I am St. Peter's successor. Welcome me; do not despise me. Welcome me for what I am. I am the Vicar of Christ. I am speaking to you on His behalf and

so I beg you to have respect not so much for me as for what I am saying and announcing. I do understand what is this Church which has the mission to proclaim the Lord's word with authority and confidence.

Conservatives love Pope Paul and pray for him; they would not be surprised to live to see him canonized because of *Humanae Vitae*, when it has proven to have been the last great gallant attempt to halt the destruction of Christian society.

CHAPTER 3

THE WORD MADE FLESH

So fare-wel shryne of which the seynt is oute.

CHAUCER

Catholicism is often said to be an *incarnate* religion, meaning, most importantly, that the heart of Catholicism, the reason for its existence, is the Word incarnate, the Word made flesh, "the Babe the Son of Mary." It further means that the way Catholicism apprehends its central mystery is reflected in its entire system of externals. Catholic belief is embodied in concrete form, not only through the seven Sacraments, outward and visible signs of inward, invisible grace, but through a system of sacramentals, blessed objects and actions that dispose one to acquire sacramental grace. This quality is summed up neatly by the often-quoted Latin tag—*Lex orandi, lex credendi*. Translated loosely, that means, "You can tell what the Church believes by looking at the way she prays." Or, vulgarly, "What you see is what there is."

It is this visible system of objects and actions that non-Catholics think of as "Catholicism"—kneeling penitents, chanting priests, rosaries, holy water and flickering votive lights, crossings and genuflections, wayside shrines and Stations of the Cross, crucifixes, incense, and images. They see these externals of Catholic piety not as physical embodiments of spiritual concepts but as pagan idolatry, foolish and fond superstitions.

This view points not to an abuse in Catholicism, but to a basic mistake of Protestantism. The real Protestant heresy lies not in rejection of papal authority or of any particular dogma, but in the dislike of the incarnate aspect of religion, of the Word made flesh and dwelling among us. Protestant loathing of transubstantiation, of the reserved Sacrament, of statues and holy water and silks and colours, stems only in part from a correct insistence on monotheism; it also comes from a deep distrust of the flesh that is almost Manichaean in intensity. Indeed, the reformers of the sixteenth century were charged with reviving Manichaeism, that ancient and perennial belief that matter is evil, that procreation is sinful, that it would be an unspeakable abomination for the spirit of God to enter into matter, especially in a way that would change it into Himself. Counter-Reformation polemicists called Luther "Manichaeus Redivivus," Manichaeus brought back to life. Though some of the Protestant reformers hotly denied the charge, others accepted it as praise. Since that time, whether in the Puritan fear of the flesh, or in the cold eroticism of the impuritan reaction (Hugh Hefner is, of course, its apostle and *Playboy* its scripture), Protestantism has rejected the incarnate. Cranmer's forbidding the "lifting up" or "carrying about" of the Blessed Sacrament is of a piece with the expulsion from the public schools of North America of Christmas carols and nativity plays.

Even in that strain of Protestantism that has remained most untouched by Modernism and secularism, and is closest to the Catholic view of morality, there is still a deep antagonism to the incarnate, to using the body to express the soul. For example, through involvement in the Right to Life movements, I have met and been impressed by several Missouri Synod Lutheran pastors, who are in total agreement with Catholics on the religious issues involved in the abortion controversy. They are generally invited to lead the meetings in a prayer, which they begin with the words that are among the first a Catholic learns—"In the Name of the Father, and of the Son, and of the Holy Ghost." Whereupon all the Catholics present make upon their bodies the Sign of the Cross—they "bless themselves." The Catholics make the words flesh. This is a perfect example of the nature of Catholic piety.

Strict fundamentalist Protestant bodies have managed to control the Manichaean urge, largely because they use the language of their prayers and hymns as an outlet for ecstasy. They *sing*, at least, of blood and fire and tears and the Cross. It is the liberal Protestant churches that have most completely excluded the flesh, its gestures and ecstasies. The epitome of this exclusion is a United Church wedding—no Figure on the Cross, no Holy Communion to build the marriage round, nowhere to kneel down, no mention in the instruction on the purpose of matrimony of "for the procreation of children." When I threw rice (for fertility) instead of confetti after one such wedding, I guiltily felt that I was destroying the intention of the service.

A revulsion against the flesh and its pleasures is much more a feature of Protestantism than of Catholicism. But one would not gather that from a reading of pop Catholic theologians, with whom it is an article of faith that it was the Church's hatred of the flesh and sex and women that led it to make such unnatural and impossible marriage laws as the ones reiterated by *Humanae Vitae*. Actually, the opposite is true. *Humanae Vitae* is a restatement of the excellence of procreative love, of the pattern of generation. It is the liberal Protestant churches that have eagerly taken up the anti-life position. It is Catholic Mother Teresa who is fishing babies out of dustbins in Calcutta and urging life upon them, while United Church ex-moderator McClure is performing one female sterilization a day as his mission work in Borneo. It is in character that he should also deny miracles.

The Catholic Church does not forbid the pleasure of the flesh. She knows that there is no point in a man's fasting in Lent unless he finds food and wine delicious; that there is no value in chastity unless sexual pleasure is a good thing and hard to renounce; that there is no virtue in getting up early unless one uses the early hours to pray or go to Mass. The United Church's prohibition of wine, with its approval of abortion, is the essence of Manichaeism. The even tenor of life in my town was broken periodically not by our Irish bishop thundering about all the out-of-wedlock babies but by the decendants of the Reverend Mutchmor come to forbid bingo. His co-religionists would, under his direction, lay a charge against the operators of bingo games; the Mounties would burst in and stop the abomination; Christian purity would return to Corner Brook, and the Rev. Mutchmor would fly back to his lair in Upper Canada, that dark realm where it was a sin to enjoy yourself. We thought it very odd.

It is Catholic to rejoice in wine and food and music, in sexual union and the fruit of the womb. The wake is Catholic; the funeral parlour is not. The Church may be a Scarlet Woman; she will never be a Bunny girl. It is the Catholic Churches—Roman, Eastern, and Orthodox—who wait up all night by candlelight to greet the born and risen Lord. It is Catholic to give presents at Christmas, and Protestant to deplore that giving. A long time has elapsed since the Puritans first forbade merrymaking at Christmas, plum puddings and carollings and the holly and the ivy, but it seems as if they are about to triumph at last in forbidding public observance of the Birth. They tried to make us feel guilty about present-giving and commercialism, they stopped nativity plays in public schools, they kept carols off the radio and crèches out of public places, and the Christ child off Christmas cards. Finally, this past year, when the energy crisis allowed them to turn off Christmas, actually and symbolically, a sigh of relief went up all over North America as the Christmas angels went out, one by one. (And *now* for the Star of Bethlehem.) The moderator of the United Church contributed his mite by damning the ancient carols as crude and primitive theology. Come Easter, he will probably be ready, like one of his predecessors, to deny the physical resurrection of Christ.

Catholicism believes in the Incarnation and the Resurrection. It has always celebrated creation and therefore hated Manichaeism. From the beginning, the Church has fallen upon it with more zeal than charity whenever this heresy has raised its head. St. Bernard of Clairvaux and Pope Innocent III devoted themselves to the extermination of the Albigensians, while admitting that they led purer lives than their Christian neighbours. But the Albigensian denial of the goodness of creation and generation was so wrong that no personal holiness could excuse it. The Church suppressed the Jansenists in spite of their edifying lives. And most recently, in the closing years of the second Christian millennium, when an upsurge of Manichaeism is feeding a quite hysterical hatred of procreation and a bitter distrust of man and his works to which many of her sons have succumbed, the same wise old Church, earth-mother and Bride of Christ, has asserted again, in as solemn a setting as she could arrange, that there is hardly anything material, not even technology, that cannot be used to praise God and to make men holy. In her task of "championing the godlike seed which has been sown in man," she means to go on offering him access to the Paschal Mystery through the flesh, through fasts and feasts, through saints and their images, through the Mother and the Maiden and the lullabies of Christmas, through colours and music and the most beautiful "sacred furnishings" she can create.

Whether she will be able to do this is open to question. In the decade since Vatican II, there has been an attack on Catholic piety as enthusiastic and as thorough-going as that of the sixteenth-century reformers. This attack is not surprising, considering the self-admitted Protestantism of the spirit of Vatican II. Nothing Catholic has been spared: not altar, not Tabernacle, not statue, nor chalice, nor Mass Book, nor vigil light, nor novena. Before the ink was dry on the *Constitution of the Sacred Liturgy* an iconoclastic frenzy seized even the most conservative priest in the most obscure parish. I have not, in the last ten years, been into a single Catholic Church that has not obviously been torn apart by the tempest and shoddily and tastelessly renovated. This assault had been fueled by the same three reforming impulses that shaped the catechetical and liturgical revolutions: the genuine belief of some reformers that they had discovered something better than the old which they were zealous to share, the nervous despair of those who had lost their faith and wanted to bring the whole structure down quickly, and the ecumenism of both.

About the faithless reformers, whose name is legion, there is little one can do but pray for their souls. But if the

Catholic Church is to survive as the comfort and help it used to be to great numbers of people, the Catholic must question the correctness of the assumptions of the *believing* iconoclast and put up a fight for the Catholic externals—for the sacramentals and devotions, for the symbols, for the physical, tangible, *incarnate* side of Catholicism. This aspect of Catholicism must not be discredited and driven out of the Church. It will not perish, because it satisfies a basic human need, but it will turn to paganism or, worse, to secular superstition, to astrology, spiritualism, and devil worship.

One further reason, perhaps not very admirable but natural enough, for the dislike that liberal Catholic intellectuals feel for the externals of Catholic piety, is that it is only fairly recently, at least in North America and England, that any significant movement of Catholics from lower working class to the middle class and the intelligentsia has taken place. The Irish labourer's daughter, the Italian immigrant's son, upwardly mobile through the channels of convent, seminary, and college, at last acceptable to the WASP élite, are embarrassed by the peasant pieties that go with membership in the Catholic lower class. The rosary beads, the plaster Madonna, the Last Supper painted on velvet, are social stigmas every bit as damning as a lower-class accent in Britain, or the ownership of a snowmobile in Canada.

I had a little taste of this WASP condescension when I married an English Protestant and went to live with him at an Ontario private school which was a Low Anglican foundation. At the welcoming cocktail party, one of the master's wives, the one renowned for getting drunk quickest, ended her introductory conversation with me by shouting: "Listen, everybody! John has married a Hail-Mary Catholic!" All the embarrassed courtesies that followed could not conceal the Orange Ontario shudder, the recollection by all those present of the superstitious, extravagant, wild Irish girls who had been their parents' servants. I wasn't at all embarrassed, for I *was*, and *am*, a Hail-Mary Catholic. I had never heard the phrase before, but it is a good one. It conjured up for my WASP friends a picture of an ignorant woman, afraid of ghosts and priests, hung with amulets, breeding like a rabbit, having her children christened with unsophisticated haste, and behaving indecorously at funerals.

That is the way, too, that the liberal Catholic élite sees the unreconstructed Catholic, and goes far to explain the revulsion liberals felt for *Humanae Vitae*. Many liberals, unlike the Bourbons, learned nothing during the Council years, and forgot everything. Somehow, they started believing all the Protestant libels, and instead of defending Catholic positions, as earlier liberals like Frank Sheed and the Catholic Evidence Guild had done, they began to write books like *Objections to Roman Catholicism*, which scorns Catholic "magic." Liberals now believe, or affect to believe, that pre-Conciliar Catholics really did worship statues and relics, and thought that medals and scapulars had magic properties. They also, on sounder evidence, insist that Catholic pious practices often seemed to non-Catholics to be idolatrous; but that is a different thing, and it is a distinctly liberal post-Vatican II doctrine that the answer to non-Catholic misunderstanding of Catholic practice is to get rid of the practice rather than to try to explain its significance to the outsider.

In the early days of ecumenical fervour at the beginning of the sixties, it was common, at least in large cities, for synagogues and Christian churches to invite groups from each other's congregations to come and be introduced to their symbols. It made for an interesting evening, but had very little value in bridging religious gulfs since the introduction was necessarily so superficial. But at least in the beginning it was not a dishonest exercise. It was a genuine attempt to explain deeply held beliefs through the symbols peculiar to them. It was limited in value because it very quickly encountered the real religious differences that a friendly showing of treasures could not heal—that what is merely a memorial symbol to the Protestant is an actual sacred Reality to the Catholic; that the Jew firmly believes that those friendly Christians are unhappily involved in a fraud or a delusion; that the Christian thinks that his Jewish friends have deliberately shut their eyes to their Messiah and refused to continue their history as the Chosen People of God.

These are dangerous waters to get into in any ecumenical

venture, and the Catholic liberal knows very well where the rocks are and that no amount of careful steering will avoid them forever. If he cannot bear to abandon his pentecostal Vatican II hopes for ecumenism, he has to be dishonest and take refuge in what the Council's *Decree on Ecumenism* calls a "false irenicism, in which the purity of Catholic doctrine suffers loss and its genuine and certain meaning is clouded." He has to pretend that the rocks are not there, and he does this by following the non-Catholic charts. He says that the Church was misguided in the past and has now returned to a purer revelation.

In the case of Catholic pieties, the liberal longs for a return to a Christianity that does not need to baptize pagan superstitions, but is mature enough to throw away all crutches in coming face to face with God. As a writer in the *Tablet* said lately, liberals believe that medals and scapulars and devotions are Catholic debris, and it is time they were thrown into the garbage can. When a liberal hero is caught indulging in a Catholic superstition, his disciples loyally hush it up. You will not read, in liberal hagiography, of John XXIII's devotion to Our Lady of Loreto, nor Teilhard de Chardin's to the Sacred Heart of Jesus, two sentimental Catholic devotions that are so lower class now that to join in them would be much worse even than owning a snowmobile.

It is only since the Council that Catholics have started worrying about what non-Catholics think of them. Before the Council, if a Protestant refused to accept a Catholic's explanation of his practices, the Catholic would have said: "Well, that's your loss." If a non-Catholic thought that the Catholic was idol-worshipping, then the *non-Catholic* was in error. It would not have occurred to the Catholic that a proper remedy would be to abandon his devotional trappings in order to avoid scandalizing Protestants. Generally, it never entered his head that he was misleading anybody.

Protestants, some of them anyway, did attribute magic powers to Catholic blessed objects. Perhaps I am wronging them, never having given much thought before to what Protestants felt about medals, etc. Perhaps they simply hoped that Catholic belief would extend to them in a "Help thou my unbelief" benevolence. Once, when I was a child, a devout aunt came back from the shrine of St. Anne de Beaupré bearing enough St. Anne's Oil to give several ounces to each of her relations. My mother, a most undevotional Catholic, shoved it away somewhere, since one could not very well throw it out or fry potatoes in it. At that time, tuberculosis was still endemic in Newfoundland, and one of our Protestant neighbours had just learned that she was the latest in her family to get consumption. Since she had watched the others die one by one, she was terrified. Someone told her about the St. Anne's Oil, and she came to my mother for some. My mother, charitably not passing on her skepticism, gave it to her.

The form with a sacramental of that sort is to trace a small sign of the Cross on the injured part, which in Lizzie's case was a spine and lungs full of T.B. For no reason, we assumed she would know the form. But Lizzie, full of some sort of odd strong faith and hope, rubbed herself all over with the oil, chest and back, and tied herself up in a shawl. And Lizzie, if not miraculously then certainly inexplicably, got better. She really did. We were so surprised, all of us skeptical Irish Catholics, and so amused. "That's grand stuff, May," she said gratefully, bringing back the empty bottle. "Can you get me some more of it?" I can still hear my mother laughing.

Being Irish Catholics, we recognized that Lizzie's recovery was a sardonic comment on our lack of faith by whatever member of the Church Triumphant, St. Anne presumably, was moved by Lizzie's hope and felt like teaching us a lesson. The point I want to make is that a Catholic using that St. Anne's Oil would have used it correctly, as a symbol, by tracing a Cross with it and requesting the intercession with God of the saint in whose honour it was blessed. My mother's Protestant friend, on the contrary, ignorant of Catholic theology, used it incorrectly, as a magic potion. I do not believe Catholics do, or did, use Catholic sacramentals as magic charms. Even the most ignorant peasant can see through the icon to the saint behind it and to the God with Whom the saint will be a powerful pleader.

Catholic addiction to sacramentals has always trod a fine line between devotion and idolatry. Chaucer satirized the selling of pillow-cases as "our lady veyl"; Martin Luther swept tons of relics out of German churches; a bishop at Vatican II begged that the whole mass of relics, "Our Lady's milk" and all the rest, should be decently laid to rest; and liberals try every year to prevent the demonstration of the liquefaction of St. Januarius's blood. Periodically, there are furious bouts of iconoclasm, like the post-Vatican II episode. Probably this one won't succeed in tidying up Catholicism either. Certainly it has not had much encouragement from the Council, for the official Church is extremely philosophical about the use of objects as sacramentals. The Church decided long ago that if you can't lick them, you baptize them. "There is hardly any proper use of material things which cannot thus be directed toward the sanctification of men and the praise of God," said the liturgical *Constitution*. Far from destroying traditional sacramentals, the *Constitution* proposed adding another layer. Elements from initiation rites in mission lands, "when capable of being adapted to Christian ritual," may be "admitted along with" traditional Christian baptismal rites. As a matter of fact, "anything in these peoples' way of life which is not indissolubly bound up with superstition and error the Church studies with sympathy and, if possible, preserves intact." It is wonderful to hear that old, tolerant voice still, in this savage century when technology and Americanization are levelling cultures and urging upon the world the richness and diversity of "true" civilization.

The Church has been adapting rituals successfully from the beginning. Pagans accustomed to bow deeply to the rising sun god continued, in Christian Churches built to face the sun, to bow to "the Orient from on high" on His altar; shrines of Artemis were reconsecrated to Mary; the multitude of Frankish country deities were canonized and went on occupying their shrines; the magic charms were blessed and assigned to various members of the Church Triumphant for attention. Yet Catholicism is not a syncretic religion. It did not embrace pagan symbols in order that as many people as possible could accept Christianity. Rather, it taught that elements of truth could be found in pagan practices, truth that pagans, though still bound by original sin, had discerned without revelation by the natural law. St. Paul wrote that even Gentiles, "which have not the law," sometimes "do by nature the things contained in the law." Initiation rites foreshadow baptism, and fertility rites are an intuition given to pagans of the shape of the great Christian Mystery. As St. Paul proclaimed to the Athenians who had raised an altar to "the unknown God," "Whom ye therefore ignorantly worship, Him declare I unto you."

Catholicism has in common with pagan religions the fact that it is intimately connected with the country, with fertility and increase, with seasons and harvest. It is not just by historical accident that the chief symbols of Catholicism are water, fire, beeswax, oil, ashes, wood, wheat and bread, vine and wine, linen and frankincense—natural substances and fruits of the earth to remind us how elemental religion is to man. For since man belongs by his body to the natural order of creation, is dust from dust and to dust with it, religion can put him in touch with God only through the created world. There may be other patterns of creations in the limitless universe, but the pattern men on this one small planet know because it is written into our members is that of seed, birth, increase, death, and rebirth. The Bible tells us we are made in the image and likeness of God. That must mean, that for this part of His creation, on earth, He reveals Himself in the natural image of generation.

The tremendous picture of the creation of the world in Genesis shows the Spirit of God moving over the black deep, leaning upon it with warmth and light, incubating creation, quickening life to be fruitful and increase. Man, created in harmony with the rest of creation, lives in a garden, but by disobeying God causes a breach in nature that destroys the perfection of his relationship with God and with other created things. Harmony is destroyed; the disorder Adam begins is passed on to all his descendants; we call it original sin. And when God comes to repair the breach in nature, He comes of necessity in the image of earth's creation—incubation, birth, life, death, rebirth. The archetypal religious myth is the death and rebirth of the fertility god. Christianity teaches that Christ came in the fullness of time, in the manner that the pagans had glimpsed through a glass darkly, to heal Adam's injury to nature. Christianity both fulfilled and destroyed the pagan fertility myths. Christ's death and resurrection, His dying no more, restored the initial harmony of creation, frees us from original sin, and gives back to man the certainty of resurrection.

Christianity is a most satisfying explanation of the human experience. It is a "world hypothesis" of such scope and adequacy that it has been received through the ages by all sorts of men with relief and delight. Anyone who reads the Christian poetry of the Anglo-Saxons is immediately struck by the ecstasy with which those religious pagans embraced a better explanation of the universe than the one they held. Suddenly, the seafaring had a goal; suddenly, human life was no longer like that of a bird who flies into a fire-lit hall from the howling darkness outside, lingers for a moment, but must fly back again into darkness.

To say that religion must be intimately linked to the earth and the seasons is not the same thing as saying, as critics of Catholicism now do, that the Church's message is outmoded since it was developed to deal with a rural culture and has not adapted to an urban technological culture. The question is raised as to whether the Church can survive the technological explosion of the twentieth century, and whether it has anything of use to say to the apartment-dweller in New York, London, or Toronto. The various denominations are desperately trying to devise new forms of ministry to overcome the alienation said to be suffered by the isolated, programmed, big-city dweller. Some of these—shoppers' drop-ins, community centres, parish councils, block Masses—are on the whole laudable efforts to re-create community for people who have moved away from their own.

Critics of the Church's efforts in the secular city suffer from what C.S. Lewis called "chronological snobbishness." They seem to think that urban problems are new, that no one was ever cut off from his community before in the history of Christianity. Yet Christianity flourished in, and spread from, great populous cities—Rome, Constantinople, Antioch, Ephesus, Alexandria, Florence. The history of religion in these cities would suggest that urban culture itself is not necessarily inimical to Christianity, as we have come to think.

In the cities, it is true, men are removed from the immediate apprehension of natural processes. They do not plant and tend and harvest. The seasons do not matter so much. In the city now, a man may live and work in buildings with no windows and an artificial climate. He may rarely see the sky and may never get rained on. It is becoming increasingly difficult to live in harmony with natural processes. Yet it is also becoming increasingly clear that man must improve his relationship with the earth or perish. The very recent ecological movement, wrong-headed as it often is, is not merely the sentimental self-indulgence of comfortable urbanites. It is a good example of the natural law working among the Gentiles to urge them to live according to the laws built into creation by God. The churches may have stopped teaching people that man must follow the natural law or perish, people may automatically tune out religious voices in this post-Christian era, yet the natural law instructs even the most secular urbanite that there is a necessary religious relationship between men and the earth. He will replace the Christian symbols with secular ones. He may express his connection with generation and resurrection by baking his own bread, buying a bicycle, growing his own carrots, joining a commune, eating Granola. The pity is that he has forgotten, and there is no one to remind him, that harmony with the earth is an image of harmony with God, that "as we have borne the images of the earthy, we shall also bear the image of the heavenly."

The duty of the liturgy is to remind man of the harmony of generation and regeneration, especially in the city, to enrich with symbols life naturally impoverished. That is why the liturgy uses pastoral symbols, not because it is trapped in a pre-industrial frame of mind. Technology ignores the seasons; the liturgy must therefore recall them. The liturgical year is bound to the seasons. It begins, like life, with the expectation of a birth, in Advent. The light of Christ appears in darkest mid-winter. Christ dies and is buried like the grain of wheat and rises to become "the first fruits of them that slept" (I Corinthians 15).

The date of Easter is tied to the turn of the year in the

spring; Easter occurs on the first Sunday after the first full moon after the spring equinox. There is a move to fix the date of Easter, a move which, sadly, the Council approved, "provided . . . the brethren who are not in communion with the Apostolic See give their assent." There is an attraction in all Christians celebrating Easter at the same time, but it would be a pity to untie it from the spring full moon and the spring equinox, the symbolism of which, so complex and so primitive, so before and beyond language, enriches the "spring-like fullness of the Paschal Mystery." The Orthodox, who take their Easter symbolism extremely seriously, are not likely to agree anyway. (Their Easter is also tied to the date of Passover.) We have the prospect of another Easter controversy.

The Catholic liturgy, far from being under the spell of a beautiful but outmoded pastoralism, has from the beginning used a most sophisticated symbolism to translate the natural into the supernatural, not by a slavish representationalism, nor by a bow to pagan animism, but by subtle abstraction. Therefore, to teach about generation and increase and the goodness of creation, the Catholic liturgy does not need to bring vegetables and cows into the sanctuary. The Harvest Home is Protestant. I have never seen a pumpkin in a Catholic Church. The Church is not talking about crops, nor even primarily of thanksgiving for their abundance; she is talking about the religious relationship of man to creation, and through creation to God.

We should remember that when we talk of Catholic liturgy, we are talking of the formal religious practice of the cities, of Jerusalem and Rome and Constantinople, not of the villages of the Appennines or of Asia Minor. When the Church refers to sheep, she means souls, and her symbolic meaning is immediately clear. Thus, it was an unintelligent tampering with symbolism when the "Church of the Catacombs" group of liberal bishops at the Council voted to use wooden croziers—those symbolic shepherds' crooks bishops carry to denote their pastoral authority over the Church. Wooden crooks are for real sheep. The ornamented, stylized crozier the bishop carries is symbolic, not bound by an antiquated rural way of life. You shouldn't be able to use it on real sheep.

In like manner, when the Catholic liturgy recalls the seasons, it does so by the colours of the vestments: the green of growing things to symbolize hope; red for fire and blood, for the summer ardour that makes love and courage hot; snow white for innocence and joy; black for the death of living things in winter, and for the darkness of the grave. Many Catholic priests have taken to celebrating Mass without vestments. This, too, is a serious liturgical error in a religion with a Paschal Mystery of death and rebirth. It also seems a mistake for the Church to change from black to white vestments for the Requiem Mass. One sees why it was done, because death for a Christian should mean joy, because for him "death is swallowed up in victory." But there must *be* death before there is victory, before mortality can put on immortality. It would make a more successful symbol if the priest could begin the Requiem in black vestments and change to white at some point during the Mass, probably after the consecration, thus making the point that it is Christ's death that ensures the Christian's resurrection. There used to be a good deal of changing from one vestment to another during solemn functions; a change of chasuble during a Requiem would take only a moment and have real import.

The change from black to red vestments weakens the Good Friday services in the same way. On this one day there is no consecration—the priest and people communicate from Hosts consecrated on Holy Thursday. There is, therefore, no real Mass on Good Friday, though it is called the Mass of the Pre-Sanctified. On this one day, Christ's Church does not recall His Resurrection, but only His death. After the service, the altars are stripped and the tabernacle door flung open to show that Christ has gone away into the emptiness and blackness of death. An extraordinary feeling of desolation hangs over the Church on Good Friday; only a few years ago it used to hang over the whole community as the sombre excitement of Holy Week built to its Easter climax, all gold and lilies. The bell does not sound on Good Friday—a wooden clapper gives harsh tongue. And as one walks home from evening Stations of the Cross, the heavy Paschal moon hangs low as it hung over Gethsemane and Golgotha. It seems a mistake to change the Good Friday colour, even to the martyrs' red. And it is a tragedy to have lost *tenebrae*, the great dramatic night office of Holy Week.

If the liturgy does not remind modern urban man of birth and death and sin and forgiveness and resurrection, what else will? The city is no more wicked now than it was twenty centuries ago; what makes it more difficult for man to see his Creator now is the marvellous technological progress of the last century, which has encouraged us to hope that we can, after all, make a perfect world without God's help, a lasting city here on earth. It has taught us to disbelieve in original sin, free will, and the natural law. Yet it has not succeeded in making us free and happy. Instead, it has become a runaway monster. We are terrified of it and powerless to stop it.

Blake called material, technological progress the Tent of Science. It is intricate and even beautiful, but it shuts us off from the sight of Eternity. Only a few years ago, materialism, supported by technological omnipotence, was so confident that there was not a social science or philosophy lecture room that did not ring with hopeful predictions about the end of religious superstition, the curing by chemicals of "sin," the end of war. Five years ago, people were still saying that the computer would soon end poverty and greed, because it would produce a surplus of goods so cheaply that everyone could have as much as he wanted. Original sin was to be removed as a factor in the human equation.

Yet now we are close to despair. The professor who jeered at students who held to a belief in free will is now lecturing on how quantum physics disproves determinism. Ivan Illich tells us that it is our use of energy that corrupts us, and that we could overcome the effects both of original sin and of technology if we would reduce our speed to fifteen miles an hour, that is, to the mechanical speed of the bicycle. Dedicated young feminists at the University of Toronto run this cartoon in their newspaper: a sky full of birds with the caption: "Ladies and gentlemen, welcome to Birdcommunity Flight '74. I have good news and bad news for you. The good news is that we are making excellent time. The bad news is that no one has any idea where we are, or where we are going, or why." Liturgists took the *Dies Irae*, the great ominous hymn about the Day of Wrath, Doomsday, out of the liturgy just as the Massachusetts Institute of Technology gave a date for it. Only Catholic liberal reformers are still cheerful about the case for progress.

There is a general feeling that something has gone seriously wrong, and the chosen villain is technology. Yet, because this age has lost sight of the religious springs of human existence, it blames the wrong things and proposes the wrong solutions. It identifies as the illness something that is only a symptom. For example, there are good grounds for seeing the present energy crisis as a symptom of breakdown rather than as a cause. A respectable body of opinion testifies that there is no world shortage of fossil fuel and that North America is importing as much as it used to. In the same way, we stand in overflowing supermarkets; we read of surplus peas and peaches being dumped, and we worry about the food shortage. One is tempted to conclude that we *want* our materialistic, technological society to collapse before it shuts us off forever from our eternal life. But, hating technology, we know nothing better than to turn to it for solutions. More and stronger chemicals to inhibit procreation, better and more efficient methods of abortion, weightier and more expensive computerized government control agencies. These remedies compound the illness, but they are the best blinded men can devise.

The Church can, if it will, offer a better cure. She can say, settle for daily bread. Mortify your appetites. Give away what you thus save. This is not the time to broadloom the convent or the rectory, to put air-conditioning into the church, to flirt with population control.

Sadly, even Catholics, steeped from childhood in resurrection symbolism, lose heart in this old Catholic answer. Father Adrian Hastings, whose well-publicized sympathy with Frelimo terrorists qualifies him as an authority on First World misdemeanours like bringing on the energy crisis, writes in the *Tablet*: "If the clergy throughout the country encourage the continual lighting of countless candles . . . then it seems certain that the same Church will show less concern for a great many other issues." He is wrong, in the alienated neo-Manichaean way. It is not by cutting down on its liturgical symbolism that the Church will help either the energy crisis or the profounder crisis of loss of nerve in the West. On the contrary. The Catholic response to this situation should be to turn off the television set but turn on the Christmas angels, to stub out the cigarette and light a candle before the Blessed Sacrament, to put away the car and walk to Mass. If there is an energy crisis, this will help end it; it will do wonders for our spiritual crisis, too.

The Church should not at this time be abolishing the obligation to fast. Catholics are not going to fast voluntarily, but if one's bishop said: "Friday is to be regarded as a day of strict fast and abstinence. Put the money you do not spend on food, drink and entertainment on that day into the collection plate on Sunday and I will use it for the Church's charities," the Catholic would then see an incarnational reason for going hungry.

Though one is loath to use the debased phrase, the Church must "celebrate life," not by abolishing liturgical ritual, but by enriching it. The most poignant cry of modern alienated man, brutalized by technology, is that of Arthur Miller's salesman: "Attention must be paid!" To his life, to his work, to his death. The Church's liturgy must pay that attention. In a life-denying age, it must praise life. The new liturgists have got off on the wrong track. This is not the time to forbid infant baptism, but to baptize every baby and have a party to celebrate its physical and spiritual birth. This is not the time to frown on the First Communion dress or breakfast, or the happy wedding or the cheerful wake, or the parish suppers or the public religious processions. The Church must make a liturgical fuss over all the milestones in her children's lives. Attention must be paid by the liturgy, because the city and the government and the multinationals won't pay it.

The Church's Council intentions were encouragingly Catholic and incarnational and celebratory of life and death. How they have been put into practice is a different matter. Not unnaturally, many of the priests and scholars who are implementing the liturgical reform are infected by the anti-incarnationalism of their Protestant models, and like them, opt for the wrong solutions. They reject the older earth-related symbolism in favour of the most abstract of symbols—the word. This produces a change in the *lex orandi*, the rule of prayer, which inevitably alters the *lex credendi*, the rule of belief. The word is infinitely manipulable; it can either replace a symbol or alter it out of recognition. (It has been fascinating to watch this happening. A whole theory of liturgy could be composed from a study of four short texts: the old Latin formula for the distributing of ashes on Ash Wednesday, its original English translation, the gutted ICEL version, and the alternative abstract formula recently provided. I shall give them without comment: the Latin: "*Memento, homo, quia pulvis es, et in pulverem reverteris.*" Its English: "Remember, man that thou art dust and unto dust thou shalt return." The ICEL rendering of that: "Remember man, you will return to dust." The new alternative formula: "Turn away from sin, and believe in the Gospel.")

Like the Reformers and the Albigensians, the new liturgists are People of the Book. Involved in this is not the old bibliolatry, but a reverence of the word itself as abstract symbol that has less and less to do with Scripture. At Mass, the Book is carried about and paid reverence to in the manner that used to belong to the Blessed Sacrament. The bells, incense, vessels, and candles that used to honour the Sacrament have had to yield place to a flock of microphones, so that every syllable can fall weightily upon us. It is not so much the revealed word of God that is being idolized as the word symbol itself, the absence of incarnation. The word has become a pure icon and the extent to which it has pushed out other symbols is extraordinary. The New Mass is one long stretch of words, anybody's words. All other symbolic features, gestures and appeals to the senses of smell and sight, are minimized. The body has little to do. The sermon—sorry, the homily—is longer and more dramatic than the Canon.

The word alone, no matter how eloquently packaged, is not a nourishing enough symbol for most people. Stirring nationalist rhetoric must eventually sum itself up in a flag; codified law puts on a judge's robes. Flag and uniform are icons, as the crucifix for the Catholic and the car for the secular American.

To feed everyone on a liturgy barren of any symbol but the

word is to starve most. This explains, I think, why Protestant churches have dwindled steadily while a church like the Russian Orthodox, with so much seemingly against its survival, *has* survived.

If the Church's public prayer reduces its appeal to the senses and relies increasingly on the letter, it will become arid. Catholics will lose the conviction that something important is happening in the liturgy, but they will certainly not do without the symbolic. They will hang their houses with Christmas lights, little secular sanctuary lamps, affirming the resurrection of the body. And they will protest the loss of the body's involvement in the liturgy by a descent into pentecostal frenzies. They will seek out charlatans who offer anything mystic and beyond meaning.

If the priest is to help his city flock see past technological despair, he needs an incarnational liturgy. The word made flesh, the Word Incarnate, is what he has to give. This is the moment to baptize everyone in sight, light all the candles, burn all the incense, send us off with a grand melodious Requiem, take the people out and bless their cars, boats, lawn-mowers and highways, say Mass with every splendour, sing all the carols, walk in procession down all the main streets, fast on the fast days, feast on the feast days, keep holiday on the Holy Days. And instead of locking up the church, he should encourage his people to guard it by their presence, to light a candle, to go to Confession, devotions and Benediction.

Some months ago, our parish had a whole day of Exposition of the Blessed Sacrament, a rare occurrence since the Council. Coming into Church in the evening for Benediction, one could sense at once the serene control which the Blessed Sacrament exposed exerts over its surroundings, the sort of contented suspension that holds someone who is regarding a glowing sunset. In the centre of the altar, transforming the bare table into a throne, stood the Monstrance, the golden vessel shaped like a sunburst which is used during Exposition. In the centre of the Monstrance is a little round glass case that opens to admit the large Mass Host, like a sacred locket. Incense curled up fragrantly around the Word made Flesh, the candlelight shone through It. And at Its Feet, turned off and bent flat to the altar as if in defeat, was the microphone, the word of technology, lying like a dead, gleaming snake.

The people knelt a little apart from each other, as a Catholic congregation always does unless coerced into closeness. Unselfconsciously intent, they looked with grave longing at, and through, the Monstrance window, through the veil of Flesh, in the prayer of silent regard. Hands wrapped in a silken scarf, the priest traced a huge slow sign of the Cross over us with the monstrance.

And we said: "Blessed be God."

CHAPTER 4

A GARDEN ENCLOSED

Nuns fret not at their convent's narrow room.

WILLIAM WORDSWORTH

They said to me, "Come, Spouse of Christ"; and I walked up the chapel aisle, wearing a bridal gown, and in the sight of God and the congregation was betrothed to the King of Heaven and earth. "*Eructavit cor meum verbum bonum,*" I sang. "*Dico ego opera mea regi.*" "My heart hath uttered a good word; I will speak of my deeds to the King." "Behold how good and joyful it is," they rejoiced as I left the chapel, and "*Te Deum laudamus,*" as I returned, having laid aside all bridal ornament and dressed myself in enveloping black, face hidden by a veil, hands buried in wide sleeves. All the glory of the King's daughter is within. A garden enclosed is my sister, my spouse. "*Ecce quam bonum, et jucundum, habitare fratres in unum,*" they carolled approvingly as I walked out among my sisters into my new community. "Behold how good and joyful it is for brothers to dwell together in unity. It is like the ointment," they remarked, "the precious ointment that ran down upon the beard, the beard of Aaron."

It sounds better in Latin. But the message of this ceremony of reception into the novitiate of an order of semi-cloistered teaching nuns came over loud and clear. I had, like

Mary, chosen the better part, which should not be taken away from me.

I had never wanted to be anything but a nun. No, not true. I had wanted to be a martyr like St. Tarcisius, but since there was unluckily no persecution in Newfoundland, I had, like Teresa of Avila when the Moors let her down, settled for next best. If I couldn't be St. Anne of Corner Brook, virgin martyr, I still could, like Teresa, go off to Carmel or the nearest equivalent of it.

This response was not uncommon among Catholic adolescents of a certain temperament at the end of a convent school education. The desire for martyrdom, for the grand gesture ending in a glorious death, was a logical result of years of pondering the lives of martyrs, or rather their deaths. At school, the nun would each day write at the top of the blackboard the saint from the Roman Calendar whose feast day it was, and we would read his life and ask his protection during the day. Generally the saint would be a martyr—St. Sebastian, pincushioned full of arrows; St. Agnes, refusing to be married to anyone but Christ and losing her head for her fidelity; St. Maria Goretti, closer in time, stabbed to death while resisting violation, crying, "No, it is a sin. You will go to hell." Or if he was not a martyr, then he would be someone who had died spectacularly to the flesh, like St. Francis of Assisi, not the wet sixties version, but the man whose flesh was torn by his rolling in thorns to chasten it and by the mystical Stigmata, the man who was in love with Sister Death.

The new catechetics finds this predilection for martyrs and martyrdom distasteful, to say the least. Sick, really. If a martyr washed in the Blood of the Lamb ventured into the Canadian catechism, he'd get rushed off to Father Lafreniere for sexual counselling. Its St. Francis is the Franco Zeffirelli version, who would not make the most self-indulgent modern feel uneasy. But the new catechists are wrong about martyrs as they are about most other catechetical matters. The Catholic delight in martyrs was not sadistic or masochistic. It was romantic. What attracted the generous child and adolescent was not the blood but the gallantry, the sheer *panache* of those splendid men and women standing like shining arrows before their powerful tormentors, making earthly power look pitiful by the eloquence of their defiant deaths. It was the *beau geste* that ravished us, not the welter of blood at the end. All for love, and the world well lost.

There was a very strong element of romanticism in Catholic education, but it was not unhealthily enamoured of violence and was not just useless daydreaming. The Catholic romantic yearned towards heroic virtue on earth and an eternal crown in Heaven. An example of the sort of story we delighted in was the one about the Forty Martyrs of Sebaste. We never tired of this one. Before most of the saints got the heave-ho in the recently reformed Roman Calendar, this feast fell on March 10, while the landscape outside our classroom window was still piled deep in snow. The nun would read the laconic account from the *Lives of the Saints*: "Under Licinius, forty soldiers of the garrison of Sebaste (Armenia) were exposed on a frozen pond for refusing to sacrifice to idols. All persevered but one, whose courage failed him and who perished in a bath of tepid water prepared for him. But their guard, inspired by grace, took his place and expired with them, so there were forty martyrs still. They suffered A.D. 320."

From this raw material we got a gorgeous drama. The little band of Christian defectors on the ice. Their former companions watching their agony with a mixture of sympathy for their plight and anger at their foolishness. The fire leaping high in the dark cold. Then one of the soldiers of Christ, defeated by his suffering flesh, crawls ashore to rejoin the soldiers of the Emperor. From the shore, another soldier sees forty angels descending above the dying Christians, each carrying a glowing crown. But now there are only thirty-nine in the running for crowns, and the fortieth angel hovers disconsolately. The watching Roman suddenly stands up, throws down his weapons with a clash, strips off his greaves and boots, and without a backward glance at fire and comrades marches across the ice to join the thirty-nine. "So there were forty martyrs still"—and one relieved angel. The Christian who crawls ashore expires in his tepid bath.

That story is very powerful stuff. There is absolutely nothing in the Canadian Catechism about Christ or His saints that seizes the imagination with that force. I do not for a moment, with all respect to a fine old legend, think that the replacement martyr was attracted by the crown that was going begging. He was caught emotionally by the gallantry of the Christians, and spiritually by a longing for that great good they saw that was worth such a price.

All these heroics did not in any way obscure the person and message of Christ. Rather, they made clear that union with Christ was so desirable that the Christian was moved to heroic action to attain it. And the way to such a union was through the Cross. The Christian must be crucified, and he must, as St. Paul said, glory in his crucifixion. He must lose his life to find it.

This was perfectly clear to the first Christians, and the chance of literally dying for Christ was generously provided to them by an establishment that held an exactly opposite world view from the Christian one: eat, drink, and be merry for tomorrow we die, as opposed to die daily for tomorrow we live. It was in many ways easier to be a Christian before Constantine made it legal than after. It is easier to die once by the sword than to die over and over again, bit by bit; easier to submit to an external sentence of death than to decide how to kill one's own concupiscences.

Anyway, that is why I entered the convent, inspired by the martyrs, to lose my life and find it. That, too, is why an extremely difficult vocation was able to draw and hold able young people, whose numbers grew throughout this century even though universal education might have been expected to turn them towards careers in the world, now that the Church is no longer the only career open to the clever poor. It explains why the young people of the sixties found the Berrigans so attractive, though as martyrs they were rather second-rate. Daniel Berrigan even compared himself and his brother with the Jesuit martyrs of Elizabethan times, spreading the Faith, eluding the police, breaking the law and suffering for it, and all with such gaiety and wit. The young, and the not so young, looked at Dan and Phil and saw Edmund Campion. No matter that the Jesuit martyrs must be spinning in their graves at the thought of Father Phil and Sister Liz being married by an ex-Benedictine and having a baby. No good pointing out that Elizabethan priest holes didn't come equipped with television cameras and compliant nuns. The Berrigans *were* prepared to go to jail for what they believed; they *did* actually go to jail for several years. Catholic memory, theirs and ours, gave them a glamour that poor Protestant William Sloane Coffin won't acquire in a lifetime of fervent civil disobedience.

The sort of religious education that produced the fierce and simple Catholic response to Christ's call to take up one's cross and follow Him came to an abrupt end in the early 1960s. Catholic children simply are not programmed that way now. The old pattern has been shattered, and the new one, if there is one, is not working. It should not, though it does, surprise the ecclesiastical authorities that the young do not repair to convents or monasteries anymore. They obviously do not want whatever the monasteries are offering. Or, more exactly, whatever it is that the ardent young want, they know that the post-Vatican II monastery has stopped offering it.

A serious generation gap exists within the Church, and oddly enough, it is the young who answer the old lures—the exotic ritual, the transcendental, the mysticism, the lonely, brave confrontation with God, and the austerity and sacrifice —while the middle-aged enthusiastically push meaning, intelligibility, participatory democracy, accommodation with the world and the flesh, easing of restrictions, ecumenism, updating, and homogeneity. And all the fed-up young novices have rushed off to Hare Krishna and the Maharaj Ji, and the Process Church and Pentecostalism, where they can wear religious habits, live ascetically and pray ecstatically.

When close upon Vatican II the religious orders began to modernize their dress, an American bishop, treated to a fashion show by one such order, made what must be the sick Catholic joke of the century. "Build more buildings," he said, "because when the young women see your new habit, they will storm your convents for admission." The storming, alas, has been all the other way. Perhaps it is unkind to remember this against the poor man. Perhaps it was just the clumsy gallantry of a priest unskilled in complimenting women. But I think it was much more a profound error in judgement than a polite social fib. It was an early revelation of a confusion about the direction and end of the whole Catholic institutional effort that has become very obvious in the decade since Vatican II. The Church has forgotten *why* nuns are in convents. The ranks of religious grow thinner day by day, and the hierarchy, the bishops and religious superiors, obsessively go on applying measures that have proven to be spectacular failures. They break the enclosure of contemplatives and turn them out to roam the boutiques of Toronto. They send them away from early morning chapel to exercise and swim nude at the neighbourhood Vic Tanny. They supply funds for nuns to live alone in apartment towers. They allow them to dye their hair and enrol at Figur Magic. While every year, fewer novices come and more professed leave.

And they are not for a moment given pause by the startling success of Mother Teresa of Calcutta and her Missionaries of Charity. At a time when the nun is often the best-paid, best-dressed, best-automobiled, and most leisured Catholic woman in her parish, Mother Teresa prescribes for her nuns, North Americans and Europeans as well as the others, a life of almost savage asceticism. They each have two saris and a pail to wash them in. A cardigan sweater is their concession to a cold climate. There is no physical beauty or comfort at all in their surroundings. They sleep hard and eat the food of the poor and are denied even the solace of a fan in Bengal's sultry climate. Their prayer books are cheaply mimeographed loose-leaf. They kneel without prie-dieu or pew. When gently bred upper-class Indian girls join her order, the first task she sets them is to cut the toenails and wash the filthy feet of the human flotsam she picks up from the street. For such a girl to touch an untouchable is dying to the flesh with a vengeance. And Mother Teresa insists that it must be done gladly, that the sisters must see in this dying vagrant the suffering Christ.

If modern Catholic wisdom about updating and relating to the world is sound, then Mother Teresa's order should be empty. Actually, she is besieged by vocations. She has to turn them away. Nuns from older withering religious orders beg to join her in Calcutta and Harlem and the slums of London. I know a Sister of Loretto, the order to which Mother Teresa originally belonged, who begged to be allowed to join her in India. "No," Mother Teresa said firmly. "You must serve the crucified Christ where you are." So Sister D. is gallantly hanging on her cross in Niagara Falls, where the suffering Christ comes better dressed but in just as distressing a disguise. Mother Teresa knows that for Sister D. it is a harder place than Calcutta to suffer in.

When Mother Teresa visits a new house of her nuns, she asks at once: "Where is the Cross of Christ?" She is always taken to the chapel where a great dramatic crucifix is set up. She means, of course, more by the Cross than a worked piece of wood. If someone could go into every convent and seminary and cry, "Where is the Cross of Christ?" perhaps some meditation on this theme might lead to a reduction of the present general confusion.

Mother Teresa has a very strong Catholic flair for the dramatic. Over each crucifix is written, "I thirst," the words of Christ on the Cross. It is difficult to think of any phrase as many-layered as this one, and as applicable to the life of a religious.

I thirsted too, as a fervent novice. At one time I very much wanted to become a missionary nun. Years of reading the *Scarborough Foreign Mission* magazine in school and listening to priests back from the beloved China Mission made me fancy myself there. My superior dismissed my romanticism in the same way Mother Teresa does. I think perhaps that I was hoping that the novelty and excitement of the foreign missions might help me bear better the community life.

For the community life is, and is admitted to be by spiritual writers, a genuine unbloody martyrdom. The order I joined forbade its members to undertake any private acts of penance, like fasting or whipping oneself with the "discipline," or even the imposition on oneself of extra prayers. Novices are very eager to mortify the flesh, and we did not believe our novice mistress when she said that we would find that living the community life charitably was penance enough and to spare. She was, however, right. Anyone who wants to read the best account of the martyrdom involved in the common life should read *The Story of a Soul*, the autobiography of St. Thérèse of Lisieux. She was sainted for her sort of martyrdom, absolutely justifiably, I think. She called it "the little way of love," with the humblest of irony. The common life lived well is truly heroic.

From the moment a postulant entered a religious order she gave up her privacy. I was about to say her individuality, but that is a libel. She was expected not to destroy, but to perfect, her personality, to rid it of all un-Christian traits, to keep it under such control that it did not irritate her sisters nor disrupt community peace. For fifteen minutes every day before the noon Angelus, we sat in chapel engaged in an exercise called "Examen." This was a method of examing our progress in the uprooting of some fault or the implanting of some virtue. We marked down the arithmetical results in a little book. For example, I might have set myself to a month-long effort to be truly charitable towards my sisters. So every day I would count on my Examen calendar all my falls from grace, and my co-operations with grace, too, if any. All the sixty-five times I gave way to irritation because Sister G. sucked her false teeth in the choir stall behind mine after meals, or because Sister C. dragged a second behind everyone else in oral prayer were noted in the book. It was a funny, practical exercise and, if persevered in, successful. It did not make *me* noticeably holier, but the old nuns were as perfect as sinful human beings can be. After a lifetime of this pragmatic approach to the devout life, not only sins and faults but even mannerisms were burnt away. Old nuns did not fidget, worry, or hurry. They were grave, joyful, beautiful, and still.

An old religious maxim says that if by chance the Holy Rule of an order should be lost, then one should be able to reconstruct it by following a mature nun about and observing her behaviour. You could have done that with any one of our senior nuns. What a hair-curling document you'd get if you followed around after almost any nun from a Canadian active order today. It would give even Martin Luther pause.

The common life means just that—you live life in common with many other people. You go to bed and get up at the same fixed time; you say the same prayers at the same hours; you eat the same food at the same table. At recreation you do whatever your sisters are doing.

So you can't go to bed with a thriller, or out to a movie with a friend. That destroys community. You can't read a newspaper or have the radio or television on when everybody else doesn't want to read or listen or watch. That destroys community. And if you become a Pentecostalist, and pray with a few only of your sisters, or with a prayer group of outsiders, though you seem to be engaged in a holy exercise, you destroy community just as surely. And when community life dies, the religious order dies. The religious has come down from his cross and decided not to die daily.

The community life was a hair shirt, and it was glaringly obvious that I did not have the grace of vocation to wear it. Finally Reverend Mother took pity on me and my sisters and sent me home before I had a nervous breakdown and drove everyone else mad.

I have never regretted leaving the convent, but I have never regretted my years there, either. For though the common life was painful, it was also inexpressibly beautiful and serious. Now that it has virtually perished, it seems as exotic and unlikely as the life one might have led as a visitor on another planet. That is not to subscribe to the prevalent liberal Catholic view that religious orders, and most of the rest of the Church, were trying to live in the past. The monastic life for those with a vocation to it was as contemporary and vigorous as any other modern life-style, inestimably more forceful and satisfying than the anaemia of North American suburbia or a downtown apartment complex. It was healthy, socially conscious, fulfilling, and useful to the secular community. It had no identity crisis. It was strongly linked to all Catholic time, to the earliest Christian centuries, to the High Middle Ages, to the Counter-Reformation.

There was a magical timelessness about convent life that was the result of living in strict obedience to an ancient rule. I remember my first experience of that quality of living in a sort of eternal present, the moment when I first understood the Christian belief in the immutability of God and of His natural law. It was a few days after my entrance into the convent. We had come in from recreation, which in fine weather meant walking in the huge walled garden, up and down three sides of it, from the novitiate, past the cemetery, to the scullery and the rhubarb patch, and back again, briskly, in threes. We had made the transition from the chatter of recreation to the habitual silence of the Rule by reciting the *De Profundis*, a psalm for the souls in Purgatory, which we began as we reached the end of the path on our last turn and ended as we began to take off shawls and galoshes. Forty-five silent young women observing religious decorum, no whispering nor even exchange of glances. We sat in the novitiate common room around a long table in the order of seniority, the newest entrant in the seat nearest the novice mistress. We were all engaged in quiet handiwork, darning or embroidery, while we listened to a senior novice reading the Gospel for the day and a Patristic commentary on it.

The novitiate common room was long and narrow with a whole wall of tall windows running along one side. The pale golden sunlight of a northern fall evening slanted down upon us, the many panes refracting it in long bars upon the much polished wooden floor and tables and upon the veiled bent heads and serene recollected faces of black-habited nuns. Golden light and silence, the quiet, grave voice reading the simple Gospel words and the formal, intricate periods of the Church Father, the painstaking, untechnological work we were doing, the sense of a shared and holy purpose—it was an experience I had never had before, but I recognized it at once for what it was, a distillation of all Catholic experience. I felt that if the Blessed Virgin or a Desert Father or St. Augustine or St. Benedict or St. Ignatius or Cervantes or Chaucer should walk in upon us, they would recognize at once that we belonged to *their* period. They would understand our dress, purpose, methods, prayers, and world view. They could have joined us in reciting the psalms of the Office, have assisted at Mass and not found it strange, have listened at supper to a reading likely about or by one of them.

It was for me an insight into what the Church means when she appeals to Catholic tradition to support her authority. She is appealing not to some usage fixed like a fly in amber by historical accident, but to an elastic super-historical *now*, to a world view in which the Catholic truths are always true and Catholic recognition of them immediate.

The life we led would be contemporary with the whole of Christian time as long as it was bound to the Christian imperatives—charity, brotherly love, sacrifice, glorying in the Cross of Christ, praying always, striving for perfection, putting the salvation of one's soul before any active apostolate. Our life would, and did, stop being contemporary the moment it tried to match its life-style and goals with those of modern secular society. Relevance put the convent instantly out of step. Nuns took off their habits just at the moment when the young in our society, looking for some ideal of beauty and spirituality, put on a travesty of religious costume. When, in the interests of living like a small group of middle-class, white, western women, nuns broke community, did not turn up for evening prayers, bought smart clothes and hit the picket lines, they destroyed the rationale of religious life. It is foolish and wasteful for them to go on pretending that because they live together in the same echoing old convent they are living the religious life.

Many nuns have realized that, but instead of leaving the order altogether, they move into single apartments and live lives as private and selfish as any unmarried career woman's. This is even more false and pernicious, for there is in this arrangement absolutely no protection for the vows the nun once so solemnly swore to God, not even the sketchy protection a modern convent can offer. It is a mockery for such a woman to call herself "sister."

The community life was a practical device for the protection of vowed poverty, chastity, and obedience. The religious orders of the Church did not need reformation by Vatican II as far as the practice of the evangelical counsels by individual religious was concerned. Orders might be rich and powerful; the nun or priest was scrupulously poor, chaste, and obedient. The common life was a superb safeguard. There was little chance of becoming individually affluent and luxury-loving when the religious owned, or had "to his use," only what he stood up in, and when his salary, if any, went straight to his community's use. Likewise, for the vow of chastity. The cloistered common life, with its restrictions on privacy, letters, visits, and particular friendships, helped keep the nun's heart not empty, but free, detached, open to the love of others only through its great love, Christ.

The restrictions of the common life were all painful, and those pertaining to obedience hardest of all. The religious had to give immediate cheerful assent to the voice of the superior as to the Voice of God. It always amazed me that women with such utter power over the physical and spiritual lives of so many other women so rarely abused it. Occasionally, for the sake of our progress in humility, our novice mistress would have us repeat a task even though we had done it as perfectly as we could the first time. But generally, sense and charity kept superiors from abusing their power, and novices were never threatened or punished into obedience. It was the necessity of exacting from oneself obedience to a strict and unchanging routine that was hard. Always to answer the bell at once, in the middle of a prayer or a word. Never to shorten or lengthen prayer. Never to talk during silent times nor be silent during recreation. Never to leave one's place without permission. No wonder the religious have happily thrown it all over.

It was an impossible sort of life, unless one was helped by the supernatural grace of vocation. To try to live in a convent without a real vocation was like living in a polite but ruthless prison. Obviously, some of the people who are leaving now, years after profession, should have left during novitiate. Various things kept them there, the admiration of Catholic society, the overzealousness of their novice-masters, their parents' pleasure at having a nun or priest in the family, and, not least, the very great seductiveness of the monastic ideal, of being the Spouse of Christ, of belonging to the white-robed army who follow the Lamb whithersoever He goeth.

When I left the convent I felt, again thanks to my romantic Catholic education, like Lancelot, barred from finding the Holy Grail because of his sins, even though his heart burst in longing for it. Or like David, forbidden to build God's house after a lifetime of collecting cedar and gold for its walls. It was no good for various liberal young priests to warn me that I was being Jansenistic and that it was wrong to look upon the religious life as in any way superior to life in the world. I knew what I was losing, and so did my sisters.

I served breakfast in the huge silent refectory the Sunday morning I left. I had not been permitted to speak of my departure because departures upset novices; they used to cry for days. But, of course, everyone knew. As I went about with the huge copper kettle, all the sweet-faced nuns for once broke religious decorum, one by one raised their eyes and looked at me with such love and compassion, as if I were going alone into a jungle while they stayed safe behind. Later, I took off all the elegant old garments that had been blessed at my Reception and which I had kissed and prayed over before I put them on every morning. The habit, the cincture, the beads, the long over-sleeves, the guimpe, the bandeau, the veil. All the glory of the King's daughter. The modern clothes provided for me seemed sleazy and immodest. The part of my dowry that had not been used for special expenses was returned to me. I had to give back my crucifix.

Reverend Mother and my novice mistress kissed me as one kisses a dead face. I knelt in the oratory one last time. Old Mother Agnes rose from one of the choir stalls and kissed me.

"Goodby, Sister Mary," she whispered.

"Mother Agnes, please pray for me," I said through my tears.

"Yes, yes," she said soothingly. "It will be all right, Sister Mary."

I went down the front steps and looked back through the sleet to see the two old nuns clinging together sadly in the deep window embrasure. I was back in the World. The Flesh and the Devil I had never been able to keep far at bay; they were waiting there by the taxi for me. I had chosen the better part and it had been taken away from me.

Now, like Martha, I had to be busy about many things, even though I knew the only thing that was necessary. The layman has little time to sit quiet at the feet of Jesus. Often, he feels like a poor donkey, tied by one leg, able to move only in a small circle in a small patch of nettles. This is why the pious Catholic has always looked so wistfully towards the monastery, why he has tried to imitate its prayer life, by recitation of little Hours of Office, or by becoming a tertiary—a member of the lay Third Order of a monastery. It accounts for that most beautiful of prayers that has become syonymous with popular Catholic piety—the Angelus. When the monastery bell rang the Hours of the Divine Office for the monks, the peasant in the fields, or, where I grew up, the fisherman in his boat and his wife on the drying flakes, stood with bent head and recalled how the Word was made flesh: *"Angelus Domini nuntiavit Mariae* . . . the Angel of the Lord declared unto Mary; *Ecce ancilla Domini* . . . Behold the handmaid of the Lord; *Et Verbum caro factum est* . . . And the Word was made Flesh." The layman has had to make do with what Jacques Maritain called "contemplation on the highroads."

It is not, therefore, surprising that the laity is so scandalized, so broken-hearted, over the disintegration of the religious orders. It has been, above all, a very disheartening spectacle. If religious, with such time for growing in perfection, fall away, what hope is there for the poor donkey?

However, in a strange way, perhaps providential, the decline of the religious orders has enriched the lay vocation. For today the Church asks of the Catholic laity, especially of married Catholics, a heroism and a lifelong commitment that it no longer dares to expect of the priest or nun. All about him the married Catholic sees nuns and priests and even bishops being dispensed from their solemn vows; the layman must stick by *his* marriage vows till death frees him. It is the faithful Catholic layman with a family, struggling to keep the Church's laws pertaining to his state in life, who is perforce poor, chaste, and obedient, who has unaccountably been left to defend authority and orthodoxy. This layman, at any rate, considers the unexpected new dimension to the vocation to which most Catholics are called a great grace, a source of comfort, an aid to holiness, a share in the better part, a doorway into the enclosed garden.

CHAPTER 5

NEW LIVES FOR OLD

Scratch a monk and you'll find the devil.

PROVERB

It was raining when I revisited my convent on a fall evening in 1972, and the rain that lashed its pink stone front seemed to be the only thing that had not changed in a way of life that had been changeless for centuries. (The rain falls most of the time in that Atlantic town, sideways, with a gale from Spain behind it, so that as you toil up the hill to the convent at the top, only your back gets wet.) When I came away I was too sad to cry, too shocked by the realization that a holy and gallant way of life had vanished along with the Catholic world it had served, that the monastic life, the summit and summary of the Catholic experience, had lost both its confidence and its appeal.

The anthropologist Margaret Mead once had the opportunity of studying a Stone Age society when it began its forcible introduction to Western culture and again, twenty years later, when its primitive life style had been much diluted and corrupted. She had realized the anthropologist's dream—a perfect human experimental group, long-term, isolated, assailed by irresistible pressure from a stronger, more complex society. She had returned to find her savage New Guineans wearing Western clothes, discarding taboos and totems, grappling with technology and democracy, and feeling materialistic longings. All very right, one felt. New lives for old.

As I came away from my beloved nuns, I felt a little as Margaret Mead must have felt after revisiting her islanders. This cloistered convent of nuns, a Catholic equivalent of Mead's tribal group, reflected with exquisite precision the disintegrating effect of the process of *"aggiornamento"* on Catholic society, the substitution of one world view for another. But in this case I found it impossible to believe that the change had been for the better. The nuns were wearing modern clothes. They had broken cloister, discarded the rule of silence, and dismantled the community life. They had strenuously adapted to the modern world. But along with habit and rule they had shed their cheerful certainty that what they were doing was an unchallengeable, good thing. Perhaps what was happening to them would prove to be good—the Church's coming of age in the modern world. In the meantime, however, it was shattering. The order was in disarray, its members pouring out, and those remaining bewilderedly marking time.

There were few nuns left of the once-large congregation. The old sisters who used to occupy the top table in the refectory during my novitiate were all dead. The process of *aggiornamento* was very hard on old priests and religious; it killed them off with the bitter efficiency of a hard frost among the year's last roses. They were very like late roses, those old nuns, with the same beautiful glowing serenity, the sense of life's purpose accomplished, waiting after the long hot summer unperturbed for death. The cheeks they pressed to mine during the formal, affectionate greetings on my Reception and Feast Days had had a satiny softness and bloom, and there hung about them a fragrance compounded of uncosmeticized cleanliness, incense, beeswax, cut flowers, and prayer. The odour of sanctity. To look at them was to be reminded of that verse from the Song of Solomon: "A garden enclosed is my sister, my bride." *Aggiornamento* broke down their enclosure and radically altered their spiritual environment. The old nuns took a quick look at the new order, found it impossible, and departed with despatch for heaven.

There were no novices. Indeed, the novitiate, built with such hope in the fifties, when the order was growing faster than ever before, had been closed. Whatever lure had drawn the young and generous into a difficult and cloistered life had ceased to appeal. Perhaps, given the turmoil in Catholic education and the breakdown of a confident Catholic consensus after Vatican II, it was not surprising to find few new vocations. Still, there is always a chance that the young may come later. The most serious thing that had happened to this order, as to every religious order in the Church (with the significant exception of Mother Teresa's of Calcutta), was the mass departure of the mature women who were the active working force in every congregation. They were professed and presumably fully committed women—past the doubts of adolescence, trained in their professions, and spiritually formed in a strict novitiate—women who had taken vows of poverty, chastity, and obedience at First Profession, after several years of study and consideration—who had renewed them every year for as many as six years, with every year the option of refusing and leaving. Sometimes as many as half of any year's postulants would drop out before Final Profession, but it was extremely rare for a finally professed nun to leave. Her defection was always treated as a grave blow both to her own spiritual well-being and to that of her order.

Since Vatican II, every religious order has been faced with such multiple defections. This situation, which makes doubtful the continued existence of the order, has had an incalculably serious effect on the strength of the Church of which the religious orders have long been the task force.

In their distinctive dress, religious were instantly recognizable as the most committed militants in the Church Militant. Members of religious orders ran most Catholic schools and provided a powerful Church presence in secular society, in hospitals, asylums, orphanages, universities. The governments of mission-countries trusted them; they were incorruptible and non-political. They owned and ran newspapers, magazines, and radio stations. The Church could depend on their loyalty and energy.

Now, that hard-working corps of professionals has been

shattered. The Canadian Religious Conference in a 1973 report showed just how hard-hit the religious orders in this country have been by *aggiornamento*. In 1962, there were 59,712 women religious in Canada; in 1972, with the renewal promised by Vatican II presumably well under way, there were 44,606. The report noted that the majority of those leaving were between the ages of twenty-five and thirty-four, that is, in the bloom of their creativity and energy. Their departure crippled their orders, for although the number of religious women dropped during the decade by 25 per cent, their actual presence in society diminished much further. Thirty per cent of the remaining nuns are over sixty-five. They will naturally be giving up their public work soon, and there will be no one to replace them. In 1972, 232 young women entered Canadian convents; 1,549 left. The authorities speak hopefully of a levelling-off in the numbers leaving, but if the outward flow is slowing, it is only because there are so few left who are in a position to leave. For it is not safe to assume that those who stay do so out of an unshaken commitment to their vocation.

What has happened in Canada, and in every Western country, is a dissolution of the monasteries far more sinister than the one that took place at the time of the Reformation. More sinister and more dangerous, because this time it is being carried out from within the Church. When the English monasteries were knocked over by a king desperate for money, or the German monasteries by princes hungry for territory, even when the monasteries of Spain and Mexico were burned by fierce anti-Catholic anarchists, the setback suffered by the Church was chiefly to the physical establishment. The ideal of vowed service was not at all tarnished. Very much to the contrary. Edmund Campion, hanged, drawn, and quartered. The Charterhouse monks. The bayoneted nuns. The priests praying "*Introibo ad altare Dei* " as they mounted the scaffold. "*Vivo el Cristo Rey*," before a firing squad. The blood of martyrs is the seed of Christians. Dead so gloriously, remembered so patriotically, they were worth more to the Church than a multitude of abbeys.

I am not suggesting that the most useful thing that can happen to a convent is to be burned down and to have all its inhabitants slaughtered. But I am suggesting that persecution from outside the Church is an annoyance rather than a disaster. What is happening now to and through religious orders *is* a disaster. For incredibly, the Roman Catholic Church, at a time when its power and prestige were greater than at any time since the High Middle Ages and free almost everywhere from persecution, succumbed to some mysterious death wish, deliberately tore down the structures of religious life, and broke the hearts and lost the loyalty of its espoused lovers.

When the Church looks about today for its sister, its bride, it is likely to find that she has eloped with someone else—often, compounding confusion, with a priest.

Some nuns more energetic or more optimistic than their sisters, instead of resisting the disintegration of the old way of life, enthusiastically support it. Such a one is Sister Catharine Wallace, Sister of Charity and president of Mount St. Vincent University for women in Halifax, Nova Scotia. On April 14, 1973, *Weekend Magazine* published an admiring article on the way this nun's personal odyssey has reshaped her Catholic environment. Beside the picture of a pretty, middle-aged woman, smartly dressed, with a blue rinse and a peace medallion, Harry Bruce writes: "a gently captivating Halifax nun who has danced to a calypso beat in a Barbados nightspot, rapped with Ivan Illich and Buckminster Fuller, wears chic bathing suits on the beaches of Nova Scotia, attends cocktail parties and sometimes seems to have more male admirers than Raquel Welch." Sister Wallace has been president of Mount St. Vincent since 1965, during which time it has stopped being a college of the Sisters of Charity for Catholic girls and become a university half of whose enrolment is non-Catholic. Its rule and spirit since then have undergone the same violent swing from super-strictness to permissiveness as that of the religious orders. Fifteen years ago a friend of mine was expelled from the Mount for insubordination—she would go on walking across a forbidden piece of grass in high heels. Now ("incredibly," says Harry Bruce, as well he might), "there is an ad offering advice on abortion clinics in the student newspaper. The times, they are a 'changin'."

Sister Catharine Wallace, "the right person . . . in the

right place at the right time," drawing on that fund of toughness and persuasiveness nuns were famous for, runs a smart and successful small university and is an officer of the Association of Universities and Colleges of Canada. She is a Canadian religious who has made it. She seems to have put off the old without trauma to herself; whether younger, less firmly grounded nuns can do the same remains to be seen.

The Second Vatican Council itself was not responsible for the debacle. Its *Decree on the Adaptation and Renewal of Religious Life* is impeccable in its devotion to the ideals and practices of the religious vocation. It reaffirmed the glory and necessity of the evangelical counsels, poverty, chastity, and obedience, of the cloister and of the common life. The old priorities still held: first, the personal sanctification of each religious; second, the active ministry. Paradoxically, it was the *letter* of Vatican II that if followed might have quickened the Church; it was the *spirit*, the "spirit of Vatican II" that killed. The Council urged a return to each order's original spirit. It envisaged religious, "poor both in fact and spirit," protecting chastity by "mortification and custody of the senses" and by the common life, offering "the full surrender of their own will" in obedience, and wearing a habit which as "an outward mark of consecration to God should be simple, and modest, poor and . . . becoming."

Before the Council, every religious one knew fitted that description; now few live that way. Why? What happened? What makes elderly nuns suddenly take to dyeing their hair? Why has a nun who was middle-aged when she was my teacher left her convent? Why does Sister T. have to be taken home drunk from a party at 3 A.M.? I have suggested some reasons why religious orders no longer draw novices. And the arbitrary change of the ground rules, accepted originally after such struggle, is probably the main reason why so many older professed leave, feeling that they have wasted their strength and love. But why do so many of the ones who stay seem dedicated to the destruction of their own way of life?

The reasons for this are too many and too complex to be dealt with here. The Church will have to understand the disaffection of its vowed religious if the orders are to survive the century, and most orders are engaged in frantic introspection. There is one fairly obvious cause, the blame for which must be laid on the pre-Conciliar policies of active religious orders. The vigorous growth of Catholic religious orders after the Second World War was, in hindsight, as much a curse as a blessing. For the more the orders did, the more they were called on to do. Thus, they spread themselves too thin, and unable to resist the invitations to open new schools and hospitals, they sent their tender novices into the work, woefully unprepared. I saw this process at its beginning in my convent twenty years ago. The canons of the order prescribed at least three years closed novititate. During the first two years, the novice studied the Rule and mediated deeply upon the meaning of the vows. During the third year, a limited amount of the order's work might be done. After First Profession, the new nun was still supposed to spend more time on her spiritual formation than on the active apostolate.

That was the process that I saw break down. In the 1950s the order opened dozens of new schools and convents. The modern centralized high schools demanded that the order, content before to train most of its members in its own Normal School, while sending a few mature nuns to universities or monastic schools of music, must now send most of its young professed to expensive and secular degree programs.

The rapid expansion also made it necessary to send novices, untrained in either the religious life or the teaching profession, into the schools. Even the sacred Canonical year was broken in upon. I taught as a novice; by the time I left, all the first-year postulants were teaching. In the beginning, the Rule was strictly observed. No nun was allowed to stay late at work, engage in evening activities, or stay up at night to study. These restrictions were very frustrating, since they meant that all preparation for the next day's work had to be done in the time between after supper chapel and eight-fifteen recreation. That was clearly impossible, especially when so many of the nuns also were enrolled in university courses. Something had to give, and, alas, it was the community life, which was under such great strain that it collapsed at the first breath of the spirit of Vatican II.

An exacerbating factor was that the sixties, when so many young religious were thrust unprepared into the secular universities, was the period when the secular consensus was being shattered as well. During the sixties North America admitted that it was no longer Christian, that it no longer needed to make its legal and civil behaviour conform to the provisions of the Judaeo-Christian moral order. The religious orders cannot now resist secular liberalism when so many of their members, at the most vulnerable time in their lives, had their moral and political values fixed at those secular holy offices, the universities.

The religious calling is to the highest ideal and involves a continual struggle of mind and body. It is always open to the affliction that older spiritual writers called *accidie*, a revulsion against the spiritual life because of the effort involved in leading it. This malaise, both caused by and resulting in a lessening of faith, is endemic to the religious life, lived as it must be at full spiritual stretch. Only by wise, careful, and continuous guidance can the religious avoid it. The novices of the last twenty years or so have not had the lengthy religious formation necessary for the spiritual athlete. They all began with great fervour to lead the life indicated by their Rule; but since they were not given time to learn how to lead it successfully, they merely coasted along for a time on the example of their elders. Then, unhappily, their novitiate ardour cooled, and they found themselves in a milieu that encouraged a turning away from Catholic religious orthodox effort, with the best of support for throwing the whole thing over.

The novices of the fifties were the teachers of the sixties. They were in a position to succumb without blame to the *accidie* brought on by their own ill-formation, and the radical climate of opinion allowed them safely to instruct today's young religious in an easy infidelity. Even in the best of times, religious as a class are tempted to relieve the tedium of their lives by taking up new ideas. The religious of the last two decades, spiritually undertrained and academically overtrained, were pushovers for the new liberal orthodoxy. The radical post-Conciliar catechisms were written by very young people; thirty-five is the prime age in the new catechetical circles. By the end of the Council, their new catechisms were already appearing, not, as advertised, presenting Conciliar thought, but full of pre-Conciliar reform theology, especially of the romantic evolutionism of Teilhard de Chardin, which, though rejected by the Council, informs every page of post-Conciliar catechetics.

In February 1973, the Canadian Religious Conference published a research project called *The Thinking of Young Religious*. The publication records the answers to a series of questions on the Church and on the nature and purpose of religious life that were given by a group of young religious, formation directors, and major superiors. If it even partially reflects the thinking of the youngest members of religious orders, Catholics must not hope for anything serviceable to the Church from that quarter in the foreseeable future.

The most widely quoted sections of the publication had to do with observance of the vows. Catholics who have so often been lectured by young priests on the poverty of the Third World were irritated to learn that the survey showed, for example, that "They [young religious] will buy anything to make sure of a good party; relationships are the key thing; material things come second. Self and one's relationship to others is very important: not 'the sky is the limit', but the cost should be a secondary factor. They are critical of community poverty. Some of the young have a very high regard for poverty." That, to the struggling Catholic parent, is salt in the wound. The attitude of the young religious to "human love as a lifelong commitment to a person" is equally unedifying for the Catholic bound by his vows to a less than perfect marriage; " 'For better or for worse' means nothing for them. On the contrary, if the condition changes, then life does, too. . . . They do not want to see in advance, that they have committed themselves 'for always'." It's enough to make Donatists of us all. They consider their religious order "a hindrance to their desires to live the Gospel imperative" mainly because "those in authority are not convinced that the Holy Spirit is with the young and giving them new insights," and because "they resent being accountable for their actions and for the money they spend."

But by far the most hair-raising section of this document is the one that records the answers to the question: "What does the Catholic Church represent in the lives of young people?" ("young people" referring both to the young religious—who ranged from twenty-two to thirty-two—and to their students). What is revealed is not just discontent with the Catholic Church but a deep implacable *hatred* that is very chilling. What does the Catholic Church represent to young religious?

> It does not represent much and says nothing. . . . [It is] a structural institution caught up in a morass of unchristian mores . . . an obstacle to the opening up of life of young people today . . . archaic, authoritarian . . . formalistic . . . a bulwark of rigidity . . . a large boat crammed with structures that smother out life . . . inflexible . . . triumphalist . . . restrictive . . . an entity to which they do not belong . . . too juridical, formal, legalistic and sacramental . . . whatever the meaning of 'Church', it does not mean much to them . . . it is far from real life. They do not understand the meaning of 'Mystical Body' in its amplitude.

The best these young religious could say in its favour is the Teilhardian cliché that the Church is "a pool of information for the truth."

But perhaps those young religious feel the same towards any organized religion, perhaps their anti-Catholicism is a reaction to all the Establishment? Not at all. For the next question: "How do young people consider the other Christian communities?" drew this response:

> [They show] much interest in Eastern religions and in radical movements . . . see little difference and cannot understand why we do not or cannot worship as one. . . . [Other churches] are more human, closer to Christ and to Scripture . . . nearer to the poor . . . nearer to life . . . more

open . . . [Other churches make them feel] . . . less embarrassed.

They want inter-communion immediately. They revere the Protestant ecumenical monastic community of Taizé.

If these young religious hate their Church as much as this, they must have been taught to hate it by Catholic religious teachers because they were not taught it in their homes. Catholics of my generation, of my father's generation, and my grandparents', love the Church with all our hearts, as Mother, Teacher, and Country. Young religious and their young students, however, "do not understand the meaning of 'Mystical Body'." My grandmother, barely literate, understood it: at Mass she prayed to the Church Triumphant for herself and her family, members of the Church on Earth, the Church Militant, and for those of the Church Suffering with whose memorial cards her Missal was crammed. My father, whose Catholic school could not offer him all the years of high school, knew what "Church" meant—it meant working the Saturday shift every weekend for twenty years for a Seventh Day Adventist friend who would not work on his Sabbath, even though the Adventist then got paid time-and-a-half for working on Sunday. Yet these young people, after such all-out effort by the Church, don't know.

The Sacred Congregation for Religious and for Secular Institutions is planning to issue new directives concerning the formation of religious, and the study I have been quoting is the Canadian submission to an international symposium on the subject. If this study is reliable and representative, the Sacred Congregation has its work cut out. Will it yield to "updating" pressures and allow religious orders to continue to disintegrate? Or will it rule that, since the sanctification of the religious is more important than the apostolate, spiritual formation—the prayer part of the religious life—should get more time and attention, not only in the novitiate but throughout the lifetime of the religious? If this means scaling down the amount of work and study an order can undertake, will the orders accept the circumscription? Will the Pope take the unattractive step of requiring orthodoxy, perhaps by an oath like that against Modernism, from teachers in sensitive posts? Will the bishops clean up or close down the catechetical schools, those nurseries of dissent and heresy in the domestic Church?

Religious orders cannot, and will not, continue much longer if their incoming members hate the very Church to whose view of the service of God they are committing themselves. The Church itself cannot long survive this mutinous army of teachers. For it does not take long to spread this disaffection throughout that part of the laity that this group reaches. It is instructive and unnerving to see it reproducing. Two years ago, a young Holy Cross Father from the local high school gave an adult education series on the Church in which he expounded the theme that: "The trouble with Martin Luther was his authenticity." (He meant Luther's views were correct, not that he was really and truly Martin Luther.) This year, I was a member of a panel discussing marriage with aspirants to that state. When a young man in the audience said, apropos of *Humanae Vitae*, "Isn't the Church being hypocritical?" a Protestant on the panel said to him: "I expect you feel that way because you're a non-Catholic like me and have trouble with the teaching—"

"No," I interrupted. "You're a Catholic, aren't you?"

"Yes, I am," the boy said rather sheepishly. I would have staked my hope of heaven on the certainty that he was. Only Catholics speak like that of the Church today. He turned out to be a recent graduate from the hands of the Holy Cross Father.

Yet, black as things seem, the Catholic would be despairing prematurely if he were to write off the organized religious effort. There *is* Mother Teresa. And there is, too, a hopeful movement towards reform from inside the religious orders, which calls itself Consortium Perfectae Caritatis, from the first words of the Vatican II document on religious. It is an international organization of general superiors of orders of women religious, who accept the Conciliar documents and unequivocally support the Magisterium of the Church. It is an attempt to provide sisters with what they have lost, a community of purpose and method. The members "look like nuns." They act like nuns, too. The existence of this organization may help collect the scattered religious who are resisting the pressure to conform to secular norms and who try in their withering orders to live the Rule, shunned on the one hand by the pant-suited sister with the cute boyfriend, and on the other by the hot-eyed Pentecostalist and her conventicle.

The last time Western civilization went smash, the monasteries preserved and transmitted its accumulated wisdom. They copied it down; they illuminated it in azure and gold. This time, the monks have left it to Kenneth Clark and the television cameras to photograph the lineaments of civilization and to put the illuminations in a tin for posterity. If any. McLuhan would have something portentous to say about the significance of that. But this Catholic believes that the Holy Ghost will not allow the Church and the monasteries to go out of the civilization-preserving business. This Catholic believes, admittedly against the evidence, that the religious orders will make the right decision about what to transmit and how to illuminate it.

CHAPTER 6

SHEPHERDS AND CROOKS

It is not the people who would be the heirs of a dethroned Pope. It is some synod of Bishops; a group small enough to be insolent and large enough to be irresponsible.

G.K.CHESTERTON

The Catholic Church before Vatican II did not pretend to be a democratic institution but an hierarchical one. It believed that all power came from above, from God through Christ the Mediator, to the Apostles under Peter, and through them and their successors, the bishops and the Pope, to the universal Church. "All power is given to me in heaven and in earth," said Jesus to the Apostles. "Go ye therefore and teach all nations, baptizing them in the name of the Father and of the Son and of the Holy Ghost: Teaching them to observe all things whatsoever I have commanded you: and lo, I am with you always, even unto the end of the world." The bishops of the Catholic Church, in communion with the Bishop of Rome, thus find their duty and power defined with great clarity by Christ Himself, and after Him by St. Paul—to teach and to baptize, to teach what Christ taught, to preach it to everybody. This special duty and power makes of the bishop not a sort of super-priest or super-Christian, but the essential, unique conductor of the teaching of Christ to the Church. Nobody can usurp his place. He cannot democratically share his duty and power, though he can appoint others to help him teach and baptize, in union with him. When an American bishop recently addressed a large gathering of Catholics as "My fellow bishops," it could be nothing but an exercise in flattery. A bishop, by virtue of his Christ-appointed office, can never accept democracy as the liberal world wants it. He can never put himself in such a position, for example, as to find himself overruled by a majority of non-bishops in a pastoral council, when a matter of faith or morals is at stake. This does not mean that he must make every practical decision himself. One can envisage a bishop being overruled on an administrative or financial matter, like the building or repair of a parish facility. But one can never accept a bishop being overruled on what catechism to teach and how to teach it. It is precisely the bishops' abdication of power in instances like the latter that has caused the painful rupture between themselves and the faithful.

In the Church before Vatican II, still operating under the Tridentine reform, power was centralized in the Roman Bishopric, the Papacy, to an extent that deprived the other bishops of some of their rightful freedom of action. That was necessary in a time when whole hierarchies were succumbing to the pressures of the Reformation and the only way Rome could ensure the teaching of sound doctrine was to exercise strict control over all its principal teachers. Each bishop was personally responsible to the Holy See, to which he had to report regularly in personal *ad limina* visits. This system served the Church well, for it preserved her against incalculable odds, so that she is here in the late twentieth century with her ancient doctrines intact and her hierarchical structure still in useful operation.

Nevertheless, the system had its drawbacks. It preserved orthodoxy, but it subtracted from the bishop's freedom in his own diocese. Closely watched by the papal delegate to his region, he tended to act more as a senior functionary than as an Apostle, and he turned his energies to administration, fundraising and building, a legitimate part of his missionary duty, but one that often had too great importance placed upon it.

Also, perhaps chief of its demerits, the system of necessity caused to grow up in Rome a huge overbearing clerical bureaucracy to administer the vast amount of work, much of which could have been done at diocesan level. Everything had to be referred to Rome, dispensations, annulments, many appointments. This overcentralization produced the logical results—callousness to individual hardships, delay, resentment, legalism. For example, a dispensation for a mixed marriage might be obtained at a diocesan level, but permission for the annulment of a marriage had to come from Rome. It always took years. The bishop was powerless to speed it up and the delay caused untold anguish. Even the most obedient Catholic boiled with resentment at watching a close relative wait throughout her childbearing years for an annulment that came too late. Surely this, in a reformed Church with trustworthy bishops, was unnecessary. (The other side of this objection, though, is that in local marriage courts since Vatican II, there has sometimes taken place a rubber-stamping of annulment decrees, to find a way round the Church's teaching on the indissolubility of marriage.)

The huge central bureaucracy is called the Roman Curia. Before Vatican II it administered the universal Church. But bureaucrats are bureaucrats, ordained or not, and working for the Church does not necessarily improve fallen human nature. The Roman courts did on the whole administer justice, but there were always the charges that a rich Catholic could get speedier justice than a poor one. Some of these charges were true. A rich man can get everything more easily, except, as Christ told us, admission to the Kingdom of Heaven. That comes "hardly." The ordinary Catholic layman, however, lives his life without a brush with the Curia. Probably he couldn't name one member of its many congregations.

It was the bishops who bore the brunt of Curial highhandedness. A bishop, used to being treated with reverence in his own diocese, was often treated in his dealings with the Curia as an ignorant, probably heretical, colonial, and sent home chastened with his orders. The bishops loathe the Curia. The Curia distrusts the bishops. Both attitudes have a good deal of foundation.

The bishops hoped to break the power of the Curia at Vatican II. They didn't succeed. They pruned it a little, squashed the Holy Office (which watched for heresy) and the Index of Prohibited Books. But bureaucracies are self-perpetuating. Also, of course, in a universal Church some strong central administration is necessary, and it is always going to be difficult to control its growth. The bishops, since Vatican II, have set up a rival power structure to the unsubdued Curia, national groupings of bishops strong enough to resist Curial direction. As might have been expected, these national conferences of bishops have quickly developed Curias of their own, no more sensitive to the feelings of the laity than was the Roman version. Today, in most countries, half a dozen vigorous, "progressive" bishops direct episcopal response.

That is why, when a Catholic wishes to express disagreement with episcopal policies, he has to direct it at one of the members of the small powerful liberal oligarchy which has succeeded in enforcing its concept of what a post-Vatican II Church should be on the Church in Canada. He will most likely direct his fire at one of the two Bishops Carter, or at Bishops Plourde, Remi de Roo, Power, or Flahiff. These bishops are ubiquitous. They pass the presidency of the Canadian Catholic Conference from one to the other, chair the committees, attend the synods, issue the press statements, write for the Catholic press. Bishop de Roo masterminded the Winnipeg Statement and led the delegation on abortion to Parliament (I'll be discussing both events later), Bishop Alexander Carter forced through the Winnipeg statement and took the celibacy issue to the 1971 Synod, Bishop Emmett Carter is chairman of the International Committee on English in the Liturgy with the last word on things liturgical. Bishop Emmett Carter will also attend the 1974 Synod at which Bishop de Roo, not an official delegate, will serve as consultant to the Canadian delegation. The Catholic layman's view of this post-Vatican II situation is that the Curia has simply moved closer to home.

The issue of contention here is not that the bishops are not ruling democratically while pretending that they are. The last thing most Catholics want from the teaching Church is democracy. In this sense, post-Vatican II bishops are no worse than bishops were in the bad old days when they so often irritated the laity by their single-minded devotion to fund-raising, and their rudeness and contempt for both lesser clergy and laity.

Nobody ever referred to our pre-Vatican II Bishop, for example, without including the words "the old devil." ("Do you know what he said to me, the old devil?") He ran the whole Catholic show in his diocese; he was on all committees, issued all communications and ran the school system. In his capacity as school board, he received from the government the salaries of his teachers and paid them out at his own convenience. Once, he set out in September for Rome (by way of Ireland; he went to the dentist by way of Ireland), for his *ad limina* visit, leaving no power of attorney, so none of us was paid until his return in December. The fact that he returned unscathed casts considerable doubt on the power of prayer.

He was intolerant and inflexible. I was teaching for him when I became engaged to a Protestant, so I naturally went to offer to resign if he felt my example would influence my Catholic students. After submitting to the remonstrance I felt he had a right to give, I asked if I might introduce my future husband to him, so that he could see that it was unlikely that the marriage would take me out of the Church. He refused, on the grounds that he could not trust himself to behave civilly. The old devil. I don't know whether to be glad or sorry that he lived long enough to see his successor officiate at the marriage of one of his diocesan priests (laicized, i.e., returned to the lay state and forbidden to practise his priestly ministry) to a parishioner.

One would think there must be some medium between those extremes of episcopal behaviour, but there doesn't seem to be. The difference for Catholics like me, of course, is that we approved of what our bishop did. We just didn't like the way he did it. He was a good bishop, a pious and learned man. He built dozens of churches and schools, and was always in both, teaching. His liturgy was splendid, he heard confessions, he kept an eagle eye on catechism and catechists. He was good to the poor and the missions. The confident Catholicism flourishing today in his diocese is a tribute to his piety and energy. We felt he believed what he was teaching. Few Catholics now ever see their bishop. Many think the bishops have betrayed Catholic orthodoxy in their new catechisms, and destroyed Catholic belief by new liturgical procedures. Remembering the fearless, orthodox old devils, they wonder what the new breed is up to? Do the bishops still believe what the Church taught as lately as Vatican II? Why did they waffle on *Humanae Vitae*, hesitate on the abortion issue, support a change in celibacy at the Synod, approve Communion in the hand, force on parents a hated catechism? What can explain the sudden *volte face*? Not, one concludes, Vatican II. It isn't at all surprising that some Catholics have embraced a conspiracy theory, and have simply decided that most bishops have become Communists. No other theory, they think, can support the evidence.

But one does not need to subscribe to a conspiracy theory to explain episcopal behaviour. The fact seems to be that since Vatican II bishops have been in a state of confusion about the proper way to exercise their authority both in the Church and towards society in general. Again, this does not seem to be the Council's fault. The two Conciliar documents that deal with the role of the bishop in the universal Church—Chapter III of the *Dogmatic Constitution on the Church*, and the whole of the *Decree Concerning the Pastoral Office of Bishops in the Church*—give the bishops no new powers and add no new duties. The primacy of the Pope, the Bishop of Rome, is restated, "in order that the episcopate might be one and undivided." This primacy does not take away from the position of the bishops in whom "Our Lord Jesus Christ . . . is present in the midst of those who believe." The Pope and the bishops constitute "one apostolic college," which acts in concert for the good of the Church. But, states the *Dogmatic Constitution on the Church* (III,22):

> the college of Bishops has no authority unless it is understood together with the Roman Pontiff. . . .The Pope's power of primacy over all, both pastors and faithful, remains whole and intact. In virtue of his office . . .

the Roman Pontiff has full, supreme and universal power over the Church.

The Pope may act alone. The bishops may not act without the Pope. When bishops teach in communion with the Pope, the faithful must obey them.

The bishops of the world collegially ratified all this unequivocal teaching on the nature of authority in the Church. They were given by the Council some of the reforms in the administrative structure that they had hoped for, more participation through frequent synods, and the creation of territorial episcopal conferences. Likewise, bishops were expected to extend decision-making in the practical affairs of the Church to the clergy and laity. The synods take place regularly; episcopal conferences have been formed. The pastoral councils, however, are in limbo.

Only the Dutch bishops put into practice the Vatican II suggestion of a National Pastoral Council, and its first sessions so nearly produced a schism that it frightened not only the Dutch but every Catholic hierarchy. It is unlikely that the experiment will be repeated, even though the Canadian bishops in 1968 approved the plan for a National Pastoral Council to assist the Canadian Catholic Conference. The last thing bishops want is the laity telling them what to do, or helping to elect them. That is not at all what they mean by co-responsibility or dialogue. What they want is to be free of Roman shackles, and to run their territories under a small oligarchy, the day-to-day paper work being done by a consenting liberal group of *periti* and middle-class intelligentsia. That is the reigning definition of "collegiality."

The conservative laity, in spite of its historic reverence for the bishop, is quite clear on his duties and prerogatives. They know what they want from him: that he teach the Faith in communion with the Pope and preserve and defend it. Only their conviction that the bishops have not on occasion acted with the Pope and tradition could move conservative Catholics to remonstrance and opposition. Liberal Catholics, too, expect much from the bishop, though they want him to lead the Church in a different direction. All in all, bishops are having a bad time of it lately, tossed between two camps, and both liberal and conservative Catholics think they deserve it; the liberals because they think the bishops have stifled the spirit of Vatican II, the conservatives because they think the bishops are too cowardly to uphold doctrinal and liturgical order. It is not, however, necessary to feel much sympathy for their predicament; bishops are *supposed* to have it difficult—it's in the contract. They can, as St. Paul says, expect to be reviled, spat upon, thrown out of the synagogue, and crucified. They are supposed to preach Christ in season and out of season, in spite of tribulation, distress, famine, nakedness, danger, persecution, and the sword. They are anointed to be, as St. Ignatius of Antioch exclaimed as he was thrown to the lions, "the wheat of Christ, ground by the fangs of wild beasts to become bread agreeable to my Lord!" They are a light set upon a candlestick, a city upon a hill; whatever they do cannot be hidden.

The early Church took this literally. All of the Apostles except John, scores of bishops, and nearly every pope of the first three and a half centuries were martyred. When, halfway through the fourth century, Christianity became legal and respectable, the routine martyrdom stopped. Since then, except for the occasional sport, bishops as a class have exhibited more caution. Whenever there has been a well-mounted attack on the unity and orthodoxy of the Church, by the Arians, the Albigensians, the Reformation, the French Revolution, or post-Vatican II neo-Modernism, the hierarchy has immediately fallen flat on its collegial face. Only St. Athanasius, Bishop of Alexandria, refused to capitulate to the imperially supported Arian establishment after the Council of Nicaea. Only one English bishop, St. John Fisher, refused to sign the Act of Supremacy at the beginning of Henry VIII's break with Rome. "Dumb dogs!" thundered Pope Innocent III at the Provençal bishops who fostered the laxity that allowed Albigensianism to flourish.

Bishops do very well proclaiming the word *in* season; it's the out-of-season work they dislike. Being thrown to the lions eventually gets rather wearing. And the lions today, the liberal establishment which controls the media, secular and Catholic, are a lot harder on the nerves than the ones Bishop Ignatius encountered. The arena lion at least offered a glorious martyrdom; the liberal lion is more likely to laugh at the bishop's claim to deserve such importance, yawn at his pronouncements and demand the right to vote him out of office.

The liberal lions were kindly disposed towards the Canadian hierarchy from the beginning of the Council. It had already begun to establish for itself a reputation as one of the most "progressive" hierarchies in the world. A delegation of bishops that employed Gregory Baum as its most influential *peritus* at the Council was obviously deserving of approval. As the Council progressed, the Canadians improved their image.

Cardinal Léger of Montreal was one of the leading liberal figures at the Council, speaking always to warm applause. His speeches on the liturgy and on marriage were called "bombshells" by Rynne and the press. In the latter speech, Léger pressed the Council to change Church teaching on marriage, to get away from the theology of primary and secondary ends, and to allow contraception in individual acts of intercourse as long as the marriage itself remained open to procreation. He expressed his deep concern for the faithful, "often among them some of the best [who] encounter daily difficulties, search for solutions in accord with their faith, but do not find comfort in the answers given them." He urged the Council to find new answers. In the event of course, the Council did not have the chance to follow his advice, since the Pope decided, as was his Vatican II-supported right, to make the decision on contraception by himself. Nevertheless, the image of a progressive hierarchy bound against its will by Roman inflexibility remained, and the ground for the later Canadian episcopal resistance to *Humanae Vitae* was laid.

The bishops had a lovely time at the Council. It was an extended holiday from the thankless job of running a diocese. They lived luxuriously in Rome in the company they are most comfortable with, other bishops and administrators. The press catered to innocent vanity. The apathetic, or irritable laity was far enough away so that the bishops could, as Rynne quotes Bishop Alexander Carter, descant on "the sin of clericalism" without qualms. Bishop Emmett Carter, writing in the *Catholic Register* recalled those years wistfully. He was one of the "young Turks" who, defying the rules, earned Cardinal Ruffini's displeasure by applauding during the speeches. One such burst of applause greeted the cutting-off of the microphone of blind, aged Cardinal Ottaviani during his speech on the liturgy, an action which shamed the old priest so deeply that he refused to attend the sessions for two weeks. The Canadians were also members of "the Church of the Catacombs," a group of bishops devoted to living Gospel poverty. According to Rynne, they fired their chauffeurs (who thus got an opportunity to practise evangelical poverty at first hand), decided to use wooden croziers and pectoral crosses, and instigated a move to pass around a basket at a Council session to collect the episcopal rings. Someone's good taste prevailed, however, for this latter gesture did not take place.

Nonetheless, for all the larking about, the bishops in sacred solemnity did reiterate and promise to uphold the entirety of Catholic doctrine transmitted through the ages. It was a truly extraordinary feat—explicable only by the direction of the Holy Ghost—that these modern men performed, in the teeth of secular society in which they lived and to which they must return after the Council. They told an incredulous world that they still believed in angels and saints, devils and hell, heaven and purgatory, original sin, the Immaculate Conception, the perpetual virginity of Mary, her assumption into heaven, the Incarnation, death and resurrection of Christ, the infallibility of the teaching Church. They told the world further that they meant to instruct it in justice, in respect for the dignity of human life and in Christ-like generosity. When one is out of charity with the bishops, one ought to remember that, and rejoice in their steadfastness. In these great pronouncements, the Canadian bishops shared.

No wonder they came home full of the pentecostal spirit. Even bishops who had not quite grasped what was happening felt that they were now expected to behave differently from their pre-Conciliar pattern. The new stance did not involve any giving up of power, all that noble talk against clericalism notwithstanding. Their rapid and ruthless dismantling of the liturgy (Bishop Emmett Carter boasted in the *Register* that the Canadian bishops were the only hierarchy to provide the whole vernacular New Mass at the first possible legal time), and their imposition on every Catholic school in Canada of a radical new catechism were examples of a clerical totalitarianism that would have impressed Torquemada.

Most Catholics were not expecting a new democracy. If the bishops had proceeded in solidly Catholic directions, no matter how new and post-Vatican II their methods, they would have been spared the reproach of the laity. What happened was that many bishops accepted the liberal interpretation of the spirit of Vatican II, and moved in liberal directions. This was easier to do because it brought pleasant approval from the liberal Catholic and secular press. Since Vatican II, in a number of important issues, the bishops have acted in ways to which a large part of the laity took violent exception. I will consider several of these in this chapter: the introduction of the Canadian Catechism in 1966, the Winnipeg Statement on *Humanae Vitae* in 1968, the Canadian delegation's stand on the celibacy question at the World Synod in 1971, and the conduct of the abortion issue, from 1967 through today. Because the last issue is the one of which non-Catholics will probably have most knowledge, and with which they have been deeply concerned themselves, I shall deal with it first.

It was particularly unfortunate that this issue should have been given to the bishops to resolve just at the moment when they were most uncertain how to balance the claims of the Church to moral certainty with respect for the pluralistic character of modern society. They floundered on the abortion issue not because they were uncertain about the hideous sinfulness of abortion but because they were unsure how to proceed in making this clear to non-Catholic government and society. Nowhere can it be seen more tragically how their understanding of the Council's *Document on Religious Freedom* paralysed their rightful pastoral instincts than in the abortion issue.

Catholic laymen are the main force in the various pro-life organizations, but their great regret is that they came so late to the battle. Every Catholic awakening to the abortion issue asks: "Why weren't we fighting it earlier?" The answer, simply and sadly, is that we were not led to it. We took the confusion about procedure to be symptomatic of a doubt among the bishops about the immorality of abortion. When they did not urge Catholics in the medical and legal professions to exert pressure through their professional organizations, or Catholic media people to put the Catholic arguments, when they did not strongly suggest that the Catholic laity—46 per cent of the population of Canada—should rise up and forbid the government to loosen the abortion law, many Catholics assumed that the Church was changing its mind about abortion. This was not so, as the Catholic press kept pointing out. But the Catholic didn't hear it from his bishop until too late. If liberalized abortion was as serious a matter as the Catholic press seemed to think, and if the Catholic Church was, as the secular press kept charging, the only opponent, the Catholic thought he ought to be hearing about it more urgently—as, for example, by a sermon from the bishop himself in every parish in the diocese.

Catholic bishops do not approve of abortion; they did not in 1967. One should recall the timing of the Omnibus Bill containing the abortion legislation. 1967 was Centennial year; the Catholic Church had wholeheartedly joined in the celebration of Man and His World. Cardinal Léger was deeply involved in the preparation of the ecumenical Christian Pavilion at Expo, special collections for which were taken up in most parishes. (This collaboration even made it into the *Canadian Catechism*, Book V, *Building the New Earth*.) Then Justice Minister Pierre Trudeau was, as the press kept calling him, "a sophisticated Catholic intellectual." Furthermore, he was a *French Canadian* Catholic intellectual, which was better fashion. The bishops hoped for great unspecified things from Trudeau. They were caught by his glamour; he was the Canadian John Kennedy, in the line of charismatic political Catholics.

One should remember, too, that in 1967 the "spirit of Vatican II" was blowing strong, and the bishops' instincts were much cramped by it. They would rather not have had a relaxed abortion law, but they did not any longer know how to resist acceptably. Pius XII in 1948 had threatened Italians with excommunication if they voted for atheistic Communism, and he thus saved Italy from a Communist takeover. Probably everyone in the West approved his action then; it was unthinkable to do anything of the kind in Canada in 1967. In 1973, a recovering Canadian episcopate publicly restated the Canon Law that anyone who procures, performs, counsels, or undergoes an abortion is automatically excommunicated. They could not bring themselves to say this in 1967.

The story of how sophisticated, intellectual, Catholic Pierre Trudeau used the bishops' own statements against them in pushing through the abortion legislation is humiliating. Especially sickening is the fact that he got away with it. To this day, the ordinary Catholic accepts the picture of Trudeau as an enthusiastic pro-lifer, not responsible for the carnage that followed the law he personally rammed through Parliament.

From its inception, the Canadian bishops rightly concerned themselves with the proposed changes to the Criminal Code which together made up the Omnibus Bill (or the Bill des Fesses, as the French called it). In 1966, the Canadian Catholic Conference made a statement to the Commons Standing Committee on Health and Welfare on the subject of allowing the sale and advertisement of contraceptives. Their brief asked and answered two important questions: Are Christian (read "Catholic") legislators bound to vote for laws which forbid what the Church forbids? Are they bound to oppose laws which permit what the Church forbids? Justifying their reasoning by extensive reference to the Vatican II document, the *Church in the Modern World*, they answered *no* to both. "The Christian legislator must make his own decision." Making it clear that not opposing a change in the law did not imply approval of contraception, and urging that personal freedom be ensured in any government family planning program, they concluded: "We do not conceive it as our duty to oppose appropriate changes. . . . Indeed, we could easily envisage an active co-operation and even leadership on the part of lay Catholics to change a law which under present conditions they might well judge to be harmful to public order and the common good."

This statement was welcomed by J.M. Forrestall, MP

for Dartmouth-Halifax East as a "long-awaited and much-needed guideline to Catholic legislators like myself, who have been greatly perplexed over this problem for a long time."

Although the bishops specifically excluded the issue of abortion from their ruling about the duty of a legislator in a matter like contraception, their statement was quoted again and again when the question of liberalizing abortion came up. Early in 1967, the bishops were invited to present a brief on this matter as well, the date set for their hearing being December 19.

Suddenly, Trudeau moved to table the Omnibus Bill, containing the abortion legislation, before the recess. The Commons Standing Committee, informed of this, asked the unsuspecting bishops to postpone their appearance until January 22, and in the December 19 meeting voted an interim recommendation to legalize abortion. On December 21, Trudeau tabled his Bill, announcing to the press that evening that he was doing it on a recommendation of the Committee (which by now should have heard the Catholic Church's views) and that he anticipated no trouble in getting it through Parliament quickly after Christmas.

On December 22, a Canadian Press story describing the reaction to Trudeau's move as "generally favourable" quoted Father Edward Sheridan. S.J., a member of the bishops' committee that prepared the brief to Parliament, as being in agreement with what Trudeau had done. The story was not denied. There was no official reaction from the Canadian Catholic Conference. However, on Christmas Eve, Father John Mole, OMI, the information officer for the Catholic Hospital Association of Canada, preached a much-publicized sermon from the Church of the Resurrection in Ottawa, calling Trudeau's action in "putting the weight of his office on one side before the other side has been heard" dishonourable, and accusing him of wanting Canadians "to celebrate the massacre of the innocents by Herod rather than the birth of Christ."

Even though they were smarting under Trudeau's contemptuous dismissal, the bishops did not want to embarrass him. When episcopal pressure on the Catholic Hospital

Association did not persuade it to apologize to Trudeau, its vice-president, André Moisan, announced that Father Mole "had expressed a personal opinion," and he again stated the bishops' views on pluralism, legality, and morality: "*Dans notre société pluraliste, il est normal que les lois soient neutres. Autoriser une chose n'est pas l'imposer. Chacun est libre de se servir de cette autorisation ou de l'ignorer.*" (*Le Devoir*, January 3, 1968.) Obviously, Father Mole's days as information officer were numbered.

The bishops, rightly indignant about Trudeau's actions, refused to submit their brief after the Christmas recess. Instead, they issued a strong pastoral declaration calling abortion an "unspeakable crime," the words Vatican II had used about it. It had begun to dawn on some of them that Trudeau didn't give a damn what the Church thought and was simply using them to lend respectability to his legislation.

Nevertheless, on March 5, 1969, a delegation from the Canadian Catholic Conference did appear before the Standing Committee. It was led by Bishop de Roo and included three of the Winnipeg Statement *periti*, Naud, Sheridan, and Daly. All these men believed that the Catholic view and the view of the secular state were not in serious opposition, that Catholics should not try to make their views prevail in the name of Catholic moral order, but, through civility, reason, and dialogue, help the state make its decision. Said Bishop de Roo: "We are here on your invitation to try to help with a complex and difficult question. We come therefore in the spirit of dialogue. That is, we do not feel that we have the whole answer. We do not want to impose a particular point of view."

The Canadian Catholic Conference seemed to be suggesting that the Catholic view was just one among a number of acceptable solutions. Not so the Catholic Hospital Association. During an earlier appearance before the Committee, a delegation including Father Mole had established that there was a particular Catholic point of view, which held that human life is equally valuable at every stage of its development. The Committee recognized the uncompromising nature of this stand and pointed out that other Churches had lately retreated from it, and that therefore the Catholic Church was trying to impose its own morality on Canadian society in this particular instance.

Why, asked the Committee, during the Canadian Catholic Conference's appearance, if the bishops did not want to make their Catholic view on abortion prevail, did they not follow their own 1966 statement to Parliament on birth control. At that time they had allowed Catholics to co-operate in changing a law they judged harmful to the public good, even though many of them thought the change was against the law of God. Why might not Catholics feel equally free to weigh the evil to society of illegal abortions against the evil of liberalized abortion and decide for the latter?

Throughout the debate on abortion, the bishops' 1966 statement on contraception came back to haunt them. The Canadian Catholic Church, though believing divorce and artificial contraception to be against the law of God, did not oppose the liberalization of civil laws governing them. Why didn't it take the same position on abortion? Because, said the Canadian Catholic Conference delegation, liberalized abortion law would be against the public good. How did the Church know that? Why, if divorce and artificial birth control are against the law of God, are they not also against the common good? Did not this mean that the Church had decided there were no absolutes? That the Church might come to regard abortion in the same light as society regards divorce and birth control?

And if the Catholic legislator accepts that morality evolves, is he morally bound to oppose liberalized abortion? "In the final analysis," said Bishop de Roo, "he must follow the dictates of his conscience." He added that the legislator's conscience must be well informed, and he must legislate for the common good.

What emerged from the various debates on birth control, abortion, and the common good was that the only absolute is conscience, formed by evolving social opinion. The bishops, with their distinctions between private and public morality, morality and legality, and a Catholic's duty as a Catholic and as a citizen, unwittingly directed the large number of Catholics in the Liberal Party to obey their leader and vote for what they truly believed to be against the law of God. Again and again the Catholic MPs expressed their relief at having been so directed. By the time the Omnibus Bill came to a vote, Pierre Trudeau, now Prime Minister, once again quoting the bishops on freedom of conscience and the difference between legality and morality, refused to allow a conscience vote on the abortion legislation, making it a party issue. Only one Catholic Liberal voted against it.

Probably there was little St. Athanasius himself could have done to change the minds of the Parliamentary Committee, composed of such religious liberals as Stanley Knowles and Grace MacInnis. But the bishops might have made themselves clearer on what the right use of conscience is for the Catholic. When five years later they reminded us that "to follow one's conscience and to remain Catholic" one must obey the Church, it was far too late to have a delaying effect in the abortion issue. They might have explained to us why it was wrong in a pluralistic society for Catholics to seek to make their views prevail by various sorts of pressures, but why it was all right for small liberal pressure groups within the Canadian Medical and Bar Associations and the media to press relentlessly for a radical change in Western legality and morality, all the while charging the Catholic Church with obscurantism and bigotry. They might have had a few all-night sessions about whether they really want to divorce legality from morality.

But they did not, and we did not. When the abortion legislation was dropped with the end of the Pearson government the hierarchy made no move to make it an election issue. This is when, as Catholic citizens, we should have acted. We should have made it clear to our Catholic intellectual and Liberal hopefuls that we would vote against them if they continued their plans to force on us a package deal with abortion smuggled in. As it was, an official Catholic silence fell. Catholics were not led to battle. Trudeau, triumphant, had only Réal Caouette to deal with, than whom no more unsophisticated, old-fashioned, rural, pre-Vatican II Catholic exists. With wit and filibuster, Caouette and the Social Credit fought the legislation in Parliament. He got no support from the Catholic establishment—he was the wrong sort of French Canadian Catholic, and he was dismissed as an embarrassment by a Church come of age in the Just Society. But ordinary Catholics won't forget; at a massive anti-abortion rally on Parliament Hill in 1973, there was not a bishop nor any mention of one; however, English Catholics carried signs that said: "Thank you, Réal Caouette!"

Perhaps the most charitable explanation for the Canadian bishops' trailing behind the laity in this matter is that they took bad advice from people who told them that their visible presence in the abortion row would hurt the cause. That is what happened in England where Cardinal Heenan took the advice of MPs like Norman St. John Stevas and kept silent. The Cardinal bitterly regretted it, as he has said on a number of occasions, most recently in the *Catholic Herald*, February 2, 1973: "The Catholic Church deliberately made no pronouncement against the Abortion Bill because we were told by politicians that if Catholics did so it would confirm the humanist argument that only Catholics object to abortion. We all know what a terrible thing that abortion law is." He has said that he will not make the same "strategic mistake" about euthanasia.

The Canadian bishops perhaps made the same strategic mistake, though one wonders why they don't worry about their support hurting other controversial causes, like the grape boycott for instance, La Causa itself.

For on the very day, November 3, 1973, that the pro-life groups across Canada had arranged a national Festival of Life, with a march on Parliament Hill and a lobbying of MPs, a Cesar Chavez solidarity celebration and march, sponsored by Toronto's Archbishop Pocock, took place in St. Michael's Cathedral, Toronto. On the Hill, however, there was no official Catholic presence. But although there were not more than half a dozen priests, there were more than 2,500 laymen. The St. Michael's Boys' Choir turned up, complete with piano and blue with cold, and sang valiantly; there was one splendid stout French Cistercian in full ancient habit, who gave the whole thing a Canterbury Tales' flavour; one young French Canadian priest gave a beautiful, formal blessing; there were a couple of priests in civilian dress.

Recently a pro-Morgentaler speaker sneered at "all the Roman collars in evidence on the Hill." We found that too ironic—we had been raging at the scarcity of them. One of the Roman collars belonged to an Anglican, defying his Church's soft official stand; one to the priest who had delivered the Christmas Eve broadside.

Ironic, too, is the accusation that the Catholic Church pours money into the pro-life cause. The Canadian Catholic Conference turned down a formal request for help from the Alliance for Life, the umbrella organization for the pro-life groups. Several bishops, and more parish priests, contribute generously as individuals, but the abortion fight is run by the laity at great personal sacrifice. And that is a splendid grace from God on the laity and they rejoice in it.

I do not want to be unfair to Bishop de Roo, or to Bishop Emmett Carter, who did in 1968 urge Catholics to write to the government over the abortion issue. He, and the other Canadian bishops, have never wavered on the fact that abortion is, as they put in in their 1968 Pastoral, "an unspeakable crime."

Bishop de Roo did his sincere best before our secular Parliament. Had he spoken with the tongues of men and of angels he probably would have had no more success. Nevertheless, "we are here simply to bring our little contribution in the spirit of dialogue to help as best we can with the grave responsibility that rests upon your shoulders" may be found a little wanting in the true apostolic ring.

There are times, like this abortion issue, when a bishop must say to the men who govern his society: "If this embarrasses you, or hurts the Church politically, I am sorry; but I am an Apostle and I must tell you that what you are doing is against the law of God." He might quote Bishop Irurita of Barcelona, who, addressing the government on the institution of the Spanish Republic in 1931, said to it: "You are the ministers of a king who cannot abdicate, who cannot be dethroned because he was not enthroned by the votes of men. Men did not place the crown on his head, men will not take it off. Everything falls after a time . . . thrones collapse and royal crowns roll in the mud. Alone, the kingdom of Christ remains standing . . . because it is guaranteed by the word of God." Bishop Irurita was speaking out-of-season; in 1936, he was shot with the approval of both sides.

One gets very impatient with the curious embarrassment, or perhaps the fear of wounding other Churches who are soft on this issue, which keeps the Canadian hierarchy from carrying their convictions into the political scene. After all that has happened, I couldn't believe my eyes when I read that the Canadian Catholic Conference had joined the United, Anglican, Lutheran and Presbyterian Churches, the Canadian Division of the Rabbinical Assembly and the Canadian Council of Churches, in "a rare direct intervention into the political scene" (*Catholic Register*, July 6, 1974), to pin down candidates on their stand on "the rights of native peoples, equitable food distribution, political prisoners, trade, aid and development policies, Canada's response to political refugees and the moral responsibilities of governments," *and did not once refer to the abortion issue*! Their intervention, so near to the election, got saturation coverage in Canada. Catholic members of pro-life groups who had been working so hard to influence politicians towards a pro-life stand, gnashed their teeth at such an opportunity lost. They took it as a gratuitous slap in the face that the abortion issue was so pointedly omitted, probably because the United Church wouldn't have let it in.[1] We listened to the Canadian hierarchy's spokesman, Father Everett MacNeil, general secretary of the Canadian Catholic Conference, saying that "between December, 1972, and December, 1973, the price of hamburger jumped thirty-five per cent, wieners . . . thirty-seven per cent . . ." and how in Sri Lanka the cost of imports had risen very much. *Wieners? Sri Lanka?* What about the inflation of the abortion statistics, the drop in the price of Canadian human life?

"Father MacNeil told the *Register* that the joint presentation was the result of continuing dialogue among the churches on the moral aspects of governments and corporations." If that is the result, perhaps it is time the

Canadian Catholic Conference stopped dialoguing and took up unpopular unfashionable causes again.

The same ecumenical selectiveness among social issues continues. In St. Michael's Cathedral, Toronto, you can read a recently installed banner, a vast expensive stretch of linen that demands: "ARE WE PREPARED TO ASK OUR POLICY MAKERS TO: GIVE GRAIN FOR CREATION OF WORLD FOOD BANK . . ." on through five more demands to Parliament on behalf of farmers, workers, and poor nations. If there is anywhere in the Cathedral a mention of the scandal of abortion, it will be on some small notice stuck up in the vestibule by a lay Right to Life supporter.

Or you may add your name, along with Father Everett MacNeil's, Father Gregory Baum's and the usual others to a petition against nuclear weapons. The large expensive ad in the Toronto *Globe and Mail* was no doubt paid for in part by the Canadian Catholic Conference, under whose joint sponsorship it appeared. One waits to see the Canadian bishops draft a statement against abortion and invite the Canadian Council of Churches, Dr. Floyd Honey, the United Church, Gregory Baum and all the usual others to endorse it. One suspects that the bishops don't do this because they know quite well how unlikely support from ecumenical quarters would be.

Embracing unpopular causes may get a bishop eaten by lions, or, worse, jeered at by the liberal press. But it disturbs Catholics deeply to have the bishops trail in the abortion issue and lead in the "radical chic" cause of Cesar Chavez. Whatever Chavez' merits, a row between two American unions is unlikely to enlist Canadian Catholic sympathies. Bishop Emmett Carter recently publicly endorsed the boycott of Canadian supermarkets which sell non-Chavez groceries, on the grounds that "we are our brother's keeper." Several Toronto priests were arrested for picketing. Yet he advocated no boycott against doctors and hospitals who do large numbers of abortions, politicians who support it, newspapers who press for abortion on demand. Obviously, there are brothers and brothers. Bishop Carter assured us himself that he was "never one to espouse the more popular causes" and, further, that for him the nature of leadership "was well summed up many years ago in the *Daily Worker* by Peter Morin's 'A leader is a fellow who follows a cause.' " The layman can only ponder episcopal priorities and hope his leaders will choose the right cause to follow.

As far as the abortion issue is concerned, the laity cannot reproach the bishops for holding an unCatholic position, even though they may want bishops to act more energetically. With another of the issues in which many Catholics find themselves at odds with the bishops, the question of the Canadian Catechism, it was a different matter. The introduction of this catechism caused the first breach between conservative Catholics and the episcopacy, with the former charging that there was nothing Catholic about the catechism, and the latter ignoring all protest and forcing it upon every Catholic elementary school child in Canada.

The Canadian Catechism is usually known under the name of the first book in the series—*Come to The Father*. It is a monument to "the spirit of Vatican II" and the spirit of the secular world in the sixties. The anti-dogmatism and anti-intellectualism, the cheerful trust in technology, the belief that everything is changing rapidly for the better, the easy ecumenism, the rejection of the past, the hopeful humanism of the catechism, all belong very much to the last decade. The series looks very out-of-date and shabby already. It was written when Council euphoria still hung headily about. Bishop O'Byrne, still defending it in 1974, saw it as "perhaps the sole printed instrument throughout our country that did implement the spirit and theology of the Council."

The spirit, yes, as the *periti* bottled it for us; the theology, no. And that was the complaint of many parents and parish priests, and also of some at least of the bishops. Reverend Henri Routhier, retired Archbishop of Grouard-McLennan, and Reverend Leo Blais, former Bishop of St. Paul Diocese in Alberta, both published severe criticisms of the catechism, not however, until after their retirement. Complaining parents were ignored, or treated with contempt. To every parental charge that the catechism watered down or omitted essential Catholic doctrines, the stock answer was that the parents simply did not understand the new approach and had not imbibed the spirit of Vatican II. "What is there to understand?" enquired the parents, having ploughed through the thousands of vague long-winded pages. "And what about the *letter* of Vatican II?"

We could not understand how the bishops had ever let the catechism get past them. One of them told me that most bishops hadn't done more than glance at it. They had (unwisely) trusted the priests and laymen whom they had appointed to write it, and when it was published it would have been too embarrassing to admit that they had been hoodwinked. As Rosemary Ruether and other reformers have said, the area of children's catechetical materials was the one in which the reform, the "new consciousness," of the second reformation has had the most success. In Canada, oddly enough, the triumph was much more complete than in any other country. Not even in the United States, where Catholic liberals seem much more radical, have the new theologians managed to impose one radical new catechism on the whole of the country, and managed to get the bishops to forbid Catholic teachers to use any other. No such monopoly prevailed in pre-Vatican II education.

The catechism looks very good on the surface—charmingly illustrated, no expense spared. There are, in fact, a number of good things to be said for it, but, as in the case of the new liturgy, I do not feel the need to defend it. And for the same reason—the whole episcopacy and the huge powerful rich catechetical empire that has grown up around religious education since Vatican II have been doing so with great fervour for eight years.

The bad things about it have been listed and documented in several excellent studies by laymen and priests.[2] These found that the catechism does not teach the commandments of God, the precepts of the Church, the Sacramental Presence of Christ, original sin, the Immaculate Conception, the Virgin Birth, the assumption of Mary into heaven, the divinity of Christ, the infallibility of the Pope, the hierarchical structure of the Church, and most of the Sacraments. It does not present traditional Catholic teaching on the Sacrifice of the Mass. It manipulates scriptural texts in a shocking way to make them fit its own ideology. It is man-centred and humanistic.

The series is generally charged with omission rather than with heresy. But it seems fair to say that a Catholic catechism which does not in eight years mention the Presence of Jesus in the Blessed Sacrament in every Church does not believe He is there. These are strong charges. Parents, some teachers, and many parish priests, have gone on doggedly making them.

Finally, the bishops have set up a commission to evaluate the catechism. Conservative Catholics don't look to it with much hope since it is composed of some of the same people who wrote it. Moreover, Bishop Paul O'Byrne, head of the Canadian Catholic Conference's committee on religious education, again charging parents with lack of understanding and failure to grasp the spirit of Vatican II, recently stated firmly: "This is our book and we don't want any other. The basis of this series is that it really reflects the teaching role of the bishops." (*Catholic Register*, September 28, 1974.) If that is so, parents have little to expect from a revision. And, since Vatican II recognizes parents as "the primary and principal educators" of their children, Catholic parents may have to reconsider their allegiance to the Catholic school system. That is not meant as a threat, but as a lament.

It would be easier to deal with the bishops if they *were* villains, or Communists, or heretics. What infuriates Catholics is the bishops' committing themselves to some liberal reform and then in the face of a surge of rage (always unexpected) from the laity, either revoking it or saying they were misquoted. That is the line they took in the two other controversies I will discuss: their action over *Humanae Vitae*, and their synodal behaviour on the celibacy issue. When things got a little hotter than usual for the bishops, with both liberals and conservatives enthusiastically taking up the all-season sport of bishop-bashing, Bishop Emmett Carter wrote an Apologia in the *Catholic Register* (April 28, 1973). He felt that the humility of his "band of brothers" had prevented them from defending themselves, and was, he said, amazed by Catholic criticism of the bishops' actions, especially over the issues of *Humanae Vitae* and clerical celibacy. He defied anyone to find the slightest disloyalty to the Holy Father in either response. There had been, he claimed, "an incredible misreading" of the Bishops' Statement on *Humanae Vitae*. Anyone "who can read analytically" must see that the Winnipeg Statement had supported the Holy Father's teaching.

But how much of a misreading actually took place in these incidents Bishop Carter recalls? Let us take first the Canadian bishops' reaction to *Humanae Vitae*. For two months they said nothing official.[3] Then, in the last week of September, 1968, after a general assembly in Winnipeg, they issued a statement that said that Catholics who could not accept *Humanae Vitae*, or who accepted it but could not practise its teaching, "may be safely assured that whoever honestly chooses that course which seems right to him does so in good conscience." This open sesame was embedded in a good deal of pious talk about how unified in love and faith the Canadian bishops were with "the Bishop of Rome," but the central point was immediately clear to everyone, Catholic and non-Catholic. The Toronto *Globe and Mail* for September 28, 1968, reported: "The Roman Catholic Bishops of Canada yesterday recognized that Catholics could in good conscience practise birth control even while they upheld the Pope's condemnation of birth control as the general norm of conduct for the Catholic Church." And the *Western Catholic Reporter* said contentedly: " 'The issue' is now over in Canada. Catholics are free to use contraceptives if their informed conscience so prompts them. . . . The statement is the most liberal and positive interpretation of Pope Paul's encyclical . . . yet issued by any national hierarchy. It stands in direct opposition to the rigid, legalistic, interpretation [i.e., supporting the Pope] of the encyclical enforced by Patrick Cardinal O'Boyle, Archbishop of Washington, D.C." It was also sharply at variance with the "rigid, legalistic" (i.e., loyal) response of England, Ireland, East Germany, Mexico, Japan, Spain, Italy, India, and the whole Third World.

The bishops had spent the two months between the publication of the encyclical and their Winnipeg meeting (according to the *Western Catholic Reporter*[4] and Douglas Roche) listening: to the Catholic Physicians' Guild of Manitoba, to 351 members of the Western Canadian Conference of

Priests, to fifteen directors of departments within the Canadian Catholic Conference, to eighty-two Catholics in Dialogue, to the "all-important Canadian Institute of Theology," and to fifty-eight of the "Cream of Antigonish," all of whom disagreed violently with the encyclical. This listening apparently left them no choice, for as the *Western Catholic Reporter* remarked, "with the integrity of so many of the protestors irreproachable, the progressive bishops were able to discern the Holy Spirit speaking to them through the people." That sentence is the most perfect definition of the liberal elitist "spirit of Vatican II" mentality ever written.

The Winnipeg assembly praised itself for having used "Vatican II procedures" in the preparation of its statement on *Humanae Vitae*. As at the Council, a Theological Commission, under Bishops Remi de Roo of Victoria, B.C., and André Ouellette, Mont-Laurier, Quebec, prepared a schema for discussion by the plenary session of bishops. After several all-night sessions this commission was deadlocked: the liberal Bishop de Roo, who wished the statement to say simply that Catholics might follow their informed conscience, was opposed by his co-chairman, Bishop Ouellette. After an eight-to-three vote against Bishop de Roo's position, the draft statement sent to the bishops for discussion contained this declaration: "We are at one with the Holy Father in his teaching and pastoral concern about conjugal love and responsible parenthood." This statement was an unequivocal support of *Humanae Vitae*, no matter how many pastoral qualifications surrounded it. Before the Council this outcome would have been accepted as decisive. What intervened now was the new disorder created by Vatican II—the power of the *periti*.[5]

The *periti* objected to the proposed statement, with its full support of the traditional teaching. "We think it would be a pastoral disaster," they said, "inevitably dividing the bishops from pastors and people." And they prevailed. The bishops stormed at each other, and some even walked out. But when Bishop de Roo's position won by a single vote, other bishops fell in line. A two-thirds majority was achieved and the statement was amended to read:

We are in accord with the teaching of the Holy Father concerning the dignity of married life, and the necessity of a truly Christian relationship between conjugal love and responsible parenthood. We share the pastoral concern which has led him to offer counsel and direction in an area which, while controverted, could hardly be more important to human happiness.

Then followed the "good conscience" provision and the definition of an informed conscience as one in a "spirit of openness to the teaching of the Church."

The bishops, in releasing this Winnipeg Statement to the press, said that their interpretation "goes to the heart of the Pope's thought." "Perhaps it does," wrote Douglas Roche doubtfully. "But there is no mistaking the fact that the Canadians have taken a position distinct from the encyclical—as the encyclical was legalistically interpreted."

If, as Bishop Emmett Carter now says, the Winnipeg Statement "received an incredible misreading," why did a fair number of bishops, in a position to read it properly, vote and rage against it? And why did they go home to speak against it in their dioceses, reiterating the Pope's teaching, saying, as Archbishop Carney did, that the statement needed "clarification"? Why was a statement worked on by so many experts allowed to be so widely misleading? Why, if the statement were just another in the series of hierarchical endorsements of *Humanae Vitae*, did Bishop Alexander Carter cite it as "an historic moment for the Church in Canada"? Either the Winnipeg Statement meant what everyone took it to mean at the time, and what, on the fifth anniversary of the encyclical, the *Catholic Register* still thought it meant; or, as Bishop Emmett Carter charges, only he and the *periti* "can read analytically."

It should be said, in defence of some of the Canadian bishops, that it takes a wily man indeed to outsmart the liberal stranglehold on every issue. Witness the liberal ruthlessness of this incident at the Winnipeg meeting, as reported in the *Western Catholic Reporter,* October 3, 1968: "The progressive nature of the statement would not have been possible without the strong chairmanship of Bishop Alexander Carter... who is steeped in the meaning and process of the Conciliar life. As late as Friday morning, when a bishop made a last-ditch effort on the floor to water down the statement, Bishop Carter firmly ruled him out of order." That is exactly what happened to Cardinal Ottaviani at the Council, and that is how consensus is achieved. Nevertheless, brave bishop, gallant last-ditch effort. But last-ditch bishops ought then to proceed to identify themselves to the laity. We could do a lot for each other. The risk of giving scandal to the laity would surely be no greater than it is under the present consensocracy.

From its publication, the Winnipeg Statement embarrassed the bishops. Six months later, a "clarifying statement" was made "to make sure that such interpretations would have no other basis than a false assumption" (Bishop Emmett Carter). This had no effect. Finally, after five years of bishops defying anyone to find the slightest disloyalty to the Holy Father in the Statement, and laity charging the bishops with Protestantising and dereliction of the Catholic faith, the bishops mended their fences in the only possible face-saving way. On December 12, 1973, they issued a tough, traditional statement on the formation of conscience, which repeated the earlier teaching that a Catholic must follow his conscience, *but*, and it was a large Catholic *But*:

> To follow one's conscience and to *remain a Catholic* one must take into account first and foremost the teaching of the magisterium [Pope and bishops teaching in unity]. When doubt arises due to a conflict of "my" view and those of the magisterium the presumption of truth lies on the part of the magisterium. "In matters of faith and morals, the bishops speak in the name of Christ and the faithful are to accept their teaching and adhere to it with a religious assent of soul. This religious submission of will and of mind must be shown in a special way to the authentic teaching of the Roman Pontiff, even when he is not speaking *ex cathedra*." (Lumen Gentium, 25) And this must be carefully distinguished from the teaching of in-

dividual theologians or individual priests, however intelligent or persuasive.

The Canadian bishops, twice quoting the Petrine Promise on the indefectibility of the Church, regretfully moved out from behind the leadership of the "Cream of Antigonish" and other assorted *periti*.

The bishops' behaviour over *Humanae Vitae* provided the most serious point of disagreement with the conservative laity, for it was a matter of irreformable teaching. The issue of clerical celibacy raised the hackles of the laity for a different reason. A celibate clergy is a Catholic discipline that conceivably could be changed, by a decision of the united magisterium. What the laity particularly objected to in the Canadian bishops' handling of this matter at the synod was the attempt to deny that they had advocated change.

Bishop Emmett Carter in his defence of the bishops says again that they were misquoted and misunderstood:

> The world tends to accept what it wants to accept. The celibacy issue was even more curious. In fact, it was incredible. Because here was no question of subtlety or carefully analyzed statements. The blunt fact is that in spite of a report of a committee of theologians urging a somewhat different stance, the Canadian Bishops by an overwhelming vote endorsed the Pope's position on maintaining the traditional discipline on celibacy for candidates to the priesthood. The bishop-delegates to the Synod . . . were mandated to uphold that position. And they did so faithfully.

That passage says that the Canadian delegation at the 1971 synod did not urge any change in the Roman Catholic Church's traditional rule of a celibate clergy. This layman is not going to say that a bishop is not telling the truth. Perhaps the best way around my Catholic block is to suggest that he has left something out of his account. For while the Canadian bishops at their pre-synod meeting in the last week of September 1971 voted that men who were already candidates to the priesthood must accept celibacy, they also voted, by sixty-one to twelve, that they would recommend to the synod that married men should be permitted to become priests, not thereafter being bound by the celibacy rule. Bishop Alexander Carter at a press conference at the end of this meeting said, according to the *Western Catholic Reporter*, that "he would be surprised if the Synod did not come to the same recommendation as the Canadian Bishops, for the Canadian Church is in the mainstream of progressive development." Bishop William Power of Antigonish (home of the Cream), the incoming president of the Canadian Catholic Conference, asked whether this step opened the door to future changes in the Church's law of celibacy, such as allowing candidates for the priesthood to choose between marriage and celibacy both before and after ordination, answered: "I guess so."

The bishops' own communications office released a series of taped reports from Canadian bishops at the synod to be used at sermon time in parish churches. I heard Bishop Alexander Carter say that celibacy had served an historical purpose, but that its time was past, a married clergy was a good idea whose time had come, and he confidently predicted that the synod would agree with him. The Toronto *Globe and Mail*, in a November 9, 1971, editorial, headed CANADA'S REFORMING BISHOPS, had this to say:

> This presentation of Canada as epitomizing the progressive factor at the Synod was not accidental. The Canadian delegation had carried the battle for reform in a number of important areas. Most Reverend Alexander Carter, Bishop of Sault Ste. Marie, was, with Leo Cardinal Suenens of Belgium, one of the most urgent in recommending a change in church law with regard to priestly celibacy. The Synod said a massive no. But significantly the vote on a recommendation to permit the ordination of married men while counting 107 nays, also counted the startling number of 87 yeas, which is considered to have left the door open for papal initiatives toward the ordination of men already married in cases of serious shortages of priests.

The *Globe* also praised Cardinal Flahiff of Winnipeg for raising the question of a "possible role for women in the ministry or better, in the ministries, of the Church." "It is a very important act of leadership which Canada's bishops have given the Church and the world," approved the *Globe*.

Observers at the synod noted how vigorously the Canadian bishops lobbied for support for their position, which Cardinal Conway of Armagh called the domino theory and which Bishop Power had already admitted to be so intended. Yet Bishop Emmett Carter insists that the Canadian bishops upheld the traditional discipline on celibacy. *Someone* is being misquoted.

It may seem unfair to judge the entire Canadian Catholic Conference of 115 bishops by the activities of a handful of prominent prelates. But that is what one must do as long as they all allow themselves to be moved against tradition and their own instincts by the forms of democracy, as if a two-thirds majority makes anything true. Individual bishops in private conversation with Catholics will admit to serious reservations with conference decisions, but they feel bound to keep public silence until retirement, as in the case of Bishops Routhier and Blais on the catechism. Or as in the case of Archbishop Dwyer formerly of Portland, Oregon, who, when he was finally unbound from the consensocracy of the U.S. Bishops' Conference, produced the most eloquent and scathing attack on the new liturgy that I have read.

Nor is it correct to suggest that all Canadian bishops are equally distrusted by the laity. Bishop Ryan of Hamilton, Ontario, retired recently to the great sorrow of most of his flock. Until his retirement, he had run one of the most conservative dioceses in Canada. He had provided for the regular celebration of the Novus Ordo Mass in Latin, forbade Communion in the hand, resisted the new catechetical ideology as much as he could, refused to allow sexologist Father Lafreniere into his diocese, and chivalrously saluted the Blessed Virgin publicly every year. One can only feel the deepest sympathy with such a great bishop, seeing his whole life's work in jeopardy in the uncertain times ahead for the Canadian Church. Also, many Catholics remember with gratitude their bishop's charity to them during hard economic times, in the matter of jobs and financial assistance. Most Catholics can reproach their bishops principally for their present invisibility and timidity.

Perhaps because of the pressure within the Canadian Catholic Conference from the majority of conservative bishops, there is lately a discernible moving to the right among the English Canadian bishops. In 1974, the Toronto Archdiocese set up a natural family planning clinic to instruct Catholics and non-Catholics in safe, licit, natural methods of birth control. Late, but better than never. They also at the same time choked off the funds of that committee of the National Catholic Council of Social Services which uncleverly went on with the old line and wanted to set up family planning centres which would provide information on all methods of birth control. The committee had to go out of existence. The Toronto Archdiocese likewise pledged itself and its resources to help any woman who felt driven to the expedient of abortion through social difficulties. And there is, as mentioned, the review of the catechism.

The main reason for this move to the right is that the sort of progressivism that the bishops embraced, the liberalism of the administrative layer immediately below them, the academics, the Catholic civil service, lay and clerical, has turned out to be a busted flush. The dissenters leave the priesthood, the Church, or both, one by one—Bonnike, Bader, Phil Berrigan, de Rosa, Pfuertner, Hebblethwaite, John Cogley, Valsecchi. The reforms empty the churches and seminaries. Even the great Conciliar liberal prelates, Léger and Suenens, seem to have lost heart. Whether exasperated by the slowness of the reform process, or disillusioned by the failure of what seemed to them so hopeful, they have abandoned the liberal mainstream. Léger has retired to the fierce Catholic simplicity of a mission to lepers. Suenens has become the leading figure in the Catholic charismatic movement. Incredibly, the 1974 Charismatic Conference at Notre Dame University, Indiana, found this man, so fierce at the Council about Catholic pieties and disciplines, lending his prestige to a faith-healing service during which, as the *Nation-*

al Catholic Register reported, more cures were performed in an hour than in a hundred years at Lourdes. (A barker led the proceedings, shouting, "A lady in a red dress has been cured of breast cancer . . ." etc.) Tell it not in Gath.

Bishops in normal times are very pragmatic men. Perhaps they have simply decided that their future is more secure with conservatives, bad-tempered though they may be, for the time. Because the conservative Catholic, much as he dislikes his bishop, will always insist on that bishop's necessity and authority. He knows that "No bishop, no Church." The bishop knows too, that it is easier to lead people temperamentally disposed towards obedience and respect for lawful authority.

The shift to the right does not seem to hold for French bishops, who are either more foolhardy or more optimistic about human nature. The French Canadian Church is prostrate, after introducing every possible European innovation. Yet progressive French Canadian prelates go on progressing. In March 1974, Archbishop Plourde of Ottawa announced that when one of his parishes loses its priest, he will turn the running of it over to the laity, who will, when necessary, marry, baptize, conduct the liturgy, and distribute Holy Communion. And this not in mission lands but in *Ottawa*, which is full of underworked religious priests with the time to be mischievously involved in adult re-education and sex education. At this late date, Archbishop Plourde must be able to predict what may happen in his priestless parishes. The parish councils, liberal to a man, will arrange adventurous liturgies that the conservatives won't be caught dead at. Traditionalists will turn up with a "Massing Priest" and have the Tridentine Mass. One group will lock out the other and get an injunction forbidding use of the Church. Both groups will go to law over possession of the property of the parish. The bulk of the laity will abandon Catholic practices. It will be very instructive.

For better or worse, Catholics are stuck with their bishops and bishops with their Catholics. On the principle of forgiving trespasses so that we may be forgiven, laymen will have to forgive the bishops for dithering over *Humanae Vitae*, abortion, and celibacy, even though the laity hasn't committed those particular trespasses. We must be grateful that in auspicious times, the bishops saw to it that we were given the Catholic faith, indelibly. It was they who made us confident and intransigent. Now, in an inauspicious time, we will defend the faith in the way they taught us, until they are feeling fit and apostolic again.

CHAPTER 7

THE CREAM OF ANTIGONISH

Marriage and conjugal love are by their nature ordained toward the begetting and educating of children.

GAUDIUM ET SPES. THE CHURCH IN THE MODERN WORLD.

VATICAN COUNCIL II

It is very likely that the religious event that will be remembered by posterity as the most important of the twentieth century will be, not the Second Vatican Council, nor the Papacy of (Good) Pope John XXIII, but the issuing of Pope Paul VI's encyclical letter on the regulation of birth, *Humanae Vitae*. If there is anything left at all in a hundred years of what we now call Western civilization, *Humanae Vitae* will have helped to preserve it. If by our present abuse of technology, our social engineering enthusiasms, our callousness towards human life unborn and ailing, our society will have been reduced to ruins and slavery, any man who still believes that human beings are "free and responsible collaborators of God the Creator" in "His design of love" will have nothing but the support of this beautiful statement to hold by. Its affirmation of the sacredness of the union between man and woman and God and creation will endure through all the Dark Ages, even though priests who should be teaching it now, while there is time, are flirtatiously "into" Marx and Marcuse and Mao with their students. I could not find one Catholic high school where this latest Catholic teaching on marriage has managed to find a place among the courses on sex education and popsicle-Marxism. Still, in a hundred years, as now, *Humanae Vitae* will be "a sign of contradiction," a symbol of the Catholic perception of the world, a rallying point for the loyal and a take-off point for dissenters.

Its publication on July 29, 1968, brought about the first great post-Conciliar challenge to papal authority. It was inevitable that a confrontation would come as soon as an issue worth an all-out trial of strength presented itself. If one accepts the Holy Ghost's guidance of the Church, one will not think it coincidental that *Humanae Vitae* was the test case, reiterating as it did the Church's teaching on the transmission of life, her right to so teach, and the duty of the Catholic conscience to accept it. Probably *Humanae Vitae* would have sparked little opposition if it had appeared in 1960, and the Pope is often blamed for hesitating for several years between the final report of his commission and the issuing of the encyclical, particularly since it was well known that the commission had come out overwhelmingly in favour of a change in existing Church law on birth control, and dozens of theologians writing in both Catholic and secular press were confidently predicting change. The delay added to the confusion of the laity, and there seems no doubt that many Catholics began to practise artificial birth control in anticipation of a relaxed ruling. In the absence of papal direction, they took the opinion of such reputable Catholic figures as Archbishop Thomas Roberts, s.j., and Redemptorist theologian Bernard Häring, who, writing during the Council years, shattered the theological and episcopal consensus on contraception.

However, though the Pope's delay exacerbated the conflict, a speedy reaction to his commission's conclusions would not have prevented controversy unless he had agreed with those in favour of change. "The spirit of Vatican II" was not going to agree with the confident statement in *Humanae Vitae* that "no believer will wish to deny that the teaching authority of the Church is competent to interpret even the natural moral law. It is, in fact, indisputable." The theologians, quite out of control since Vatican II, were claiming superior competence and authority to interpret both, and a showdown over primacy was as necessary as it was inevitable. That it *was* an encounter between papal authority and the "spirit of Vatican II" was made clear by the virtual passing over of the bishops in the quarrel. Pope John had reserved for papal decision the delicate issues of priestly celibacy and birth control, appointing a pontifical commission to study the latter, and forbidding Conciliar discussion of either. Pope Paul had expanded this commission from six members to nearly sixty, announcing that, with its help, "We hope soon to say our word, supported by the light of human science," which many people not surprisingly took to mean that he meant to permit use of the Pill. During the fourth Council Session, though the bishops worried at the edges of the question, they could not discuss it openly, and were, furthermore, forced to include in Schema 13, *The Church in the Modern World*, four papal amendments, though they soothed their hurt pride by changing the wording. For example, for the suggested "contraceptive practices," the bishops substituted "illicit practices against human generation," as part of the Schema's list of evils that wound marriage. They saw their formula as "open-ended."[2] The Pope closed it in *Humanae Vitae*. Also, just as *Humanae Vitae* had by-passed collegiality, so the revolt against it by-passed the bishops. It was the theologians who revolted; the bishops' conferences, with soft spots like Canada, rallied behind the papal pronouncement.

Likewise, the bulk of the laity was unconsulted, and there is nothing the matter with that if you accept, as most Catholics do, the Church's claim to competence and authority. Even by 1968, most of the laity would probably have accepted, even if disobeying, *Humanae Vitae*, with the exception of that handful of "literate Catholics," who, as John Lynch assured us, "at the present time can recite a litany of authorities, whether real or alleged, who have publicly expressed such doubts." In Canada, both the middle-of-the-road *Catholic Register*, which expressed the official line, and the lively, liberal, independent *Western Catholic Reporter* were initially prepared to say,

"Well, that's that." "Undoubtedly," said the *Register* on August 3, 1968, "the Holy Father's authoritative statement, even if not dogmatic, requires of the loyal Catholic full religious assent"; and on August 17, "It remains only for us as loyal Catholics to accept his ruling, coming as it does from the supreme teaching authority." And the *Western Catholic Reporter*, somewhat surprisingly, echoed the *Register*: "Unless we acknowledge the right of the Pope to teach this way and the duty of Catholics to follow his teaching until such time as it may be changed, we forfeit the primacy of the Pope, a primacy which Christ instituted in his selection of Peter." Interesting, too, was the *Western Catholic Reporter's* appeal to the Petrine Promise, something conspicuously absent from liberal papers from that moment.

The encyclical was "a relief," said the president of the Catholic Women's League, while a typical letter to the editor of the *Register*, August 31, rejoiced that "a new Moses has arisen in our midst in the person of Pope Paul."

Though both papers later changed their tune when Canadian liberals took courage from the American dissenters, the first response was to accept and obey. When the Catholic Women's League president hailed the encyclical as a relief, she was speaking for that large group of laity, lower middle class, parish and family oriented, not university educated, who are far more representative of Catholic society in general than Joanne Dewart, Laura Sabia, or the St. Joan's Alliance of Catholic feminists. Most of the laity were not expecting change and were shocked and surprised by the well-organized vehemence of the outburst within the Church itself.

The secular reaction *was* expected and did not worry Catholics much, though it was difficult to see why non-Catholics were so wrought up about it. When the encyclical was released, I was living on the sixth floor of an enormous apartment building. Getting into and out of it with four small children, one in a pram and one in a stroller, was an energetic exercise, and on that July evening I was extricating my brood from the elevator as the newspapers were being delivered. We clamoured along behind the newspaperboy, and as he dropped his papers by each door, we saw this headline— POPE BANS

PILL—in the type used to declare war. The Catholic Woman's League lady was right; I felt a mild relief, but not enough curiosity to bother to pick up a paper before we reached our own door. However, as each of our neighbours came out one by one, stooped, and read the headline, they *all* made a rebuking comment of some sort. (We were the only practising Catholics in that section.) The United Church minister who lived opposite popped out and said how sad and bad it was for ecumenism, population, Christianity, and the baseball scores. And my husband and I kept saying in surprise, "But what were you expecting?" Could they have imagined that the Church was going to change something she had been teaching without interruption for nearly two thousand years?

But if the laity didn't anticipate the row, the Pope did. The letter said:

> It can be foreseen that this teaching will perhaps not be easily received by all. Too numerous are those voices—amplified by the modern means of propaganda—which are contrary to the voice of the Church. To tell the truth, the Church is not surprised, to be made, like her divine founder, 'a sign of contradiction,' yet she does not because of this cease to proclaim with humble firmness the entire moral law, both natural and evangelical. Of such laws the Church was not the author, nor consequently can she be their arbiter; she is only their depositary and their interpreter, without ever being able to declare to be licit that which is not so by reason of its intimate and unchangeable opposition to the true good of man.

The Pope was expecting trouble, and it did not take long to develop. Its centre was the Catholic University of America in Washington, and its instigator Father Charles E. Curran. On the day of the publication of the encyclical, he managed to get a copy from Rome, then rounded up some theologian friends and prepared a dissenting statement. In an attempt to get as many "name" signatories as possible, Curran and his friends spent all night on the phone. The tally by morning was eighty-seven, Bernard Häring being the prize catch of the phone-a-thon. Curran called a press conference at the Mayflower Hotel in Washington and released the statement which asserted the right, and duty, of the theologians to dissent from the "authoritative, non-infallible" teaching of *Humanae Vitae*. It criticized the encyclical for not recognizing the new view of the Church "suggested" by Vatican II, for not involving bishops and laity in the decision-making (*this* from theologians who had strained every nerve to beat the bishops to a pronouncement), and for using natural law arguments which these theologians had decided were inadequate. Their verdict: "As Roman Catholic theologians, conscious of our duty and limitations, we conclude that spouses may responsibly decide according to their conscience that artificial contraception in some circumstances is permissible and indeed necessary to preserve and foster the values and the sacredness of marriage." This manifesto was later circulated widely and attracted over 600 signatures, though most of them were of unknowns.

Almost as shocking as the incitement of the laity to disobedience was the staggering impropriety of the manner of carrying out the protest, the excited all-night telephone session, and triumphalist tone of the press conference, and the sheer *indecorum* of the whole affair. Canon law does not, admittedly, rule that theologians must have good manners, but academic propriety might have been expected to operate in a matter as delicate and likely to give scandal as a dissent from an encyclical of such solemnity and importance. Men who since Vatican II had been proclaiming so self-righteously the freedom and excellence of their scholarship might have waited a little for study and reflection. As it was, many of these scholar-theologians allowed their names to be put to a statement condemning a papal letter they had not even *read*. They behaved through that night less with the prayerfulness and caution of Catholic scholars than with the excited foolishness of sophomores on a panty raid. The layman's mind boggles.

Naturally, Canada, following as usual the American lead, was influenced by the Mayflower Statement. The green light was given to dissent. In a signed editorial in the *Catholic Register*, August 10, 1968, P.A.G. McKay wrote, "The encyclical, quite frankly, disappointed and distressed me personally." Romeo Maione, director of the Canadian Catholic Organization for Development and Peace, agreed: "My preoccupation, too, is our relationship with other Churches. We're swimming against the current now." The Canadian leaders of the Christian Family Movement, which a few years before had been so devoted to implementing Church teaching on marriage, signed a protest about *Humanae Vitae* addressed to Archbishop Pocock of Toronto. Catholics in Dialogue, a group based in St. Michael's College, Toronto, wrote the *Register* disagreeing with the early editorial that Catholics must loyally accept Pope Paul's ruling, had a phone campaign to enlist support, and placed ads in the three Toronto daily newspapers and on radio and television to find out what people thought of *Humanae Vitae*. These asked:

1. Do you think that the recent papal encyclical has settled the question of contraception for all faithful Catholics?
2. Do you think it is possible for a Catholic to practise contraception in good conscience?
3. Are you satisfied with the way in which the Church's teaching authority has been used in dealing with the question of contraception?

They announced that 94 per cent of those replying voted No to the first question, 80 per cent voted Yes to the second, 91 per cent voted No to the third. This group's activities, and those of a similiar group in Ottawa, are credited with having a decisive effect on the Canadian bishops' Winnipeg Statement on *Humanae Vitae* (if anything connected with the Canadian bishops can be said to be "decisive").

The ordinary Catholic, who still cherished the sentimental notion that Catholic newspapers and colleges were bastions of orthodoxy, was alarmed by this hasty dissent. Many Catholics wavered; they were humble enough to feel that it was impudent to accept something against which so many confident, educated voices were raised. It was a bad time for faithfully practising Catholics. Their sacrifice and loyalty began to look foolish in their own eyes.

Catholics recovered though, and began to fight back. At that moment, the liberal-conservative split became irreparable, and the conservative counter-revolution took heart. It was at this time that Catholic organizations like Credo and Catholics United for the Faith were formed to give moral support to bishops like McNulty of Buffalo, or Cardinal O'Boyle of Washington, who suspended priests who taught against *Humanae Vitae*. Clear at last as to the issues at stake in the post-Conciliar struggle, these groups and others like them addressed themselves from this time, with evangelical vigour, to restoring doctrinal, liturgical, and educational order.

One of the things that helped *this* conservative Catholic get her second wind was the remark of a Canadian bishop on a group of dissenting professors. Some fifty-eight of them at St. Francis Xavier University in Antigonish, Nova Scotia, had issued a protest against the encyclical. Now St. Francis Xavier used to be a moral power in eastern Canada, a vigorous, loyal Catholic university, which genuinely, and successfully, tried to carry out the social teachings of the Church long before other colleges got into the act. Everybody respected it, so naturally the bishop was impressed by dissent from such a quarter. He wouldn't take it lightly, he said, because these men were "the Cream of Antigonish."

It was one of those ice-cold, reality-restoring remarks, like "But the Emperor has no clothes on!" Perspective was suddenly restored, one's sense of humour reactivated. *The Cream of Antigonish.*

It is not likely that one Catholic in a hundred thousand, whether or not he accepts the encyclical, can give solid theological and philosophical reasons for doing so. Most cannot tell whether, or why, the Pope's or the theologians' arguments are correct. Though I absolutely accept the encyclical, I cannot convincingly answer the question why a temporal barrier to conception is allowable and a spatial barrier forbidden. That is, I am convinced by the papal arguments for the licitness of taking advantage of the natural, God-willed infertile period in a woman's monthly cycle to space or prevent children for serious reasons. To take advantage of this temporal barrier is to co-operate with God's arrangements. This, as Professor

William Marra of Fordham University puts it, is within the scope of creaturehood. It is to act as steward, rather than as master, of the process of uniting with God to create a new man with an immortal soul. Whereas, to interpose a mechanical or chemical barrier is to assume dominion over a power that is not ours alone.

This seems to me to be beautiful and right. I realize, however, that some Catholics do not find this argument convincing, and that, ultimately, it is a question of an argument from authority. I am predisposed to accept it because of its source; dissenters are likewise predisposed to reject it for the same reason. This was made quite clear in Canada by the statement of one of the St. Michael's College protestors, Albert Wingell, assistant professor of theology: "The main concern of our group was the possibility that people and priests might accept without question the view of the *Register* editorial that the papal encyclical deserved complete and unquestioning obedience."[1]

Most Catholics do not have the competence to defend or reject *Humanae Vitae*. They don't need it, either —philosophical and theological analysis is the theologians' business. Catholics who accept the dissenters' conclusions do not do so because they are overpowered by the irresistible logic of the case presented. They want to practise artificial birth control, they want to feel comfortable about it, so they appeal to a sympathetic authority. The question for the non-theologian is not whether the Pope uses natural law arguments correctly, or rides roughshod over collegiality. The question is whether one is going to line up behind the Pope and two thousand years of Christian tradition, or behind the "Cream of Antigonish." As far as conservative Catholics are concerned, there is no contest.

Much has been made by dissenters to the encyclical of the fact that *Humanae Vitae* was not proclaimed as an *infallible* document, that is, as an *ex cathedra* declaration of the Pope with the force of dogma. Because it was not thus defined, they seem to be saying, it may be rejected without penalty. However, the Church does not teach that Catholics need obey only infallible pronouncements. Technically, papal infallibility did not exist until 1870, when Vatican II defined it, yet obviously, infallible dogmas (doctrines one must accept to be a Catholic) existed before then. The Second Vatican Council, in its *Dogmatic Constitution on the Church*, stated what sort of obedience Catholics owe to non-infallible teachings:

> This religious submission of mind and will must be shown in a special way to the authentic magisterium of the *Roman Pontiff even when he is not speaking ex cathedra*; that is, it must be shown in such a way that *his supreme magisterium is acknowledged with reverence, the judgements made by him are sincerely adhered to*, according to his manifest mind and will [which] . . . may be known either from the character of the documents, from his frequent repetition of the same doctrine, or from his manner of speaking. (My italics.)

Humanae Vitae, though not proclaimed as an infallible dogma, had all the requirements to be "sincerely adhered to." It was a document of the most solemn character, repeating a teaching the Church has always, with a continuity and unanimity achieved by few other doctrines, proclaimed—that is, the intrinsic evil of artificial contraception, the sin of irreverence committed by the assumption of control over the process of the creation of human life.

Therefore, Catholics who accept *Humanae Vitae* do not do so simply out of blind Catholic patriotism—"the Pope right or wrong." They are convinced that his teaching is correct on this issue because of its weight and continuity. They think that to decide whether his argumentation is perfect or not is out of their province. They believe that the Holy Ghost would not allow his teaching to be wrong in a matter of this gravity. Many conservatives, remembering the Pope's early billing as a liberal, believe that he would have changed the teaching if he could, but that he physically could not—they conjure up a picture of the Pope with sweat on his brow trying to write, "Yes, you may!" while the Holy Ghost holds his pen hand so that out comes in firm strokes "No, you may not!"

Not being a theologian, I have nothing new to add to the

arguments for *Humanae Vitae*. There are, however, several non-theological points to be made about the case against it. John T. Noonan, who wrote the definitive book on the history of the Church's teaching on contraception, charges *Humanae Vitae's* arguments with "internal inconsistency." People who accept the encyclical may be willing to agree with Noonan, yet consider this inconsistency irrelevant. Naturally, one would like the Pope's arguments to be watertight, but if they are not, it need not affect the truth of what he is saying. To make use of a secular analogy—a city councillor might say: "Mugging and raping are wrong because they dry up evening business in the city centre and keep away tourists." The inadequacy of his reasons does not mean that his conclusion that mugging and raping are immoral is not true. Accepting the truth of *Humanae Vitae* though not its methodology does not involve a Catholic in a retreat from reason. If watertight arguments are necessary to preserve an eternal truth, the Catholic trusts that the Holy Ghost will make them available to Catholic theologians.

Another argument of the same kind is that *Humanae Vitae* is bad law because it is widely disobeyed. A liberal Catholic will quote a poll finding that 70 per cent of Catholics practise artificial birth control; this, they say, shows that the Church's laws on marriage are wrong and that Catholics *think* they are wrong. But a poll-finding indicates only that a number of Catholics are breaking a Church law, not how many of them are doing so because they think the *law* is wrong, therefore leaving them guiltless, and how many still admit the law is right, and *they* are being disobedient. Some Catholics commit fornication and adultery. Probably 100 per cent of Catholics tell lies. Yet it is unlikely that many of them will want to say that the sixth and eighth commandments are examples of bad laws. This "bad law" argument is often used by secular liberals, when they are urging the liberalization of drug or abortion laws. Since they have never, to my knowledge, used it about traffic laws, which 100 per cent of Catholics *and* pagans break, one may entertain the possibility that it is valid only for sins and crimes the liberal wants to commit with a restful conscience.

A further source of dissent with *Humanae Vitae* is the

Pope's argument from the natural law. It satisfies me, and though I am not equipped to defend it on Curran's or Häring's level, I am sure the Pope has an infinitely greater chance of being right than Häring or Curran. He certainly has a much greater claim to be assumed correct by the laity. One of their objections that is accessible to criticism is the one that sneers that if, as the Pope says, artificial contraception is against the natural law, isn't it odd that only Catholics can see this? Apart from the fact that Catholics believe that "the teaching authority of the Church is competent to interpret even the natural moral law," whether non-Catholics believe or not, is it really true that *only* Catholics believe that it is intrinsically wrong to separate the unitive from the procreative aspect of marriage?

Until fairly recently, 1930 to be exact, all Christians professed to believe it. In August of that year, the Anglican Church, in the *Lambeth Declaration*, gave its grudging approval of birth control, recommending abstinence as the "primary and obvious method," and condemning conception-control when it was undertaken for "motives of selfishness, luxury or mere convenience." (Partly as a reaction to this move, Pius XII issued on the last day of the same year the great encyclical on Christian marriage, *Casti Connubii*.) The Orthodox Churches, so long without an ecumenical council, are divided on the issue. The traditional teaching is the same as the Roman Catholic. The Pope got important support from influential Orthodox Patriarch Athenagoras of Constantinople, who said: "I agree absolutely with the Pope [who] could not have spoken otherwise. Holding the Gospel in his hand, he seeks to protect the morals as well as the interests and the existence of the nations." Metropolitan Chrysostom of Piraeus said: "While I am by no means a lover of the papacy, I feel the need to commend the encyclical." Metropolitan Nikodim of Leningrad agreed.

Hundreds of millions of Asians and Africans, Hindus and Moslems, are still strongly opposed to birth control, to the despair of international agencies, who are trying for the best of Western motives to curb Third World fertility.[3] Catholic liberals, who appeal to Third World wisdom on so much else, are silent on this manifestation of it. And every guidance counsellor, social worker, and doctor is acquainted with the maddening young women who come to them pregnant, who knew all about contraception, but who felt that to use it was unloving and unnatural. They usually, nowadays, are murderously unwilling to accept the consequences of their instinctive response, but that is a different matter. All the expensive energies of public school sex education programs, planned parenthood apostles, population control experts, drug company salesmen, cannot force the young to separate the unitive from the procreative in sex. It is the primary urge that defeats them, not the ignorance or the laziness of the young.

The instinctive response to the impulse to co-operate with the Creator is a part of the working of the natural law that must be obvious not only to Catholics. Even a city garden in the spring, bursting with delighted procreative energy, proclaims that the primary purpose of sexual union is procreation. A pair of sparrows, single-minded, selfless, directed by instinct through their tiny roles in creation, gives a most poignant lesson on the nature and purpose of conjugal love. We have it from Christ that men are of more worth than many sparrows, though one sometimes wonders why. We are both blessed and cursed with the gift of reason; God expects us to use it to raise marriage from a purely biological to a spiritual level. "The Church," remarks *Humanae Vitae*, "is the first to praise and recommend the intervention of intelligence in a function which so closely associates the rational creature with his Creator; but she affirms that this must be done with respect for the order established by God." Therefore, the Church, looking out into the cosmic garden, where it is always spring, tells us that it is *orderly* to take advantage of "the natural rhythm immanent in the generative functions," and *against order* to introduce something which is "intrinsically disorder" into the marriage act. But original sin makes it difficult for man to appreciate the "great beneficent realities" of the divine law. It is harder for fallen human beings than for sparrows to make "visible . . . the holiness and sweetness of the law which unites the mutual love of husband and wife with their cooperation with the love of God, the author of human life."

Though it took a papal order, Vatican II reasserted the traditional Catholic view of the nature and purpose of marriage. After a good deal of wrangling, the bishops produced a typical Council compromise paragraph which either (a) reaffirms the hierarchy of ends in marriage, or (b) denies it, according as to whether it is interpreted by (a) Cardinal Browne, or (b) Gregory Baum. It says:

> Marriage and conjugal love are by their nature ordained toward the begetting and educating of children. Children are really the supreme gift of marriage and contribute very substantially to the welfare of their parents. The God Himself Who said, "It is not good for man to be alone" (Gen. 2:18) and "Who made man from the beginning male and female" (Matt. 19:4), wishing to share with man a certain special participation in His own creative work, blessed male and female, saying: "Increase and multiply" (Gen. I:28). Hence, while not making the other purposes of matrimony of less account, the true practice of conjugal love, and the whole meaning of the family life which results from it, have this aim: that the couple be ready with stout hearts to cooperate with the love of the Creator and the Savior, Who through them will enlarge and enrich His own family day by day. Parents should regard as their proper mission the task of transmitting human life and educating those to whom it has been transmitted.[4]

It went on to add that Catholics might limit the number of their children, for reasons and by methods permitted by the Church, and it praised the "gallant," who trusted in God completely, accepting "even a relatively large family" generously.

Many theologians objected that this traditional teaching put an impossible strain on Catholic marriage, and that God does not ask the impossible of His children. Even bishops said this as if it were axiomatic, as they expressed their anguished concern over the sufferings of the laity. That argument irritated this layman very much, as a working of the liberal élitist mentality that has so taken over the Church. There was no attempt to explain why the teaching should have suddenly become intolerably hard to bear in the last ten years, nor why the laity of the late twentieth century should be frailer than those countless millions of the Church Militant who practised it faithfully throughout the Christian centuries. Nor did any cleric think twice about using the cliché that God does not ask the impossible of man, and wonder if perhaps He *does* come fairly close to asking it. *Does* not God ask the impossible of Christians? Was Christ joking when He told us to be perfect as our Heavenly Father is perfect? To love our neighbour as ourselves? To sell all and give to the poor and follow Him? The Apostles were so appalled by the difficulty of the Christian teaching on marriage that they glumly said to Christ that it would be better not to marry at all. One must remember that the Christian revelation has always seemed, to the Greeks, madness.

The truth is that liberals (whether they are bishops like those who pressed for change at the Council—Léger, Alfrink, Suenens— or parish priests) do not expect nobility from the laity. They do not think it is necessary or possible for the ordinary Catholics to be "gallant" in the sacrifices involved in Christian marriage, or anywhere else (with the possible exception of the collection plate).

This condescending indulgence is very different from love. Liberals hate the laity; they think there are too many of them in the Church, that they hold back its evolution by their primitive theology. When you love someone, you do not expect him to be weak and ungallant. You expect, or at least hope, that he will be brave and clever and not settle for second best. It is not love when a liberal priest tries to remove from the layman's life the Cross of Christ.

Since most clerical objectors to *Humanae Vitae* were not only celibate but also rarely in touch with the laity through Confession, it is perhaps understandable that none of them suggested that the very qualities necessary to observe the

Church's teaching—unselfishness, self-discipline, trust in God, respect for women, an eschatological orientation of married life—might be just those necessary to preserve the stability of Christian marriage. Certainly, they could find little evidence to support their claims that the practice of artificial birth control made marriage happier and less strenuous. The Christian churches that permit it, and the secular world in general, show every day a rising percentage of divorce, desertion, abortion, and infidelity. They did not entertain the possibility that Catholic marriage was relatively free from these ills precisely *because* of the difficulty and sacrifice involved in it.

Of a piece with the liberal clergy's condescension to the laity is the stupefying callousness towards women in particular implicit in their championing of artificial methods of birth control, especially of the Pill. Liberal priests love the Pill, partly because originally they hoped that it would provide a way out of urging sacrifice upon the laity, latterly because they are infected with their society's despairing hope that technology will solve all mankind's problems, Nothing, not even a "folk" Mass, infuriates me more than men pushing the Pill, and I am simply not responsible for my behaviour when that man is a priest. For the Pill represents all that is most hateful about modern society—the enslavement of human life by technology, the treatment of fertility as a disease, the sanctioned rampant selfishness of sex without responsibility. The Pill, as both the Pope and some wiser Women's Libbers have pointed out, makes possible, even laudable, the most appalling male selfishness. The Pill frees a man even from the restraint that fear of the consequences exerted over him. It has removed society's concern for the protection of young innocent women. As any high-school counsellor will admit, it is now open season on girls. If I were a member of the Women's Liberation Movement, I would stump the country against it.

In the first conversation I ever had about the Pill, more than ten years ago, I expressed my horror that men would so casually wage chemical warfare on the women they said they loved, and drew that rejoinder that was so annoying at the time: "Oh, that's because you're a Catholic." But yes, I guess it *is* because I'm a Catholic. *Catholic* husbands and wives are expected to engage in mutual restraint as they do in mutual satisfaction. *Catholic* men should think it a sin to place their lover under the most hideous daily bondage to technology. *Catholic* women are too spirtually liberated to submit to it. Neither will Catholic women, when a male contraceptive chemical is developed, expect their husbands to use it.

That's the way it used to be before the theologians liberated us. Not any more. Lately, I was a member of a marriage panel (an experience I do not intend to repeat), as part of the preparation for marriage of young people. The idea was that half a dozen experienced married couples would share their insights with the aspirants to holy matrimony. Inevitably, birth control came up, and one after the other, several dozen young Catholic men remarked casually: "Oh, she's going on the Pill," or words to that effect, their faces full of self-congratulation, their girls smiling embarrassedly beside them. I longed to say to them what I was thinking: "You miserable young S.O.B.s!" The English Protestant beside me muttered: "Bounders!" And so they were, S.O.B. bounders. I confined myself to a hot little speech, supported by a chemist on the panel, on the danger and untriedness of the Pill, and the selfishness of forcing young wives to chance it. One young man accused me of being a Women's Libber. The girls said nothing. The sad truth is that they, as well as their husbands-to-be, had been indoctrinated with the liberal dogma that science and technology are about to give man control over all creation, that he will be able to produce happiness and eliminate misery chemically, thus making irrelevant concepts like right and wrong, moral and immoral, natural and unnatural.

It is not surprising that the Women's Liberation Movement, itself an end-product of the technological revolution, should have got hold of the wrong end of the stick that they are using to beat society with. It is not by getting further into the grips of technology (Enovid's Pill to prevent conception, Upjohn's abortifacient potions to kill the product of a failure of the first technological step) that women, or men, will free themselves. The Church knows this, which is why, in this latter day, it is also not surprising to find her standing between women (and men) and the life-denying side of technology, to defend them. The Church has always fought the domination by science of human life, and much credit she has had for her pains. And now, ironically, just as the secular world is beginning to turn in horror from technology's savagery, members of the Church have taken up its praise, with that comic time-lag that affects Catholic liberals. "My brother Bishops," begged Cardinal Suenens, in urging the Church to embrace birth control technology, "let us avoid a new Galileo case. One is enough." Not at all. Better a thousand Galileo cases than one tragic capitulation to technology about the principle of generation or the purpose of human life. For once given in to, the process of enslavement is irreversible; if you once deliver control of the springs of life to technology there is nowhere to go but down into the Pit.

Reflect, counselled *Humanae Vitae*, on the consequences of methods of artificial birth control: the general lowering of moral standards, the danger of a man losing respect for a woman, "no longer caring for her physical and psychological equilibrium," the placing of a dangerous weapon in the state's hands, the possibility of forcible population control and genetic engineering. The overwhelming evidence is that the Pope's fears were justified, and the theologians' hopes ill-founded.

Even in the case of the argument against *Humanae Vitae* that carried most weight in the secular media, the demographic argument that the Pope's stand would result in a population explosion that would soon starve the world, Catholic liberals positions were quickly made untenable by the same scientific experts they had so obediently followed. When the Pope, appearing at the United Nations, urged the developed countries of the world to place more food on the table of the hungry nations rather than to try to cut down on the number of guests, a chorus of abuse from both Catholic and non-Catholic sources was raised aginst him. The huge rich American corporation Xerox (which goes in for a different sort of reproduction) even put into mass distribution in the public schools a booklet entitled *Population Control: Whose Right To Life?* containing this moderate statement: "The world must quickly come to realize that Pope Paul VI has sanctioned the deaths of countless numbers of human beings with his misguided and immoral encyclical." It went on to enquire whether the Catholic Church should be brought to an international tribunal for crimes against humanity.[5] At that time, accepted wisdom had it that the underdeveloped nations of the world, groaning under the burden of ignorance and large families, needed only birth control information and devices for a drastic drop in their birth rate to begin at once.

Yet, the most recent sociological and demographic research suggests that the Pope's solution was the correct scientific one. If there can be a redistribution of goods so as to raise the standard of living in poor, overpopulated countries, demographers now say, the population will decrease naturally. Poor people want large families. Many children make life easier—they carry water, they pump and push and pull all the devices that run automatically for us, they support parents who can no longer work.

"The whole of the population problem," writes Peter Adamson in the special World Population Year issue of the *New Internationalist*, published by Oxfam, "has been plagued by the almost subconscious assumption that poor people have many children because they don't know any better; that they would be happier and better off if they had less children; that 'we' know what's best for 'them.' The most important lesson of the last ten years has been that poor people are not stupid, that they make rational decisions about their lives; and that large families are usually an intelligent response to economic circumstances." And the conclusion of Oxfam and the Overseas Development Council, and other sources of thinking on the Third World? "A development policy and a population policy are one and the same thing, and the key to both is more equal distribution of income." Therefore, wrote the Toronto *Star* (August 21, 1974) in editorial comment on Adamson's article, "the unpopular truth that will have to be faced . . . by the World Population Conference" is that "if the rich countries are to combat world overpopulation effectively, they will have to rely less on preaching the virtues of the Pill and more on helping poor countries improve their economic position." The Pope said it more eloquently.

It turns out that in this instance Catholic liberals would

have done better to have supported the Pope than to have followed Xerox and company. Moreover, it almost makes one feel sorry for them, because in supporting the huge, mainly American effort (Rockefeller Foundation, World Bank via McNamara, etc.) to make the Third World practise birth control, they roused the suspicions and lost the friendship of the people in the world they most admire—Third World, and black American activists. For, if they meet on nothing else, the Pope, black radicals in America and Africa, Marxists in China and Latin America, and Third World bishops speak with one voice on the question of the affluent countries forcing contraception upon them, as for example, by the World Bank's tying loans to population control. "Genocide," they call it. They charge that for the rich countries population control in the Third World is a substitute for controlling their own overconsumption of the world's resources. It is less traumatic for the affluent nations to spend heavily on lowering population elsewhere than to consume less and pay more for what they use. At the same time that Catholic theologians were condemning the Pope for callousness, militant blacks in Cleveland were burning down the family planning centre in the black district and voting down government funds for planned parenthood clinics in Pittsburgh.

The Pope, reiterating the common teaching of the Church, knew that there are no new human problems, just the same old ones inherited from Adam—the greed that causes affluent countries and affluent people in poor countries to take more than their share; the vanity that makes the Congo keep a huge army, that maintains Air Mali; the corruption that cheats the poor in Pakistan. The same old problems to be solved in the same old way—by the imitation of Christ.

However, if all the criticism of *Humanae Vitae* faded away, and if all the theologians recanted, the Church's teaching on Catholic marriage would still be difficult to obey, still have for many a bitter taste of the Cross of Christ. *Humanae Vitae* recognizes the great sacrifice often demanded by its teaching, and looks sympathetically on Catholics who cannot follow it. Probably the Pope longed to be able as, Archbishop

Roberts was, to suggest the *Lambeth Declaration*'s compromise—contraception if necessary but not necessarily contraception. But the Church in proclaiming a law has to make it bind universally; though circumstances alter cases, they cannot alter laws. The Church does not see any way out of this, because she is neither author nor arbiter of the laws she proclaims. Therefore, *Humanae Vitae* could only urge Catholics who fail in observance to go to Confession, seek strength from Holy Communion, and not to give up trying.

This counsel presumably applies to Catholics who "do not wish to deny the teaching authority of the Church," want to obey the Church's law, and are sorry when they break it. Otherwise, the Church would, as critics charge, be suggesting bad Confessions (that is, where the penitent is without a firm purpose of amendment). It does not apply to Catholics who deny the authority of the Church in this matter, though one gathers that many of these do receive the Sacraments.

If a Catholic accepts the authority of the encyclical yet intends to persist in what he believes is sin, it is difficult to see how he could in good faith receive the Sacraments. If he rejects the Church's authority in a matter of this fundamental importance, it is difficult to see why he has not put himself out of that body of believers who accept the Church's competence and indefectibility.

The Church, to be coherent with herself, has to continue to teach that the love of husband and wife is the image of the love of Christ for the Church, with the same demands—sacrifice unto death—and the same reward—resurrection unto life. The difficulty of the law is matched by the sweetness of it. "This is a great mystery," says *Humanae Vitae*, echoing St. Paul. For the Catholic, the wedding ring is not the symbol of a fetter to an unnatural bondage, but an image of the pattern of redemption—the circle of natural life, promise, and expectation, birth and maturity, death and rebirth, and the infinity of supernatural eternal life—the Annunciation, the Nativity, the Passion, the Resurrection.

"The image of the earthly shall bear the image of the heavenly." (I Corinthians, 15)

The best approach to the truth proclaimed by *Humanae Vitae* is through the imagination, through poetry rather than through logic. The Bible is full of such insight, in the metaphors of vine and fruit, seed and harvest, birds and their young ones, or when it speaks of the marriage of Christ and the Church and makes that a model for the love of husband and wife. I recognize the efficacy of this sort of approach every year when the Easter symbols come round again, and also at Christmas, in the carols which surely are as inspired as the Bible. How can the fruitful purpose of creation and its parallel with the redemptive Mystery, or the sharp sweetness of obedience to the natural law, be more exquisitely conveyed than in these lines from "The Holly and the Ivy":

> The holly bears a berry as red as any blood,
> And Mary bore sweet Jesus Christ,
> To do poor sinners good.
>
> The holly bears a prickle as sharp as any thorn,
> And Mary bore sweet Jesus Christ,
> On Christmas day in the morn.

CHAPTER 8

MURDER IN THE CATHEDRAL PART ONE

They have taken away my Lord and I know not where they have laid Him.

The Catholic Church has always taken its liturgy very seriously, for, as the Second Vatican Council declared, "the liturgy is the summit toward which the activity of the Church is directed . . . it is the font from which all her power flows. . . . For the liturgy, 'through which the work of our redemption is accomplished,' . . . is the outstanding means whereby the faithful may express in their lives, and manifest to others, the mystery of Christ and the real nature of the true Church."

The liturgy—the Sacrifice of Mass and the administration of the Seven Sacraments—was fixed in 1570 for the entire Roman Catholic world by the Council of Trent. The reform of the liturgy by the Council was, therefore, undertaken only for "particularly cogent reasons." The Council laid down principles for reform, and it appointed a Consilium to carry out its intentions.

The New Mass made its debut at the Synod of Bishops in Rome in 1967. The Consilium's "normative Mass" got a less than enthusiastic reception—of the 187 bishops who voted on it, forty-three voted against it and sixty-two had serious reservations. Yet the Novus Ordo Missae, promulgated by Pope Paul by the Apostolic Constitution *Missale Romanum* in

April 1969 was the same "normative Mass," uninfluenced by synodal misgivings. On September 25 of the same year, a serious attempt was made to convince the Pope of its doctrinal shortcomings. This was the *Ottaviani Intervention*, a study by a group of theologians and liturgists accompanied by a personal appeal to the Pope by Cardinal Ottaviani to reconsider the Novus Ordo and "not to deprive us of the possibility of continuing to have recourse to the fruitful integrity" of the historic Mass, the Trent Mass.

The *Intervention* charged that the Novus Ordo had "every possibility of satisfying the most Modernistic of Protestants." It noted that the General Instruction did not mention the Real Presence, or the reality of the sacrifice, or the priest's sacramental function, or the intrinsic value of the Eucharistic Sacrifice with or without congregation. The Novus Ordo itself was no longer a propitiatory sacrifice for the remission of sins. There was in it no clear distinction between people and priest. The disappearance of prayers to the Holy Trinity made the Mass no longer a sacrifice of praise. Built-in reverences for the Real Presence, genuflections, purifications, had disappeared. The three new Canons had no special place for the Memento of the dead, and no named Apostles. Most serious of all, the running together of the words of the Consecration with the *anamnesis* ("Do this in memory of me") presented the Mass as simply a memorial. The *Intervention* did not charge the New Rite with invalidity, but said it was full of "insinuations" which would end by destroying doctrine and eucharistic piety.

Such a remonstrance from such a source had to be taken seriously. The Pope postponed for two years the mandatory introduction of the New Mass and caused the General Introduction to be extensively revised. Once again, the doctrines of the Real Presence and transubstantiation were reaffirmed; "memorial" became "sacrifice and paschal banquet" and the priest was recognized as the one "who does what Christ did." But the New Mass itself was not changed and became mandatory in Advent 1971.[1]

Nobody liked the new liturgy. The radical Catholic left disliked it as much as the schismatic right, and both have ignored it from the beginning. Its aesthetic and doctrinal shortcomings have been pointed out by the most diverse critics—Cardinal Ottaviani, Malachi Martin, Evelyn Waugh, Brian Moore, James Hitchcock, Malcolm Muggeridge. Conservative William Buckley and lapsed conservative Garry Wills can agree about the failure of the liturgical reform when they have stopped agreeing about anything else Catholic. Groaned Buckley about a Sunday Mass in New York: "I am reminded, as I am every Sunday, of what an aesthetic ordeal it has become, going to Mass, ever since the advent of the new liturgy: the dread vernacular, the conscripted responses—to think that the architects of this profanation claim to have done it *for us*!"[2]

"There is practically no liturgy worthy of the name today in the Catholic Church," said a man who ought to know, Father Louis Bouyer, the French Oratorian whose life work has been the study of the liturgy and the campaign for its renewal, whose *Life and Liturgy* and *Rite and Man* were the most popular and influential works in the liturgical movement of the forties and fifties. Obviously, a scholar like Bouyer is better equipped to justify his disgust and disappointment over this outcome of a movement that was so hopeful and confident than the ordinary layman whose participation in the prayer of the Church boils down to one hour on Sundays. The layman can't authoritatively attack liturgical errors and gaucheries; he can only recognize whether the new liturgy satisfies his mind and heart the way the old did, whether he can pray and enjoy as he once did.

One of the new liturgy's few Catholic defenders was the radical theologian Hans Küng. Indeed, his enthusiasm for it, expressed in his book on the first session of the Second Vatican Council which appeared in 1965, was for many of us an early *ad hominem* argument against the new liturgy; anything Küng liked so much was bound to be unacceptable to most Catholics. In *The Changing Church: Reflections on the Progress of the Second Vatican Council*, Küng listed his dissatisfactions with the Council: too many long-winded speeches by Italian bishops, all those time-consuming private Masses the delegates insisted on saying, the fact that his pet German biblical scholars had unaccountably not been invited.[3] The only action of the Council that won his whole-hearted praise was its speedy approval of the Constitution on the Sacred Liturgy. This document embodied every hope of the reformers, he rejoiced. It represented "a true return to the origins, a huge step forward in meeting those special concerns of Protestants: . . . a closer approximation of the Mass to the supper of Jesus, a renewed hearing of the word of God intelligibly proclaimed, active worship by the whole priestly people, adaptation of the Liturgy to different peoples."

Küng was writing after the document on the liturgy had been approved but before the Consilium for the carrying out of the Council's intentions had issued its norms. So, though we were alarmed by his interpretation of the *Constitution*, it was possible to believe that he had misread the mind of the Church. For, given Küng's avowed liberal Protestant attitudes, if he were right about what the Council had intended, then the results of the four reforms he had hailed should be these: the de-emphasis of the sacrificial element in the Mass and of the Real Presence, with the Mass becoming simply a memorial of the Last Supper; the abolition of Latin and with it the idea, which the Latin language symbolized, of a universality transcending nationality; a downgrading of the hierarchical nature of the Church; the decentralization of the Church and the increasing diversity and autonomy of national churches. Since this is indeed what has happened, it would seem that in satisfying the special concerns of Protestants, we have come close to ending Roman Catholicism, because in the area of eucharistic theology, Protestant and Catholic concerns are antithetical.

Orthodox Catholics were predisposed to trust the Council and mistrust Küng. But though one could read Küng on the Council in 1965, it was several years later before the final versions of the documents of Vatican II were available to the general public. By then the Consilium had more or less finished its revision of the liturgy and the concrete results had affected Catholics at the parish level. By the time study of the *Constitution on the Sacred Liturgy* revealed discrepancies between the apparent intentions of Vatican II and the published labours of the Consilium, it was already too late to present an orderly and considered case against the destruction of the liturgy.

The traditionalists arrived late and disorganized for the liturgical battle. The same reproach certainly cannot be levelled at the liturgical reformers who first prepared the schema, the working paper, for the *Constitution* on the liturgy to be debated by Vatican II, and then staffed the Consilium ad exequandam Constitutionem de Sacra Liturgia, the committee appointed by the Council to carry out its proposed reforms. The chief of the reformers was Monsignor (now Archbishop) Bugnini. He was Secretary of Pope Pius XII's Liturgical Commission in the days when the first liturgical changes, like the shortening of the fast before Holy Communion and the reform of the Holy Week services, were introduced. He was secretary both of the group that drew up the schema and also of the Consilium which devised the New Ordo. He is the man chiefly responsible for the New Mass and is therefore the foremost *bête noire* of the people who dislike the new liturgy.

Traditionalists vent on Bugnini all the fury that they cannot bring themselves to vent on the Pope. They will never admit to any disagreement with any of Pope Paul's actions or omissions. So though they point out that the Pope always says Mass in Latin, and wants the restoration of Latin and Gregorian Chant in the Church, yet they do not ask why he has given his permission to bishops' conferences to bring about the disappearance of both throughout the world. They will tell how strongly opposed the Pope is to Communion in the hand, and how at Papal Masses that practice is forbidden, yet they do not blame him for allowing it to become the rule in other countries. When the Pope, having allowed Communion in the hand, gave as his reason the fact that it had already become widespread through the disobedience of individual priests, they did not cry out that this sort of procedure is an invitation to lawlessness.

The Pope—and this is not meant as a reproach—is sacrosanct for conservatives. They see any questioning of his judgement as an attack on the whole doctrinal structure of Catholicism. Therefore, although they very much dislike most of the liturgical reforms, which could not have passed if Pope Paul had not approved them, they find themselves faced with the dilemma of having to admit either that the Pope erred, or that he was too weak to resist the destroyers. They choose the latter course, in practice, though they do not say "weak." They say "misinformed," or "ill-served," or "too charitable." The form is to blame Bugnini and Cardinal Lercaro for all liturgical misadventures and to pretend that the Pope does not know what is happening and that if he did he would act at once to restore order and orthodoxy.

But attempts to separate the Pope from the liturgical reform won't work. He is ultimately responsible for the state of the liturgy today, partly through an inability to restrain his subordinates, but also through a deep commitment to a renewal of the liturgy that would stress participation by the faithful and strip the liturgy of all ornateness. He explained early and often what he wanted—a clear, simple, unadorned vocal prayer that would shake people awake from the long sleep of centuries and keep them from going to sleep again. He wanted an end to the liturgy as a performance with the priest as the single actor and the people looking on silently if appreciatively. He wanted participation by the whole priestly people in the public worship of the Church. Participation, participation, that was the great tool to bring about a liturgical renewal that would renew the whole Christian position in the world. Ten years later, he is still singing its virtues, even though in practice it has proven something less than renewing. The Pope has said these things often enough to be taken seriously, and the fact that the Monsignor Bugnini of the Council is now an Archbishop and the Secretary of the Curial Congregation for Divine Worship would suggest that the Pope approves of his efforts, that Bugnini is simply, as the National Catholic News Service described him, "a quiet, methodical man . . . doing what the Pope has ordered."

It is one thing, however, to say that the Pope agreed with the reform of the liturgy, and another to charge him, as some now do, with heretical intentions, to claim that he meant to de-Catholicize the Mass. Some of the people who now most dislike the new liturgy approved warmly of the *Constitution on the Sacred Liturgy*. Küng was not the only important figure to comment favourably on it, though he seems to have been the one who most clearly understood the implications of the document and the nature of the coming reform. Perhaps that is because he is a German and it was the German school of liturgical theory that most strongly influenced the pre-Conciliar commission that drew up the document on the liturgy. At any rate, the respected elderly English liturgist J.D. Crichton[4] and the French liturgist Louis Bouyer[5] both wrote approvingly on the *Constitution* in the years between its promulgation and the actual appearance of the New Mass. "A window is opened on to a future the end of which no man can see," wrote Crichton. "We can hail the reform of the liturgy, which will make it more understandable to simple folk," he said, with that blend of condescension and naiveté which characterizes his whole school of liturgical reform. He quotes with approval this passage from the Constitution—"there must be no innovations unless the good of the Church genuinely and certainly requires them"—and adds a comment which, given the delicacy of what the Church was about in the liturgical reform and the danger of its going wrong, makes one reflect on who actually are "the simple folk" of whom he spoke. "This is wise and sane," wrote Crichton, "and removes the possibility of merely fantastic changes *of which nowadays however there would seem to be little danger.*" (My italics.)

And Bouyer, one of the most eloquent of the advocates of liturgical reform, approved on the whole of what the *Constitution* had ordered. In particular, he praised its "consecration" of the teaching of Dom Casel of the famous Maria-Laach monastery, which included these features—the revived understanding of the liturgy as "the *whole* Paschal Mystery of Christ," with an overdue correction of the great emphasis (unhealthy, according to Bouyer) on the Presence in the Mass; a turning back to an earlier, objective kind of worship, different from the medieval and post-Tridentine subjective worship; and a return to a Patristic understanding of the liturgy, rooted in Scripture. Bouyer was not as keen on the vernacular as Küng and Crichton, but his reasons were cultural, rather than devotional or theological. Apart from that,

Bouyer and Crichton praised in the reform the same elements which pleased Küng.

Küng, Crichton, and Schillebeeckx didn't share Bouyer's concern about the break with the cultural past of the West that would result from the disappearance of Latin. It is amazing how blithely Crichton can remark that "different accents and emphases will solidify into different 'uses' or 'observances,'" and not even feel a premonitory shiver. Even Bouyer was not quite as trusting as that.

For the ordinary Catholic, those years were a puzzling time. One pored over those commentaries, and told oneself that scholars of the calibre of Bouyer and Crichton would certainly be the first to detect any suspicious aspects in the *Constitution* and its applications, and one waited in the most painful apprehension for the results of the Conciliar reform.

It did not soothe Catholic fears to read that Protestants hailed the Conciliar reform, seeing in it, rightly or wrongly, the same implications Küng saw. "The Constitution on the Sacred Liturgy is so revolutionary, and so essential to an understanding of what is happening within the whole ecumenical movement, that it is important to know what it actually says," wrote a Protestant clergyman in a commentary on Vatican II.[6] As part of his explanation of the liturgical reform, he quoted at length from a work by Dr. Vilmos Vajta, Director of the Lutheran Federation of Inter-Confessional Research in Geneva:

> We have seen which aspects of the liturgy are now being newly emphasized: the renewal of the use of Scripture in the liturgy, the proclamation of the mighty acts of God, the active participation of the faithful in worship on the basis of their baptism and especially the restoration of Communion in the eucharistic celebration. As every heir of the Reformation will easily see, these are precisely the elements which are fundamental for evangelical liturgical life. For this we must rejoice. Nevertheless, our analysis of the dogmatic presuppositions of the Constitution has shown that this kind of liturgical practice poses problems

for Catholic dogmatics which have not yet been solved. This is evident in regard to the relation between the once-and-for-all sacrifice on the cross and the celebration of the present Lord in the eucharistic memorial. It is also evident in the failure to recognize clearly that the participation of the faithful in liturgical acts is a sharing through faith in God's saving acts. The Gospel requires us to continue to raise these questions. But now they have become questions which are directed at Catholic dogmatics by liturgical practice itself as this has been legislated by the Constitution.

The possibility that the faithful might consider liturgical reform to be a change in doctrine naturally occurred to some of the Fathers at the Council, in particular to Cardinal Ottaviani. During the debate on the liturgy at the Council, Ottaviani, warning against the multitude of changes urged by earlier speakers, asked: "Are these Fathers planning a revolution?"[7]

It was a good question. Ottaviani warned that too many changes would "scandalize the faithful." ("An old Holy Office saw," says Rynne.) Again, Ottaviani was right. The frenzy of liturgical change after 1964 *did* scandalize the faithful and goes on doing so.

The problems raised by Ottaviani and others, and those raised by detached Protestant observers after it, naturally lead one to ask some very important questions about the intentions of the *Constitution on the Sacred Liturgy*. Was the *Constitution* a Trojan Horse introduced into the Church? Or was it a sound and Catholic program for a moderate and necessary reform? If the latter, then what happened between cup and lip, why the continuing, the growing, liturgical and doctrinal chaos?

First of all, it is fruitless to speculate on the motives of the men who drew up the *Constitution*. Whatever one might suspect, one has only the promulgated document as evidence, and that is moderate, cautious, and contains much of the traditional teaching on the Eucharist as well as some of the happier insights of great modern liturgical scholars.

The most important element in the document was the insistence that the liturgy was the whole "Paschal Mystery" of Christ, not only the Crucifixion but the Incarnation and the Resurrection and the entire redemptive process throughout time. This concept was not new to Catholic belief, but in the past the emphasis on the Victim, the Oblation, had often tended to overshadow the other elements. The *Constitution* quotes the Preface for Easter: "Dying, He destroyed our death, rising, He restored our Life," and when the New Mass was written, this passage, with "Lord Jesus, come in glory" added, became one of the three "acclamations" to be recited aloud immediately after the Consecration. Another, to stress the same full teaching, is "Christ has died. Christ has risen. Christ will come again." They are one of the good things about the New Mass.

But the *Constitution*'s instruction on the nature of the Paschal Mystery is not very profound. Protestant writers are correct in remarking that the relation between the historical Sacrifice of the Cross and the continuing presence of Christ in the Church is left unclear despite the fact that it is central to Catholic belief. At the beginning of Chapter II of the liturgical constitution, there is a statement of traditional Catholic doctrine about the Mass. "At the Last Supper, on the night when He was betrayed, our Saviour instituted the eucharistic sacrifice of His Body and Blood. He did this in order to perpetuate the Sacrifice of the Cross throughout the centuries until He should come again." This repeats the Catholic belief that the Mass is one and the same as the Sacrifice on Calvary, with Christ offering Himself on the altar in an unbloody manner under the eucharistic species. Therefore, the Mass is more than a reverent memorial; it is a real and continuing Sacrifice. The *Constitution* speaks of "the divine sacrifice of the eucharist" with its "Immaculate Victim."

That is clear and familiar. Also familiar is the *Constitution*'s emphasis on the Mass as a meal. This, also, is where Protestant emphasis is placed. Catholics, too, have long prayed: "*O Sacrum Convivium* . . .", "O sacred Banquet . . ." But Catholics believe that eating the Lord's Supper is not merely joining with others in celebrating the memory of an act of sacrificial love. The Mass is a *sacrificial* meal. The Victim is offered, dies, and is eaten, perpetually, at every Mass and Eucharist.

The *Constitution*, having made a statement of Catholic dogma on the Mass, then goes on to explain that the Mass is only a part of the Paschal Mystery. Through Baptism as well, men "are plunged into the Paschal Mystery of Christ." Also, Christ is redemptively present in the other Sacraments, in the word of Scripture, and in the Christian assembly, "when the Church prays and sings." No Catholic will want to dispute the *Constitution's* insistence that the redemptive presence of Christs extends into every action of the Christian's life in the Church.

All this is admirable and beautiful. The *Constitution* becomes vague when it neglects to consider the question of the Real Presence of Christ in the eucharistic species—the consecrated Bread and Wine. "He is present not only in the person of his minister," we are instructed, "but especially under the eucharistic species." But the *Constitution* does not go on to explain in what *special* way Christ is present in the eucharistic species, nor whether His Presence there is different in any way from His Presence in the person of the celebrating priest or in the praying congregation. In other words, the *Constitution* scrupulously avoids the central Catholic doctrine of "transubstantiation," that when the priest says the words of consecration over the bread and wine at Mass, they become the true Body and Blood, Soul and Divinity, of Jesus Christ, only the appearances of bread and wine remaining. This Real Presence continues to exist after the Mass has ended and is reserved and adored in the Tabernacle as the Blessed Sacrament.

The *Constitution on the Sacred Liturgy* avoids this whole subject. Probably it does so because many other Christians do not accept this peculiarly Catholic doctrine, though all in some way consider "the Lord's Supper" to be the central point of Christian life. Perhaps the Council was hoping to advance the cause of Christian unity by agreeing wherever possible with other Christians on eucharistic theology and avoiding the impossible places. Evidence of this is the *Agreed Statement on the Eucharist*, a non-official agreement issued since the Council by a study group of Anglicans and Catholics on the subject of eucharistic belief. It, too, avoids the pitfalls by retreating into vagueness when difficulties loom.

This vagueness of the liturgical constitution on how Christ is actually present in the Mass is a real weakness. This may stem from the Council's assumption that we already know Catholic teaching on the Real Presence and do not need it restated. Or it may be because the men who wrote the liturgical constitution do not any longer share traditional Catholic belief in transubstantiation and wish to make our belief in it fade away. Or perhaps the vagueness is simply a result of the difficulty encountered in conveying this teaching on the "Paschal Mystery" in a short piece of legislation.

Bouyer, who welcomed the Council's embracing of the work of the great liturgical scholar Dom Casel on the Paschal Mystery, gave this explanation of the concept in *Life and Liturgy*;

> It is the re-enactment in, by and for the Church of the Act of Our Lord which accomplished our salvation, that is, His Passion and Death in the fullness of their final effects—the Resurrection, the communication of saving grace to mankind and the final consummation of all things. . . . The central property of the liturgy, and therefore, the central fact to be understood about it, is the unique mode in which Christ's redeeming act is permanently renewed and partaken of by the Church. An understanding of this mode, which is entirely different from that of theatrical or imaginative representation or from any physically realistic repetition, is the very clue to the understanding of the whole liturgy which began to be lost during the Middle Ages. And it is this clue which the Baroque period had lost so completely that it kept in view only a shell of the liturgy—a shell which was so much the more externally adorned and built over as the reality inside tended to be forgotten.

And that is not very clear, either. Neither Bouyer nor the

Constitution answer the questions: What happens at the consecration? How is the Mass *memorial* and how is it *sacrifice*? How is Christ present *generally* as in the Christian's life, or *specifically* and *really* in the bread and wine after consecration? Are we to go on believing in and adoring the Real Presence?

The Catholic cannot avoid the suspicion that to avoid transubstantiation is to deny it. The Pope, too, seems to have thought it a serious omission. He put "transubstantiation" importantly into his *Credo*. (See Appendix A.) Also, in 1965 he issued the encyclical *Mysterium Fidei*, a defence of traditional eucharistic theology because "there are some who . . . spread abroad opinions which disturb the faithful and fill their minds with no little confusion about matters of faith." This letter apparently was aimed at the Dutch theologians. It was a strong defence of the teaching of the Council of Trent on the Mass, and it insisted that the Church's traditional "rule of language," that is, theological formulas, should always be used in writing or preaching about the Eucharist.

Probably many holy Catholics could not give you a definition of transubstantiation to save themselves from the Holy Inquisition, and they care nothing for arguments about the value of Aristotelian terminology to the Church today. But every Catholic knows (or did know) that what he receives in Holy Communion is really physically Christ, and what is reserved in the Tabernacle before which he genuflects is really, physically Christ. It may not be malice, but a failure to have yet quite thought out what may very well be, in the future, fruitful eucharistic theology, that was the important weakness of the *Constitution*. This weakness was noted at the Council by Cardinal Ottaviani, naturally, who questioned the use of the concept "Paschal Mystery" and warned the Fathers to be clear theologically. It is a pity they did not listen to him. It must be seen as a lack in the *Constitution* that it left such doubt about eucharistic theology that it had to be bolstered up by such strong papal redefinitions.

The Protestant observers are right about the questions they raise. They are right when they say that Catholics have not worked out yet the implications of what so many of them are teaching. One hopes their charity will induce them to pray for us while we, in fear and trembling, *do* work it out.

It is the unresolved theological problems in the *Constitution* that account for the weakness of the New Mass. For the Mass is not only the core of the Church's existence, it is her principal teaching aid. Pope Pius XI called the liturgy, of which the Mass is the principal action, "the main organ of the ordinary magisterium of the Church." But a house divided against itself must fall, and the New Mass inherits the liturgical constitution's lack of clear definition.[8]

The New Mass has a built-in weakness that results from the liturgical constitution's ambivalence about what *happens* at Mass. Scholars who rejoiced in the constitution but now loathe the new liturgy do not see this. They put the failure of the liturgical reform down to a conspiracy of new theology liturgists who seized control of the machinery for putting the Conciliar reforms into effect. Even now, they would still vote for the reform but against the reformers.

I will quote once more from Louis Bouyer, since he is a classic example of the disillusioned revolutionary.

> We must speak plainly: there is practically no liturgy worthy of the name today in the Catholic Church. Yesterday's liturgy was hardly more than an embalmed cadaver. What people call liturgy today is little more than this same cadaver decomposed. Perhaps in no other area is there a greater distance (and even formal opposition) between what the Council worked out and what we actually have. Under the pretext of "adapting" the liturgy, people have simply forgotten that it is and can only be the traditional expression of the Christian mystery in all its spring-like fullness. I have perhaps spent the greater part of my priestly life in attempting to explain it. But I now have the impression, and I am not alone, that those who took it upon themselves to apply (?) the Council's directives on this point have turned their backs deliberately on what Beauduin, Casel and Pius Parsch had set out to do and to which I had tried vainly to add some small contribution of

my own. I do not wish to vouch for the truth, or seem to, at any greater length, of this denial and imposture. If any are still interested they may read the books I wrote on the subject; there are only too many of these! Or better, they might read the works of the experts I have just mentioned, on whom they have been able to turn their backs, even though the Council approved the essential points of their works, and added nothing of particular value to them. When one has thrown everything out, people will have to return to these sources.[9]

Bouyer may very well be right about a conspiracy, a "denial and imposture." After all, he must know most of those liturgists personally, and he is a better judge than we are of whether they are conspirators. But, though one feels pity for his disappointment, his feeling of a life's work wasted, his bitter sense of betrayal, one feels also the utmost irritation at Bouyer and scholars like him. What did they expect? It is all very well to talk pentecostally about Paschal Mysteries and their spring-like fullness, but liturgy is an *outward* sign, a public rite with words and actions. They never told us what the priest was to do and say when he came out upon the altar to celebrate this perfect liturgy. They said nothing about how he was to express that spring-like fullness, to re-create what we had lost during certain historical periods they don't like. They didn't go into the religious, the perhaps unbridgeable, distance between "Glory Hallelujah!" and *"Introibo ad altare Dei."* One is sorry for them, but sorrier for oneself, caught in destruction they brought down upon themselves and us.

CHAPTER 9

MURDER IN THE CATHEDRAL PART TWO

Go to Mass; the peace is ended.

TITO CASSINI, *THE TORN TUNIC*

Cardinal Lercaro, radical Archbishop of Bologna and president of the committee for carrying out the liturgical constitution, plunged the Church into an orgy of change well before the Council ended. Tito Cassini, in his furious little book directed as an open letter to Lercaro, tells of the utter confusion of priests and people in Bologna, caught in the flood of change. He gives one amusing example: near the end of the Mass are the words *"Ite, missa est"* (Go, the Mass is ended) and a blessing. The new version, one of three actually, is "The Mass is ended; go in peace." The similarity of the Italian vernacular to the Latin so confused one Bolognese priest that, after frantic efforts, he proclaimed: "Go to Mass; the peace is ended!" That gaffe has become the dictionary definition for the external appearance of the New Mass.

It is impossible to exaggerate the liturgical chaos of the past ten years or the misery it has caused. Hardly a month goes by, still, without some further change, either from Rome, like the new children's liturgy, or from the Canadian bishops, like the optional Creed. The peace is indeed ended. According to Pope Paul and most liturgists, it was not peace at all, but sleep, and now we must wake again to the spontaneity and vigour of the early Christian centuries. No longer are we to be awed spectators at a sacred play, but all priests together, in glad vocal assembly, at a restored proclamation of the Lord's goodness.

Yet, all over the world, attendance at Mass has declined. In the United States, Father Andrew Greeley of the National Opinion Research Centre in Chicago called the decline "catastrophic." And instead of tapering off, it is accelerating. In the year July 1972 to July 1973, weekly Catholic Mass-going dropped from 61 per cent to 48 per cent, "the most dramatic collapse of religious devotion in the entire history of Christianity."[1]

The most worrying thing about this picture is that the greatest drop was among older Catholics. In that one year, for Catholics over fifty, the percentage of those regularly attending dropped from 76 to 55 per cent. The researchers knew of "no other time in the course of human history when so many people—particularly older people—so decisively removed themselves from ecclesiastical practices."

Most of the blame for this catastrophe can be laid on the continuing liturgical tumult. These older Catholics, set in the habit of going to Mass, stuck it out for years, hoping things would quiet down. Finally, despairing about the prospects for improvement and desolated by the barrenness and unrest, they left. They won't be back for more of the same.

People, as Lenin remarked, vote with their feet. A liberal priest can empty a church like a fire alarm. However, Catholic feet sometimes vote the other way. For instance, in rundown, downtown Buffalo, New York, is a church called St. Michael's. Once the centre of a large flourishing parish, destroyed, ironically, by urban "renewal," it has now a minute parochial roll, only eight parishioners, but a pastoral staff of nine Jesuits. It has day-long Exposition of the Blessed Sacrament, every day, daily Benediction, six Masses on weekdays, nine on Sundays and *sixteen* on Holy Days, devotions to Our Lady, the Sacred Heart, St. Francis Xavier, and anyone else who comes to mind. It has Confessions several times a day, and weekly devotions for the grace of a happy death. The latest Novena drew 5,000 people daily, and there were 30,000 communicants during the period. Catholicism is not a numbers game, but numbers like this, when many churches are empty even on Sunday, cannot be ignored. St. Michael's is full all day of starved Catholics from all over the United States and Canada, absolutely fed up to the teeth with "renewal" in their own parishes. St. Michael's and its Jesuits have obviously never heard of "renewal." When did one last hear of prayers for a happy death?

St. Michael's Jesuits make the new liturgy work by embedding it in older Catholic devotions, para-liturgies and Adoration. Ironically, the new liturgy was supposed to do away with the need for para-liturgies, to which, it was said, Catholics turned because the centre of the liturgy was hollow and dead. That was an axiom of the liturgists—the liturgy was a shell, "an embalmed cadaver," decked out gaudily to conceal its poverty, empty, empty. A matter of legalistic obsession with rubrics, while prayer withered.

Bouyer once wrote that a priest had said to him that he (Bouyer) didn't really understand the Catholic liturgy because he had come to it from Protestantism. (Bouyer had been a Lutheran.) Although in view of his life work it seems daring to say so, I think that priest was right—Bouyer never saw past the rubrics. And not only because he was a convert. Misunderstanding the liturgy is an occupational disease of priests. Perhaps they are deadened by the callousness of the professional. I really believe the laity loved the liturgy more than most priests did. Certainly they are more heartbroken by its collapse. Most priests simply cannot understand why anyone wants an old Mass. And bishops simply think one mad.

The middle-aged and elderly Catholics on whom the liturgy has lost its hold found in the Old Mass devotional values that the New Mass lacks. Most of them find it hard to explain what is lacking. An older relative of mine, trying to tell me why he liked the Mass better before, couldn't put his finger on the uneasiness. "It's in the back of my mind all the time. I don't feel I'm doing anything anymore when I go to Holy Communion." And another hates the noise and tastelessness— I wish she could give her rendition of her parish's "Stompin' Tom Connors" Mass to the Canadian Conference of Bishops; it would do them good. These people, and countless others like them, are not liturgical scholars. When they go to Mass now, they feel they have suffered a tragic loss. They feel: "They have taken away my Lord and I know not where they have laid Him."

What are they missing when they say: "I liked it better before"? Cardinal Heenan, with the usual clerical underestimation of the laity's devotion, told the Pope it was just "nostalgia." But it is much deeper than that. The Tridentine Mass offered a mystery in the externals proper to the mysterious. Even a Low Mass offered a religious silence that stretched tautly like a silk web through the church, binding the people to each other, a sense of awe at being present at a Happening which was all-important and all-necessary, which did not require one's presence to happen, but which did not make one feel supernumerary when one was present, a feeling as of magnetism pulling from the Tabernacle on the altar and from the Host and Chalice raised at the consecration. I was trying to identify the feeling that is gone from Mass now and I identified it as *longing*. One *longed* towards the Mystery taking place in the sanctuary. The Mystery still takes place in the New Mass, but the longing for it has died.

I remember coming in late for early Mass in a Newfoundland town, into our modest little basement church with the school above, its pipes visible and rumbling on the church ceiling. On the porch steps leading down into it were dozens of woven wood lunch baskets of men from the mill just off the night shift. Some of these men had been unloading coal boats all night, and were filthy beyond belief. They stood at the back, humble as the Publican.[2] Their faces turned towards the altar were filled with an inexpressible longing, which shone through the dirt like a sanctuary lamp in a dark church. Probably they were too tired to pray in words, but their hearts were united with the Miracle and their bodies were saying "Amen!" It is very shameful for the modern liturgists to say of these men and the millions like them that they were not participating in the liturgy.

My father was one of these men. All his life he worked Sunday shift work. First Mass was 6:15 A.M. and the church several miles away. Before breakfast, he would walk through all weathers to Mass, home to eat, then go to the mill to work a double shift before he came home again. A man doesn't do that to be present at an assembly which is engaged in a memorial service (which is presumably why, come to think of it, Protestants don't have early services). He does it because he is pulled there by the Mystery, because he feels that while in Its Presence he can almost see through the veil which hangs between the Face of God and man, because he hopes it will, through his need and his longing, be granted to him to see, dimly now, what It promises him at the hour of his death. "I don't know if I'd do it now, girl," he said to me lately.

The loss of this feeling of mystery is the greatest difference between the Old and the New Mass. The New Mass is wall-to-wall noise, amplified by microphones and urged on to greater heights by priests. You get the irreverent feeling that you are a member of a studio audience at a give-away television show. Unconsciously, North America has patterned its liturgy on the offerings of the Box, not of the Tabernacle.

"Good morning," says the plaid-trousered, side-burned, brisk young lector. "This is the Second Sunday after Easter, and today we remember that though *we* have the light of Christ, there are many many people in the world who do not even have light bulbs. We shall now stand and read the entrance hymn found on page 32 in the script." Of course, he doesn't actually say "script"; he says "Missalette," the tacky little paper booklet which has replaced the Missal, and for which, in English Canada, Father Stephen Somerville writes prayers like the above, my memory of one of his efforts. (The blurb for Sunday, February 17, 1974, in the *Living With Christ Missalette*, ed. Fr. Stephen Somerville, proclaims: "Today is Happy Sunday.") The priest walks up the aisle, goes to the "presidential chair," and gets behind his mike. We read the bowdlerized Confiteor and Gloria. The lector, from behind *his* mike, haltingly reads the first and second readings. The priest moves from one studio mike to another, reads the Gospel, and gives the "homily" on some contemporary urgency. Then about the only "Sacred Silence" left in the Mass occurs, not even broken by background music—the collection is taken up. Now there is some audience participation, several people bring up the bread and wine—and the collection. The priest moves to the trestle table that has taken the place of the altar, and begins the "liturgy of the Eucharist" into the microphone which has taken the place of the Tabernacle. The flat church-filling Ontario voice reading the flat ICEL translation, few bells, no incense, and *such* music. The woman lector in green on green costume and a high hair-do—the "Church hostess," who may help give Holy Communion; the priest moving past the pews shaking hands like a television M.C.; the shuffling lines of communicants as in a cafeteria; the boring commercials inserted at every opportunity, before and after every action and reading, to explain what the vernacular was supposed to have made self-explanatory. It is a gruesome ordeal, and to think, as Buckley says, that they say they did it for us!

Two obvious differences in the new liturgy are the noise and vernacular. I have heard many people say, "I can't pray at Mass anymore. Everybody is making too much noise." That attitude is anathema to liturgists. Private prayer, they say, has no place in the liturgy, which is the prayer of the Church, objective, unified. All the congregation must pray it together. Out loud. They seem to think that to be valid prayer must be vocal. Liturgists think they have failed if they allow a silence to fall during Mass. This enforced participation, which was to be the great good of the new liturgy, has become its ugliest feature. Periodically, the people are berated for not praying and singing loudly enough, and for not using the Missalette. Enthusiastic priests sometimes get carried away, as witness this approving item in the *Catholic Register*: "St. Peter's, Bathurst north of Bloor in Toronto, can take a bow for subtle persuasion for this in its October 29 bulletin. 'To encourage closer participation in the Mass, pews in the rear of the Church, that is, those without hymnals, will be closed.' "

Very subtle. Very encouraging. No doubt they employ an angel with a flaming sword to bar the way. That little manoeuvre will certainly keep out any Publicans who show up.

It is doubtful whether anyone manages to pray at all, distracted as we have been during the last decade with unfamiliar hymns and prayers and translations. This generation of

Catholics probably cannot be taught to make a joyful noise unto the Lord, especially when we are not allowed to sing any of the old hymns. When our parish resurrected its choir, the congregation gratefully packed it in as far as vocal participation went. Which is not to say that they do not pray.

A second great change is the disappearance of Latin. Many, though not all, liturgists (not Bouyer, for instance) saw the Latin as a cruel barrier between the laity and the liturgy, keeping them from any "meaningful" participation and increasing the clerical hold on the Church's worship. "The fundamental gain of this Constitution," wrote Schillebeeckx, "is that it broke the clergy's monopoly of the liturgy. Whereas it was formerly the priest's affair, with the faithful no more than his clientèle, the Council regards not only the priest but the entire Christian community, God's people, as the subject of the liturgical celebration." Actually, the reverse is true. It was the priest who was bound to the Latin he often did not understand; the people followed the vernacular when they wished in their Missals. Thus, the people had freer access to the liturgy than many priests.

As in the other unrests that found voice at the Council, the liturgical revolution is clerical throughout. The people are now, in the name of freedom, delivered over to a clerical monopoly far more undesirable than any that used to exist. Every congregation is tied to its priests whims; every priest says Mass differently. Mass has become truly subjective now; it is the priest's alone.

It is very questionable whether the change from Latin has made the Mass more "meaningful" to the laity than it used to be. What the reformers wanted was not increased intelligibility, but rather a shift in meaning, a demystification of the Mass, a move towards decentralized, de-Romanized, ecumenical worship. Thus Latin, which kept the liturgy at a worshipful remove, which stood for a dogmatic, timeless, universal, dramatic view of God and the world, had to be replaced. It was the new world view, not the new or old prayers, which was to be more "meaningful."

The use of the vernacular in the Mass is a vexed question.

The argument for the retention of Latin in the Roman Rite usually centres on its symbolic value in representing the universality of the Church. Certainly, the Catholic Church lost much of its internationalism with the introduction of vernaculars. The travelling Catholic used to feel at home in Mass all over the world. Assisting at the familiar Mass in France or Italy gave one the heart-lifting feeling of being a full citizen of the Catholic world which the advent of the vernacular destroyed. I feel uneasy, an outsider, in Catholic churches in French Canada for the first time. A young Catholic I know, having attended a folk Mass in a French church in northern Ontario, responded to his mother's "How was Mass?" by the rude but accurate "Oh, it was just a Frog Mass." Sure it was; it's a WASP Mass in Toronto and a wog Mass in Lisbon. The abandonment of Latin has exacerbated all the ugly old regional and national chauvinisms.

People tend to speak of The Vernacular, as if it were a sort of super-Latin, released from the old Roman Catholic taint. In actuality, of course, there are thousands of vernaculars, and the choice of one over the other as the liturgical language is always a source of conflict. In India, in Belgium, in French Canada, it contributes to political and racial differences. In Mexico, choice of Spanish as The Vernacular excludes millions of Mexicans who speak only the major Indian tongues or, one of the hundred or so dialects. Worse, it implies the ascendancy of the Spanish-speaking element over the others.

Its devotional value is a different matter. A mystery religion seems to require a non-vernacular language to convey to its adherents that something beyond meaning, transcendental, is taking place. The exotic language, the anointed priest, the altar in the Holy of Holies, all go together. The Protestant Reformation sternly put aside the Catholic Mystery of Transubstantiation as an abomination, and opted for unadorned meaning, for the Word of God intelligibly proclaimed and nothing more. That is why the vernacular is so essentially Protestant an external, and why it does not suit the Catholic Mass as long as the Mass enshrines a Mystery. Christ Himself worshipped in hieratic Hebrew and some of the Catholic rites still use liturgical languages, like Ge'ez, the ancient language of Ethiopian mythology, that were dying out as vernaculars when Latin was young.

The abandonment of Latin is one of the reasons for the spectacular post-Conciliar growth in North America of Catholic Pentecostalism, with its own ecstatic language, beyond meaning and, dangerously, beyond reason. A young Catholic Pentecostalist explained why she spoke in tongues:

> You may ask of what practical use it is to be able to speak in another language to God, one that you have no idea as to what it means. I have found its value to lie in the totality and quality it adds to my prayer, especially in my prayers of praise to God. You've known times in your own life, I'm sure, when words just don't seem adequate enough to express what you really feel you want to say.[3]

If, as seems likely, this is a natural urge, it is sad that Catholics, denied access to "the language the angels speak," should have to seek comfort in gibberish.

It makes one feel very despairing to be refused even a Novus Ordo Latin Mass in the face of this phenomenon. For most North American Catholics have never once heard the New Mass in Latin, though we have a perfectly good Vatican II constitutional right to it. "Particular law remaining in force, the use of the Latin language is to be preserved in the Latin rites," the Council ruled. It recognized the usefulness of the vernacular in the readings of Mass, and in the administration of the Sacraments, but added, "Nevertheless, steps should be taken so that the faithful may also be able to say or to sing together in Latin those parts of the Ordinary of the Mass which pertains to them." How seriously was this meant to be taken? Küng in his book on the Council, and several Canadian bishops I have asked, say the *Constitution*'s ruling on Latin was merely face-saving with the conservatives. The feeling at the Council was that the Latin would soon disappear as bishops took an early opportunity to apply to the Vatican for the extension of the vernacular throughout the liturgy. The *Constitution* left it up to the "competent territorial ecclesiastical authority" to decide how to carry out these directives, and the bishops didn't even pay lip service to the preservation of Latin. The only regular Latin New Order Mass I know of in English Canada is at St. Mary's, Hamilton, where Bishop Ryan provided for its survival. Catholics who regularly attend a New Mass in Latin feel much kinder towards the new liturgy than those who know only the English version, which makes one think that Latin is more inseparable from Catholic worship than priests will admit.

When some Catholics recently asked a bishop for a New Mass in Latin, he answered that he would give it only if large numbers wanted it and if it did not deprive other Catholics of a Mass for which they had opted in the vernacular. He knew, of course, that the option had been his alone—the laity never had a chance to opt for or against the vernacular. It is disgraceful that no attempt was made to give the laity their liturgical constitutional rights, and worse still to charge them with disobedience for wanting them. It is likely that there would have been much less dissatisfaction with the New Mass if the *Constitution*'s blend of vernacular for the liturgy of the Word, and Latin for the liturgy of the Eucharist (that is, for the Mystery) had been accepted.

A further effect of the abandonment of Latin has been the frightful effect on the music used at Mass. The incomparable beauty of the ancient Gregorian Chant, the Western Church's own particular music, does not fit the vernacular. The Council acknowledged that Gregorian was "specially suited to the Roman liturgy, therefore, other things being equal, it should be given pride of place in liturgical services." Instead, it has disappeared, even from the cathedrals, along with the Latin sung to it, and a mixture of Protestant hymns and popular songs has been substituted. Some of the Protestant hymns are very fine and enrich our worship, especially since Catholic liturgists do not tamper with them out of ecumenical respect and all the "Thees" and "Thous" remain. I was deeply moved the first time I heard "Amazing Grace," even though it was being performed by two nuns hung with guitars. I felt it was a real hymn, written by a believer with an ecstatic sense of God's mercy. But what is one to say of the "religious songs" of Joe

Wise, beloved of Canadian liturgical workshops? They make one feel hot with embarrassment, they are so illiterate and pretentious, so expressive of the contempt of liturgists for the taste of the congregation. And what can one say of an all-out rendition of "The Impossible Dream" at Holy Communion? At least, it is better, in its longing for the Grail ideal of perfection, than Wise's "Lay with your face up in the sun." Liturgists have taken to exaggerating the difficulty of the Gregorian, and suggesting that only monks and boys with unbroken voices can sing it. That isn't so. Every day in our Newfoundland parish, we sang a *missa cantata*, and I didn't find out until I read Jungmann several years ago that "the missa cantata . . . is . . . the unbroken continuation of the presbyter mass of Christian antiquity," nor that the chant we sang it to was the thirteenth-century *Missa de Angelis*. This ancient and exquisite Mass has now perished. The out-of-date "folk" songs used at Mass disgust the mature Catholic and astonish the young, who can hear much better on their transistor radios.

The fact that the vernacular had to appear in some *official* translation was bound to raise problems. The version used in English-speaking countries was prepared by the International Committee on English in the Liturgy, for the past few years under the Chairmanship of Canadian Bishop G. Emmett Carter. Even while recognizing the difficulties of a body trying to please a number of hierarchies, it is difficult to forgive the ICEL translation for its relentless blandness, its committee English, and what Archbishop Dwyer called its "bowdlerization" of the liturgy. When St. Paul's "sounding brass" becomes a "noisy gong" and the woman rejoices that she has found her "dime" and the "blessed" are demoted to being merely "happy," and the congregation is made to ask conversationally: "Lord, who will be admitted to your tent?" you know you are in the presence of committee English. There was some point in seeking supernatural help against "the horns of unicorns," but I feel I can shift for myself when it comes to "the horns of wild bulls." This is not a matter of accuracy; it is a matter of atmosphere, of attitude to the sacred. It is a continuation, even if with the best of intentions, of the desacralization of Catholic worship. The English of the New Order Mass tried deliberately *not* to be a liturgical language; it avoided the sonorities and beauties of the Anglican Book of Common Prayer, which was composed just as deliberately to *be* a liturgical instrument, rhythmic and noble.

The ICEL bowdlerizes the Old Mass version of the centurion's prayer—"Lord, I am not worthy that Thou shouldst come under my roof; say but the word and my soul will be healed," to "Lord, I am not worthy to receive you; but only say the word and I shall be healed." The sense is the same, but the translation is doubly questionable; first, because it breaks the mental connection with the story of the Gentile centurion whose faith was so great that he did not even require Jesus's physical presence in his house to believe that his son would be cured; second, because of the fuss liturgical reformers usually make about rooting every Catholic piety firmly in a scriptural context. They made the change because they could not stand the pun on "roof"—the roof of the communicant's mouth, the roof of the centurion's house. The new translation is very genteel, given in no way to sonorities or extravagances.

Also, in the ICEL version, recent theological whims get an airing, such as the one that regards sin as social rather than individual—"the sins of the world" becomes "the *sin* of the world." The Creedal "I" becomes the communitarian "we." The translation throughout has a demystifying and flattening effect—"these gifts, these presents, these holy unspotted sacrifices," becomes "these gifts we offer you in sacrifice." "We, therefore, humbly pray and beseech Thee, most merciful Father," becomes "We come to you, Father, with praise and thanksgiving." "A holy Sacrifice, an unspotted Victim" has disappeared altogether. Serious? Yes, I think so. The flattening paraphrase that is the ICEL version represents an attempt to make the mysterious unmysterious. It is, if one wishes to preserve traditional Catholic doctrine and attitude to the sacred, a bad liturgical mistake. If one wishes to change both, it will certainly be very effective.

The usual objection to the ICEL translation is on aesthetic grounds, and it is raised by non-Catholics, as well as cradle Catholics. Charles Lam Markmann, biographer of the

Buckleys, agrees with William Buckley on the "profanation" that the new liturgy is:

> For there is nothing presumptuous, I think, in the fact that a non-communicant protests the debasement of the Latin Mass to the vernacular. The Roman Catholic Mass, like the King James Version, the Book of Common Prayer, the liturgy of the Greek and Russian Orthodox Churches, and some parts of the Sephardic service, is less the property of a closed religious group than a basic treasure of the common wealth of culture, and against their esthetic desecration it is not only meet but mandatory that all who recognize the outrage protest it. It is hardly necessary to be a Christian, or even the vaguest kind of deist, to feel one's blood run backwards at psalms or Nativity stories transposed to the literary level of a small-town newspaper.[4]

The aesthetic objection, though important, must be secondary for Catholics. A vernacular translation faces the temptation of doctrinal tinkering. Most Catholics have access to only one vernacular translation. The French version, for instance, is different in different ways from the Latin and the English. Where the Latin *Gloria* has "*Et in terra pax hominibus bonae voluntatis*" (peace on earth to men of good will), the French has "*Et paix sur la terre aux hommes qu'il aime*," and the English has "And peace to his people on earth." Three subtly different versions where there was only one before. Presumably each vernacular satisfies its own theological whims.

The *Jerusalem Bible* is the translation authorized for use in the Canadian Church (partly because it forces Canadian Catholics to buy Canadian Missalettes and Books of Worship, since the Americans use the *New American Bible*—there is no reason, the Canadian hierarchy seems to feel, why the liturgy cannot serve nationalism and finance). The *Jerusalem* is a good, clear student's Bible, but too understated for satisfying public worship. Several monastic congregations in Canada use the

Revised Standard Version; it fits better, they say, with the Gregorian.

In justice to the ICEL version, it must be said that although it may offend the cultural and aesthetic sensibilities of other English-speaking groups, it reflects with complete faithfulness the mentality, the character, of English Canada, the flat, bland, unaccented, undemonstrative, undramatic, unjoyful English Canadian genius, formed by long association with North American Puritan Protestantism, which has now turned into liberal secularism. If Mitchell Sharp had been set to write a Mass, he'd have produced something very like the ICEL one. This Mass completely suits a culture that met the recent energy crisis by turning off the angels in its cities' outdoor Christmas displays.

One unexpected advantage of the vernacular liturgy is that it makes it difficult to conceal a priest's lack of faith. The old liturgy was so undependent on the personality of the priest, or the expression he put into what he said, that one often could not remember who said Mass. Now everything depends on the warmth of the priest's faith and its reflection in his voice and gestures. It is very moving to see a faithful priest performing the new liturgy—he goes about it with the anxious concern with which one would handle a sick baby. He wraps about it shreds of the old rubric, beats his breast, keeps purified fingers together, bows at Christ's Name, prolongs the Elevation. The unbelieving priest brings to the Mass the conscious cold histrionics of the television M.C. He loves to shock the captive laity by introducing whimsical variations; he will, for instance, change all the prayers slightly as he reads them, in subtle paraphrase. It is very unsettling. One gets the feeling that he is punishing the laity because he is trapped in a priesthood that irks him.

An American bishop recently complained to a conservative Catholic society that one of its members had taken to attending the Mass of such a priest and, when he said "This is my Body," remarking in a loud voice, "I hope so!" My sympathies are often with her. When you watch a priest behaving in an antic manner at the Holy Sacrifice of the Mass, it is hard to accept that he believes in what he is doing, and it inevitably erodes one's own faith and drives one into a sort of semi-Donatism.

Father Dan Berrigan attends a "Mass of Reconciliation" at St. Patrick's Cathedral, New York. He is *not* invited to give the homily. He storms out with his disciples to celebrate a better Mass on the cathedral steps, with the hunk of bread and paper cups of wine which are *de rigeur* for radical Catholic ceremonies. The CBC-TV program "Adieu, Alouette" films a young priest and a bunch of long-haired, Indian-head-banded French Canadian kids at a commune Mass. They laugh, talk, smoke, cuddle, and pass around consecrated bread and wine. Millions of people read about Father Dan's protest Mass; millions more saw "Adieu, Alouette." All the believers were troubled and scandalized, no matter how hard they tried not to judge rashly. No bishop made a public protest.

Perhaps, in the light of certain priestly behaviour, it is unfair to blame the new liturgy for the decline in eucharistic piety. However, it was much harder for a priest to make a fool of himself and his congregation in the old liturgy, all set about as it was with safeguards. An older priest told me that he had been told in the seminary that it was a mortal sin not to wear his biretta, so it could be taken off in respect as Mass began. Legalism was one of the sins of the old dispensation, but is it a change for the better if the priest insists on saying Mass in an orange turtleneck?

Nobody, I think, would dispute that there is a great decline in the reverence that used to be paid to the Blessed Sacrament at Mass. Paradoxically, it has been accompanied by a considerable rise in the number of people who communicate every time they go to Mass. The decline was at least partly intentional. The liturgical reformers who wrote the New Mass, and issued the flood of instructions concerning the externals of the liturgy, altar, vessels, architecture, etc., were trying to correct what they considered the overemphasis on the Presence in the Mass which worked, they said, to the lessening of the elements of praise, thanksgiving, and sacrifice so prominent in the worship of the early Church. Jungmann, in his great work on the Roman Mass, describes the growth of the cult of the Real Presence from about the ninth century to the

Reformation, when the longing to *see* the Miracle produced the most extravagant and unedifying practices. The moment of the Elevation of the Host and Chalice became the climax of the Mass, people fighting to see it, coming to Church just before it and leaving immediately afterwards, going so far as to knock holes in the Church wall so they might see the Elevation when the ban of excommunication kept them out. Ten years ago, in Canada, the church bells were still rung at the consecration; I can still feel the church trembling to them. (A little while ago at the consecration, there was a sudden prolonged peal of silvery chimes. I looked up in astonished delight for their source. It was the Good Humour ice-cream man soliciting business outside the church.)

Jungmann sees the near-idolatry of the excesses of the cult as one of abuses that drove the sixteenth-century reformers into making the opposite error. Luther rejected transubstantiation as an abomination, denied the sacrificial character of the Mass and taught that the Eucharist was only a "testament," a memorial, and forbade reverences to It. The Reformers eagerly seized on the "Missa Illyrica"[5] because it made no acknowledgement of the Real Presence.

The Council of Trent restored the balance between the ends of the Mass, but the great respect for the Presence in the Blessed Sacrament remained. Modern liturgical reformers tend to consider what remains of the cult as an aberration, or at any rate, as a distraction from the full recognition of the Paschal Mystery. Also, that horror they feel towards anything that smacks of magic leads them to slash away with more zeal than prudence at delicate things.

The Real Presence was done reverence to not only by the words of the old liturgy but also by the host of liturgical practices that surrounded it. Such a violent assault on the liturgical practices has occurred in the last decade under the guise of a restoration of the liturgy that it is hard not to subscribe to a conspiracy theory and conclude that what is intended is the destruction of Catholic Eucharistic doctrine. Pope Paul thinks so:

Among those who deal with this Most Holy Mystery in

written or spoken word, there are some who, with reference . . . to the dogma of transubstantiation, or to devotion to the Eucharist, spread abroad opinions which disturb the faithful and fill their minds with no little confusion about matters of faith . . . to consign to oblivion doctrine already defined by the Church, or else to interpret it in such a way as to weaken the genuine meaning of the words or the recognized force of the concepts involved. (Mysterium Fidei)

Even if one assumes that the changes are made in good faith, even when they can be supported by historical precedent, their cumulative effect is shattering. The altar is pared down to a makeshift table. The sacred vessels no longer must be gilded inside, and may be handled by the laity. "Chalice" is translated as "cup." Various pottery vessels often replace the old gold and silver ones, which then turn up in antique shops to be ransomed back by believing priests and faithful. The three altar cloths are reduced to one. The Tabernacle disappears from the main altar, the Crucifix is reduced in size to a few inches since is must not come between priest and people, and the glittering microphone becomes the focal point. The altar rail is taken away and the sanctuary undelineated. The purifications are omitted. The white unleavened host is often replaced by an ordinary loaf, the crumbs of which are treated casually. Many priests do not elevate the Consecrated Host and Chalice. The people stand to receive Holy Communion, and may receive by hand.

Either someone has designs on the eucharistic piety of the laity, or else the clergy is disgracefully unaware of the psychological effect of what they are doing. Some months ago, I attended Mass at St. Michael's Cathedral in Toronto. St. Mike's now puts on, in place of the old Solemn High Mass, a sober, restrained, low Protestant service, with pathetic little dabs of Catholic pomp, such as an embarrassed censing of the altar. There are now no prayers to accompany this ritual, and the priest looked curiously janitorial, as he swung his incense pot as inconspicuously as possible at the altar. I had really tried hard all through Mass not to be mutinous, not to smother my prayer with anxiety. Communion time came and I felt recollected enough to receive. Just as the priest was giving me the Host, I noticed with shock that it was *brown*. Since my last visit, the Cathedral had obviously replaced the white unleavened bread with whole wheat. I went back to my place in a tumult of rage and wept bitter tears. No doubt it was foolish, but it was an instinctual unplanned response, and hard to recover from.

This sort of guerrilla attack on Catholic sensibilities happens all the time now. Probably most priests are not aware of the spiritual havoc they are wreaking. Perhaps it is largely boredom that drives them to an insensate frenzy of change for change's sake. I once asked a liturgical expert why I now had to stand for Holy Communion and he answered, "Because you used to kneel down."

Even if this hacking away at reverence for the Real Presence does not always spring from infidelity, it is frightfully dangerous and destructive. It has coarsened the religious reflexes of Catholics in an astonishingly short time. A few years ago, when a Host fell to the floor, everyone was upset and It was gathered up with much purification. With the coming of Communion in the hand, this reverence has gone. Just after the introduction of this practice, I was standing in a Communion line and a child in front of me, receiving by hand, dropped the Host. Nonchalantly, a teenager behind him picked It up and handed It back to the priest. "Like chiclets!" a woman snorted to me. For a moment I was dizzy with shock, but now I am used to seeing the Sacred Host bouncing around the floor. Lately one was found in the parking lot of our church. Nobody minded much. One hears many stories of how the new practice has made it easier to steal Hosts for the proliferating Black Masses, and one feels grateful that at least the devil worshippers still believe.

It is unnerving enough when Communion in the hand is authorized, but it is immeasurably worse in the situation where someone decides to force the issue in a place where it is forbidden and creates an ugly scene in which, naturally, the priest buckles, or where a priest, though forbidden (as in the

United States) to administer Communion by hand, does so anyway, and people receive in knowing disobedience. It takes a strong faith to survive all this.

For, whether liturgists admit it or not, people are reasoning along these lines—"I couldn't touch the Blessed Sacrament before; if I am allowed to touch it now, it cannot *be* the Blessed Sacrament." Even if careful catechesis *had* taken place before the re-introduction of this practice (which disappeared in the early Middle Ages because of abuses), it would have been largely lost on Catholics instructed under the old dispensation.

And with the question of catechesis, we have arrived at the conservative's sorest grievance about the liturgical changes—the manner of their introduction. For even if we assume, and I do not, that every bishop and priest brought to the liturgical reform a strong Catholic faith and a warm love of the Church and the laity, we can only cringe at the brutality of the methods used. The stupid, bull-headed, excited riot of change was clericalism at its worst, rampaging unchecked even by a weakened papal authority. Constant, reasonless change, unprepared for by catechesis but followed by shrill reproach if anyone protested. An extraordinary orgy of destruction took place in every parish church, beginning early in the Council years. Many priests simply closed the church for a week or two and had it torn apart. When it reopened, everything Catholic was gone, Tabernacle, Stations of the Cross, altar rail, high altar, frescoes, vigil lights, confessionals. Many people went back to find that their priest had smashed up and thrown out memorials they had placed in the church for dead members of their families—windows, crucifixes, fonts. A Polish immigrant told me that a Cross she had put in the church in memory of her mother had been broken up and had disappeared. "I guess I don't mind if he had to throw it out. It's his church. But I wish he had told me—I would of liked to just have a little piece of it to keep."

The blithe savagery with which nearly all priests went about the liturgical reform was incredible. They worked on the principle that everything that was not forbidden was compulsory. Thus, nearly every pastor demolished his high altar, set up a rickety table, and proudly stood behind it facing the people with all the self-congratulation of Little Jack Horner. There was nothing in the liturgical constitution to authorize this move; the sanction for it was found in the Instruction on the liturgy, October 16, 1964, signed by Cardinal Lercaro, which said that "it is proper that the main altar be constructed separately from the wall, so that one may go around it with ease and so that celebration *may* take place facing the people." Yet it did no good to protest; most priests are as ignorant of the history of the liturgy as are most garbagemen, but they all held confidently forth on the absolute necessity for Mass facing the people if we were to approach the purity of primitive worship. In fact, in the primitive Church, priests and people all faced one way—east—and until the orienting of the church building, when the priest turned about, the people did too, facing east with their backs turned to him.

The handful of reformers who knew this change had little historical justification duped the mass of parish priests into it for other reasons, ecumenical and doctrinal.[6] Yet not one parish priest I know of resisted the pressure, not one goes on saying Mass on the unfashionable side of the altar.

On consideration, the substitution of a plain free-standing table for the high altar is one of the most significant actions of the liturgical reform. An altar presupposes a sacrifice, a table a meal. An altar calls for a sanctuary, a table a domestic dining room. The reformers who initiated the change from altar to table knew exactly what it implied. The same Instruction that contains the suggestion for changing the altar's, and thus the celebrant's, position, also abolished the prayers at the foot of the altar, the chief of which was Psalm 42: "I will go in unto the altar of God, to God who giveth joy to my youth." Not one of these men can have been ignorant of the words of Cranmer, accompanying the Privy Council order in 1550, that all the altars in England should be destroyed:

> The form of a table shall move the simple from the superstitious opinion of the Popish Mass unto the right use of the Lord's Supper. For the use of an altar is to make sacrifice upon it: the use of a table is to serve men to eat upon. If we come to feed upon Him, spirtually to eat his

body and spiritually to drink his blood, which is the true use of the Lord's Supper, then no man can deny that the form of a table is more meet for the Lord's board than the form of an altar.

It is apparent that another attempt is being made to move "the simple" from believing in the Sacrifice. Of the same kind is the almost universal prohibition against kneeling at Holy Communion, for kneeling implies adoration and one does not adore even one's spiritual supper.

The ignorance of liturgical history was bad enough, but who will forgive the mockery, the parodies of the old liturgy by priests old enough to know better, the refusal of bishops to consider even a Novus Ordo Latin Mass, the insolent bigotry of liturgical committees? Clericalism triumphant provided that old priests might go on saying the Tridentine Mass as long as they did not say it for old laymen. Many older people died of grief, and countless others simply stay home from what was once the flowing source of all their serenity. "Anguish" is not too melodramatic a word to describe what one felt, and feels, about the destruction.

There really does not seem to have been any good reason for the brutality of the liturgical reform. The Pope and bishops said they wanted a uniform liturgy and that to go on using the old would be divisive. Yet one of the features of the reform most hailed by Schillebeeckx and others was its pluralism, the breaking away from "the rigid conformity of Trent. ("Divisive" is the word you use when you are refusing requests from conservatives; "pluralistic" is the one you need when your hand is forced by liberals.) Even the Council of Trent, under pressure this Council never felt, allowed any rite two hundred years old or older to flourish alongside the Tridentine reform. After all, it is not as if the old rite were some untried and dubious prayer. The heart of it, the Roman Canon, existed by the end of the fourth century, and it was, as Jungmann relates, put together in the fourth century by an author who incorporated into it prayers from even more ancient liturgies. The Tridentine Mass, with its ancient heart and beautiful later accretions, might have been left to coexist with the new.

Of course, when the New Mass met with such opposition, the bishops would have lost face if they had retreated and allowed the Old. Perhaps, too, they had guilty consciences over their indecent haste to abandon a Mass that presumably had shaped their priestly spiritual life, and whose beauty and necessity they had sung for so many years to their flocks. Bishops may waver on birth control and divorce and heresy, but a polite request from an obedient Catholic to have the comfort of an occasional Tridentine Mass stiffens episcopal spines like nothing else.[7] They charge one with disloyalty, which is funny, and with disobedience, which is untrue, since it is only too easy nowadays to have an unauthorized Mass of any liturgical reading from Black to Tridentine.

Catholics simply cannot understand why the bishops have so adamantly set their faces against the Old Mass. Their inability even to reply politely to a request for it has driven traditionalists to enquire into whether bishops are being honest when they represent themselves as helplessly bound by the Holy Father to forbid the Tridentine Mass, or whether they are, for once, exaggerating his authority and their own obedience. The two questions are raised: first, whether the Pope had the power to forbid the Tridentine Mass, and, second, whether he *did* forbid it and make the New Mass mandatory. They are far too complex to go into here, but there does seem to be a good case to be made that the Pope did not actually forbid the Old Mass by the Apostolic Constitution *Missale Romanum* which introduced the New. This case was most recently put by Father Paul Crane, S.J., the editor of the moderate conservative publication *Christian Order*. Until recently, Crane had accepted the New Mass because he thought it was mandatory, but in a series of articles entitled "The Old Mass: Not a Nice Story," he presents evidence which, if true, is very distrubing. He charges that part of the Latin original of the Apostolic Constitution was deliberately mistranslated by ICEL and by the French and Italian translators so that it reads as if the New Mass was henceforth to be mandatory. (See Appendix B for details.) Furthermore, he says that the translators interpolated a sentence not in the Latin original signed by the Pope, which set a mandatory date for the introduction of the new regulations, and that this fraudulent addition has now found its way into the Latin version of the Apostolic Constitution appearing at the beginning of the new Latin Roman Missal published by Vatican Press.

Whether Crane is correct or not, the point is academic. The Pope must know by now what happened and he has remained silent.

Certainly a number of bishops do consider that they have the power to grant permission for the celebration of the Tridentine rite. It is fairly easy to find a Tridentine Mass in England, Italy, France, and increasingly in America. (I am reluctant to name the Canadian and American bishops who allow it in case publicity frightens them into withdrawing it from my friends to whom it means so much.) In any case, whatever the legal situation, the legalistic unkindness of the hierarchy over the Old Mass is nothing short of a pastoral scandal.

Bishops have no one but themselves to blame for the Catholic bolt to Pentecostalism and worse. In rage and despair, some Catholics have joined schismatic groups which offer the Tridentine Mass. Some of these are sincere, though misled; some are cruelly opportunistic and milk older Catholics of all their money in return for the old prayers. Bishops refer to Catholics who join such groups as the lunatic fringe, and charge that they were always unstable, using Catholic pieties to feed their hysteria. This is liberal élitist callousness—the unstable have a large claim to the Church's kindness, and it is infinitely better to lead them to licit spiritual comforts than to drive them to the dottinesses they are now embracing. It is wrong for Catholics to leave the Church in a rage, even when denied an occasional Old Mass by a bishop who then proceeds to set up an extraterritorial parish for Catholic Pentecostalists who want to worship together outside their own parish structure. Two wrongs don't make a right; few bishops would admit the presence in this episode of *two* wrongs.

The righteous orthodoxy that leads local authorities to forbid the Old Mass is all the harder to stomach in the face of their spinelessness towards the radical in liturgy. "Eight Hundred Toe-Tap to Jazz Mass," at St. Basil's, Toronto, says a

Toronto *Star* headline. The *Catholic Register* carries a page of pictures of a "Christian Family Peace Festival" Mass in the fields, with the servers in T-shirts and peace medallions and Father Tom in a chasuble printed all over with thousands of faces. (Robert Fulford suggests, correctly, I imagine, that the chasuble is a picture of the Woodstock crowd. What else?) The *Register* later carries a picture of Eskimo Mass servers, "wearing the traditional Eskimo garment, the kusbuc." And hung with that traditional Eskimo musical instrument, the guitar.

And these Masses do not even represent the extremes of Canadian liturgy. Indeed, after one has attended a few university Masses, the above seem models of liturgical restraint. For university Masses are wild and foolish. They would embarrass a card-carrying atheist. The priests and people who take part in them have not, to paraphrase Joyce, merely lost their faith; they've lost their self-respect.

Yet, if one protests to a bishop (and this one does), one gets only a regretful admission that abuses *do* occur, and are not authorized. They are, of course—tacitly by the bishop's silence, and explicitly by the fact that they are advertised and presided over by priests in good standing.

Of raging about the liturgy there is no end, and the enraged are not going to give up and go away. Quite apart from the schismatic and near-schismatic groups like Father Gommar de Pauw's Catholic Traditionalist Movement, or the Orthodox Roman Catholic Movement and *The Voice*, the newspaper that supports it, there are large moderate groups of Catholics who want the reinstatement of the Tridentine Mass and will settle for optional use of the Old Mass by priests and people who find it more spiritually satisfying.

Una Voce International is the largest of these organizations. Its branch in England, the Latin Mass Society, scored a notable success when it prevailed on Cardinal Heenan to ask the Pope to grant what has become known as "the English Indult"—permission to use the Old Rite on special occasions. Probably, though, what swayed the Cardinal was not only pastoral concern. It was the 1971 "Intellectual's Petition," signed by a group of well-known writers, artists, musicians—Anglican, Jewish, atheist. These besought the

Pope not to "obliterate" the Latin liturgy, which they saw as the heart of Western culture. If "some senseless decree" were to order Chartres knocked down, they said, educated people, whatever their religion, would rush to its defence. But Chartres was built to celebrate that Mass which "in its magnificent Latin text has also inspired a host of priceless achievements in the arts." Therefore, Yehudi Menuhin, the Anglican Bishop of Ripon, Malcolm Muggeridge, and Kenneth Clark could claim ownership with Catholics of this rite, and the Pope would be committing a crime against the human spirit if he carried out his intention to forbid its use.

There has been no such concession to North America. Yet the Tridentine Mass persists here and there. The only public ones I know of are one in Ottawa, five in Quebec and some sixty throughout the United States. I am sure there are others.

A development that has been maturing since the Council is about to cause some interesting trouble. Anyway, traditionalists are going to find it interesting. After the Council, Archbishop Marcel Lefebvre, disapproving of many of the directives on priestly formation and liturgical practice, founded the International Seminary of St. Pius X at Econe-Par-Riddes, near Fribourg, Switzerland, to go on training priests according to the Tridentine system. It is perhaps the only seminary in the world overflowing with candidates. Though he does not name it, it is obviously the one Louis Bouyer went to investigate, and about which he writes in *The Decomposition of Catholicism*. He didn't like its "exacerbated conservatism," but he was satisfied that it was not lunatic. "People had told me that all these were merely fired-up youths, former colonialists from North Africa, etc. . . . I was able to discern that on the whole quite the contrary was true. They were young people who were perfectly sane and normal." What even "the most generous youths" want, concluded Bouyer, was "some assurance of stability." They get it at Econe.

The first priests from this seminary are beginning to appear in Europe. They are saying Mass in the Tridentine Rite and people are flocking to it. There has been no public rejection of them from the Vatican, and probably bishops will be left to deal with the situation. And that situation *will* be divisive, for these priests come at a time when many Catholics, despairing of ever finding liturgical peace again, are prepared for the first time to attend an unauthorized Mass. Recently, in London, England, a widely advertised "Teilhard de Chardin Mass" was disrupted by a group of traditionalists, who, when Cardinal Heenan refused to cancel it, recited the Rosary aloud, thus drowning out the words of the Master. Will such traditionalists obey their bishop in a showdown over an unauthorized Old Mass? Stay tuned.

This is not a happy situation, but it may move bishops to action. There are a number of things a bishop might do about the liturgy. Instead of sponsoring expensive and futile liturgical workshops which produce nothing but irritation at the parish level, he could, first of all, provide the New Ordo in Latin as the liturgical constitution says he should. In every parish large enough to support more than one Sunday Mass, one should be a sung Gregorian Latin High Mass, not concelebrated, but with deacon, sub-deacon, and all the altar boys who can be mustered. Secondly, after obtaining an agreement (written if he likes) from any people who want to arrange an occasional Old Rite Mass that they recognize that the New Mass is valid, he should permit easy access to the Tridentine Mass and suggest as suitable places for its celebration the countless lovely empty convent chapels. Third, he should throw out of his churches all the tacky paper missalettes, adding to his bonfire the Canadian *Catholic Book of Worship*, which is useless as a Vatican II Missal, since it does not contain the complete English, or Latin, text of the Mass, and since he may regret the royalties he used to collect on this book, he might collaborate in the preparation and publication of a Missal containing the entire three-year cycle of the new liturgy in Latin and English. This being a slow and expensive business, he should offer them for sale and not try to have the parishes buy them in bulk. Catholics used to buy and treasure their own Mass Books; they will do so again when a good one appears.

Further, a bishop can take stern measures against priests who introduce unauthorized changes into the New Mass, for, even though one dislikes the new liturgy, one must in fairness admit that one often blames the New Mass itself for things it never intended. There are some good things to be said for it—the fourth Canon is a fine prayer, and it's nice to have extra scriptural readings. However, the whole awesome propaganda machine of the Church has been extolling the virtues of the new liturgy for ten years and I don't feel the need to praise it here.

Even if Latin and Gregorian do regain the place they deserve by Vatican II constitutional right, even if sobriety does return, it will take a long painful time. In the meantime, the Catholic whose liturgical prayer has become for him a constant source of grief and distraction must not despair and throw in the towel. He must tell his priest and bishop, and the "liturgical team" in his parish, how he feels. The priest who is head of the liturgy committee in our deanery told me lately (as I was tearing a strip off him after Mass for trying to force the Sign of Peace on the congregation during the absence of the pastor who doesn't have it) that I was the first person in six and a half years who had complained to him about any of his innovations. Whatever happened to "dialogue"?

The Catholic in liturgical trouble must do his best not to be in a rage at Mass, because wilful distraction is a very destructive sin. I find some consolation in seeing the misery one endures at many Masses as a version of what St. John of the Cross calls "the dark night of the senses," when the soul no longer finds sweetness in prayer, when prayer itself becomes a cross, and the blooming spiritual landscape a desert waste. Visits to the Blessed Sacrament help, if you can find an unlocked church. And there is no harm either in joining *Una Voce* in its prayer: "Grant, we pray, Almighty God, that through the intercession of the Jesuit Martyrs of North America, the peace, order and beauty of the Tridentine Latin Mass may be restored to our Churches."

CHAPTER 10

A NOTE ON FAITH

In the last two chapters I have discussed what liturgists and theologians, left and right, Catholic and Protestant, have said about the liturgical changes, and I have noted the effect statisticians have indicated that these have had on the general practice of the Faith. But since, thank God, I am neither pastor nor teacher, I have to deal mainly with their effect on my own faith, and therefore, awfully, on my children's. That is enough for this poor donkey of a layman to manage.

I think it is true that a great many people have lost their faith during these ten years of change in Catholic worship. Perhaps it is also true that many of these had already let go of everything except the outward observance of their religious professions, and they did not realize this until they looked at their faith in the light that came through the broken roof of the liturgy. This, anyway, is what we are told by the defenders of the liturgical reform. This is making too cerebral a process out of faith. No Catholic will say that faith is irrational, but rather that it is supra-rational, above reason, and no Catholic believes either, that you can read or reason your way into faith. Faith is largely an inexplicable emotion, like love. It is a gift. You can dispose yourself to receive it, but like love, you must humbly wait till it comes.

If faith were not an affair of the heart, it would not be vulnerable in quite the same way to things like liturgical change. If you say to a priest, in Confession or conversation, that you find that against your will your faith has been shaken by the tumult, he will probably answer, correctly but inadequately, that if your faith were really strong, it could take such things in its stride. But it is true, too, that the fondest human love can be destroyed, as, for example, a wife can come to hate her once beloved husband if he is consistently unfaithful, drunken, and brutal to her, and worse, to her children. Likewise, I believe, I know, that my mother is indeed my mother, but if she set out, by persistent words and actions of repudiation to convince me that she is not, a trunkful of documentation would never make me feel secure again.

And it is so with the Catholic faith which most people absorbed through long contact with an unchanging Catholic ritual. Unwittingly or maliciously, the reformers have tried to do to twentieth-century Catholic belief what was done to pagan belief by early Christian missionaries. The god of a tribe resided in a tree; the missionary put an axe to its roots. Down came the tree and down came the god. You pre-Vatican II types believe that your God resides in that golden box you call a Tabernacle? Out with the Tabernacle. Out with your God. Catholics, of course, believe that the god in the tree was a false god, or rather, that pagans worshipped in him an attribute of the true God. Nevertheless, when a Catholic feels the almost inevitable stirring of doubt after the fundamental change in ritual that has occurred, he would have to be both very holy and very unimaginative not to wonder—is it true because I believe it or do I believe it because it is true? Doubt produces guilt and guilt further weakens faith, and if this process is allowed to continue, one's God is soon dead.

I have not lost my faith as a result of the changes. But it has been sorely beaten about, rather as if it has tumbled down a mile of stone steps and is lying at the bottom in a tight little ball wondering whether it is still alive and afraid to move in case another thousand steps are stretching beneath it. If I were very holy and my faith very strong, no doubt I would be unshaken by the last ten years. But I am no Job; rather, I am, and I suspect most of us are, like that character in *Pilgrim's Progress*, Littlefaith. His name is misleading. His little faith didn't keep him out of heaven; instead, he got to the Celestial City because he had, at least, a *little* faith. Bunyan's inspired allegory, especially his account of the bitter waters of doubt that close over Christian's head so very near his goal, have been a comfort to me since they have taken away my Lord, and I am having trouble finding Him.

I didn't introduce that reference to *Pilgrim's Progress* idly. It was through that sort of poetic approach that I was taught the Faith. It is not a contradiction to say that faith is at once a supernatural gift and a subject to be taught. Grace must use natural vehicles to reach men. The Catholic believes that the gift of faith is given to an infant in Baptism, but expects it to be nourished by a Catholic environment as love is nourished by constant care and attention. The catechism that I learned by memory ("by heart" is a truer term) was only the framework, the mathematical tables, the grammar, of my faith. All Catholic children learned the catechism answers, and catechists now say that is all they learned—a dry, cold legalism. That is not true. What a Catholic means by his faith is a spiritual, emotional, supra-rational comprehension and response, analagous to that produced by natural beauty, or, more closely, by certain poetry, music, or pictures. This side of faith was nourished by that much larger part of the religious program that directed its appeal through the senses and emotions. I spoke a little about it in Chapter 4. We were encouraged in a warm, personal love of Christ chiefly by examples of bravery, sacrifice and dash others had shown in His service.

Every thread of my Catholic education taught me to think of Christ as a living person, who could be met every day in Holy Communion, and who awaited my visits in the Tabernacle, under the Eucharistic Species, bread and wine no longer, but Body and Blood, soul and divinity. This teaching must have been extraordinarily effective because when, during that not uncommon crisis of faith in late adolescence, I felt no feeling of belief in God, I still believed with heart and mind in the Real Presence. I would kneel as close as I could to the Tabernacle and pray for my faith to return. That isn't logical, but faith isn't logic. Thomas Aquinas, having spent a whole brilliant lifetime working out the logic and philosophy of belief, having been granted some time before his death a vision of the Reality that was so infinitely more beautiful than the greatest scholar or poet can imagine, wrote across his labours: "It's all straw."

The preparation of children for Holy Communion was not romantic. It was strictly based on Scripture, old and new. But to this was added the emotional appeal—the story of St. Tarcisius, the young Roman kicked to death by his pagan contemporaries because he would not give up the Blessed Sacrament he was trying to convey to safety. Or of St. Imelda, whose longing to receive Holy Communion was such that the Sacred Host left the Tabernacle and came to her. We were prepared, too, through the popular Holy Communion hymns— "Jesus, my Lord, my God, my All"; "O What could my Jesus do more?"; "O Lord I am not worthy"; the Panis Angelicus, the Ave Verum—all full of the ecstacy of requited love. And the glorious prayers—of St. Ignatius: "Soul of Christ, sanctify me; Body of Christ, save me; Blood of Christ, inebriate me . . ." or of St. Thomas Aquinas, especially of him. His prayers seem to me the height of religious utterance outside Scripture. There is nothing else like the rapturous flight of his language, the perfect marriage of reason and emotion. Aquinas' eucharistic prayers are a complete instruction in the central Catholic Mystery. They are a miraculous expression of Catholic understanding of the Mystery of the Incarnation and of the incarnational quality of Catholicism.

"O marvellous sacrament in which God lies concealed, and our Jesus like another Moses cloaks His face under the creatures He has made! . . . By these Sacred Species we recognize the tree of life. Here, Lord Jesus, art Thou both shepherd and green pasture, priest and victim, meat and drink . . . strong meats full of marrow and wine purified from the lees . . . a ration for the march . . . living Bread, begotten in heaven, barmed in the womb of the Virgin, baked in the furnace of the Cross, brought forth to the altar under the disguise of the host." The domesticity of the language applied to the Word Incarnate is shocking and poignant. The clarity and sweetness of Aquinas' understanding of what he called "the central pillar of the Church," the Holy Eucharist, informed the whole of Catholic eucharistic piety. His hymns were sung at Benediction and on Holy Thursday and whenever Catholics required an act of faith in the Real Presence.

For better or worse, that is the piety of every Catholic generation until this one, when both liturgical practice and the compulsory catechisms have studiously set it aside. This understanding of the Incarnation colours the way a Catholic sees everything material. The belief that after Holy Communion we are tabernacles, that we become what we have eaten, gives us a reason for keeping the body pure and disciplined. It makes it easy to love the created world and one's own body. It helps us understand and obey the laws of Christian marriage, and respect our children because of their immortality.

Once in my life, every thread of this religious atmosphere of my childhood came together in the only experience I have ever had that might be called mystical. It took place at Mass. I was with child for the first time, feeling very sick, especially since I had been fasting from midnight as the rule then was, and debating whether or not I would go to Holy Communion. However, I did make my shaky way to the altar rail, and was glad to be able to sink down at it. The altar rail in those days was covered at Communion time with a white linen cloth which one held up under the chin at the moment of reception. The priest moved steadily along towards me, murmuring over and over the formula for communion—*Corpus Domini nostri Jesu Christi custodiat animam tuam in vitam aeternam*—May the Body of our Lord Jesus Christ preserve thy soul unto life everlasting. Just as the priest held up the Blessed Sacrament above me, my child gave a great leap, so powerful that I had to clutch the altar rail to keep from toppling over. I received Holy Communion, and I was filled with pure delight, for suddenly the picture and words of the Visitation sounded in my mind, and I shared in Elizabeth's experience. Just as Elizabeth, with child, greeted Mary who was carrying within her the Word Incarnate, "Whence is this to me that the Mother of my Lord should come to me? For behold as soon as the voice of thy salutation sounded in my ears, the infant in my womb leaped for joy," so I said as I received the Body of Christ: "How is it that my Lord should come to me?" I understood Incarnation, and the purpose of generative love, and the sweetness of the humility of Christ. I went back to my place saying the Magnificat.

It is a boring commonplace in every class on religion in a university that mystical experience is sexual in origin, the product in particular of sexual repression. The modern Manichaeans who say this have got hold of a truth the wrong way round. It is not the faculties of the body which move one to mystical joy, but the contemplation of an overwhelming mystical Reality which moves the body to pleasure. I find it easy now to believe that Saints like Teresa of Avila were lifted bodily off the ground by the force of their spiritual pleasure, or that the stigmata appeared on saints like Francis of Assisi, whose bodies were so sensitive in their perception of the suffering love of Christ. How, in contemplating the Incarnate, should the body of man *not* be violently moved to delight?

Every catechism class and religious service of my life had been leading me up to this sort of experience. All the lovely pictures of sharp-winged angels and radiant Madonnas, all the stories of saints in my school readers, all the communion hymns and motets we practised after school. The eucharistic devotions, Benediction and the Forty Hours, the fast from midnight, the early morning *missa cantata*, the hundred priestly gestures and reverences surrounding the Blessed Sacrament, all played a small indispensable part in the way I believed, and do still believe, in the Incarnation, Redemption, the Real Presence, and the Mystical Body of Christ.

What my children's generation will believe, bereft of all these things, I cannot speculate. Some time ago, I took part in a radio discussion with a Vancouver priest who was engaged in a row with his bishop. He kept saying that everything had changed in the Church since Vatican II, and when I pressed him to name one doctrine which had changed, he could not. Nevertheless, he insisted, "All you have to do is go into a Catholic church to see that everything has changed." He was right in an important way. No reading of *Mysterium Fidei* will comfort a faith whose emotional channels have been blocked up, by that assault on the externals of eucharistic piety that I described earlier.

Some Catholics have decided to regard this situation as a test of their faith, to see how it fares with all the supports knocked away. There doesn't seem to be much else to do.

Every time I see this suggestion put, it reminds me of that confrontation between Teresa of Avila and Christ. Teresa had been suffering a good deal and she complained of it to Christ. "Teresa," He said to her, "don't you know that I only treat my friends that way?" "Lord," answered Teresa, "it's no wonder You have so few friends!" Temptation to disbelief has always been regarded by spiritual writers as a tried and bitter test that can only be resisted by humble prayer and by an exercise of the will. "Thy dread wounds, like Thomas, though I cannot see, His be my confession, Lord and God, of Thee." One must decide to go on believing.

The reforms that were to make it easier to understand and believe have made it harder. I find it difficult to accept that this is the Holy Spirit working through the reformers who obviously don't believe what the Church believes. I have been puzzling as to why they should want to take away my faith, and I have come to the conclusion that the spirit working through the attack on eucharistic belief is the same dark Spirit who had designs on the faith and patience of Job. As Pope Paul put it, the smoke of Satan has entered into the Church. It makes the eyes smart and it is hard to see through it. But God allowed Satan to try Job because He wanted to give Job the chance to be perfect in faith and love. "Though He slay me," said Job grimly, "yet will I trust in Him." The Catholic will have to try to achieve something of this emotional response if he is to see the present crisis through. "The Lord gives, and the Lord takes away; Blessed be the Name of the Lord."

The layman often feels more like a donkey than like a creature "a little less than the angels." He plods along, laden and driven, with no time for contemplation, thrown husks instead of bread. But the natural world has an enchanting parable that might cheer up the plodding Catholic. There is a type of donkey that has, on its gray back, a large dark sign of the Cross. Legend says that this is because this donkey's ancestor was the one who was chosen by Christ to carry Him when he rode triumphantly into Jerusalem on Palm Sunday. One will recall Chesterton's poem about it, when the poor ass had his "far fierce hour and sweet," before he went back to his accustomed blows and nettles. The burdened Catholic layman is a donkey with the Cross on his back, the cross of having to keep vows and laws no one else is expected to keep, the cross of being fed acorns instead of milk and honey. But when he comes to appear at last before his Lord, he can lift his bewildered head and say: "See, I have been yours. See Your Sign upon my back. In this Sign I have conquered."

I know what the Church teaches about the Word Incarnate and His continuing Presence among us. I *will* to believe it, and I pray for final perseverance:

> O Jesus in the Blessed Sacrament of the altar, I have settled in my heart to go up to Thy sanctuary through the vale of tears, to the place which Thou hast appointed. He Who hast given the law will give His blessing. I will go from strength to strength. I will appear before the God of Gods in Sion. Lord, Whom now on my pilgrimage I receive under a veil, Lord, I believe: help Thou my unbelief.

CHAPTER 11

NOTES FOR THE
GUERRILLA CATHOLIC

Don't let the bastards drive you out of the Church.

JAMES DALY

Perhaps it is true, as Thomas Browne says, that every age feels that it is the one upon which the ends of the world have come. A Christian living now, whether or not he is expecting Armageddon, is perfectly justified in feeling that at any rate *his* world, Christian civilization, has ended. It is always difficult to set a date for an historical epoch, like the Middle Ages, like Christendom, so historians choose dates with symbolic weight. For example, philosopher Josef Pieper chooses 529 A.D. as the date of the end of pagan civilization and the beginning of the Christian Middle Ages. In that year the Christian Emperor Justinian closed the Platonic Academy in Athens, an event that Hegel called "the downfall of the physical establishments of pagan philosophy." Pagan civilization was moribund long before 529, but this action marked an official recognition of its death. In the same year, St. Benedict founded Monte Cassino, the symbol of a civilization dedicated to an opposite world view.

Future historians will hunt their symbolic moments, too. The one I choose (if I may be forgiven my Catholic bias) is the moment in 1971 when Pope Paul VI made the Tridentine

Mass obsolete. I think newspaper headlines that day ought to have read: WESTERN CHRISTIAN CIVILIZATION ENDS. Marshall McLuhan, at least sees it as the end of Greco-Roman civilization.

Perhaps, though, historians will choose a political event, in which case it ought to be the legalization of abortion on demand by Christian countries like England, Canada, and the United States. Because at that time those countries acknowledged that they were now officially committed to a world view, that is, to a concept of reality and of the nature and purpose of human life, that was radically different from the Christian. This does not mean that Christianity is dead, but that Christians admit that they are no longer able to influence the public actions or shape the private morality of their society.

There does seem to be, both in the secular and the religious world, a general uneasiness and depression about the prospects of Western civilization. The fear that technology has gotten out of control and become a Frankenstein's monster, the proliferation of doomsday-promising nuclear arms, the energy crisis real or manufactured, the failure of liberal universal education to produce liberal, world-minded citizens—all conspire towards producing as deeply pessimistic a mood among secular thinkers as the shrinking impact of Christianity does among religious. Arnold Toynbee has recently been writing very despairingly about the end of order. The Club of Rome and the Massachusetts Institute of Technology issue the gloomiest of prognoses. The MIT study "The Limits of Growth" waxed absolutely apocalyptic, even giving a definite date for Doomsday.

The religious man, in my case the conservative Catholic, is pessimistic in quite a different way. We never expected that education or technology or capitalism or politics would "work" in the way secular man hoped they would towards increasing goodness, justice, prosperity and happiness—that is, towards the kingdom of God on earth. We always found the spiritual Coúe-ism of Teilhard de Chardin—every day in every way we and God and the cosmos are getting better and better—both pernicious and mawkish. No alliance with science and liberal humanism will bring about the kingdom of God. We believe that the kingdom of heaven is within, and the kingdom of hell also; therefore, the battle is not against the bomb, or the internal combustion engine, or the multi-nationals, or wickedness in high places, but against our own wickedness, which is the only state we should seek to overthrow. For, once freed from the "rhetoric of our passions," as C.S.Lewis put it, we could by our life and work increase the prosperity and happiness of our neighbour, end war, and curb technology. It is that conviction, not a base habit of subservience, that tends to keep the Catholic obedient to less than perfect civil powers. He knows that there is no political solution to ills with spiritual causes. He agrees with the great religious and political conservative Doctor Johnson: "How small of all that human hearts endure, / That part which laws or kings can cause or cure."[1] It is that conviction too, which historically leads the Church to take Mother Teresa's way, or Jean Vanier's way, rather than the way of the revolutionary "Catholic Marxists." The way of the heart filled with love of the Blessés (as Vanier calls them) or the Poorest of the Poor (as Mother Teresa calls them) for the sake of the suffering and risen Christ, so that we may rise with Him. "Serving the poor without the Cross of Christ," said Mother Teresa, "is social work."

The Church's pessimism about the world has not prevented her from trying to make man's earthly lot more bearable while she taught him about eternal things. In the early Church the Christian lived the Gospel as best he could, took it for granted that he had little influence over the behaviour of society, and was allowed to take no part in the state's business. When Christianity became the official religion of the Empire, the Church necessarily felt that her mission could be advanced through Roman power structures. In the disorder after the fall of Rome, the Church became the only source of order in the West. She had to reinvent civilization. Extraordinary men like Pope St. Gregory the Great set the pattern for the Church's activity in society. Not of the world but most certainly *in* it. He fought, bargained with, and converted the barbarians, defended his own and the Church's estate with military vigour, and used their resources for a vast program of almsgiving to the dispossessed, collected the liturgical music which bears his name, acted as Novice Master to Europe's priests—and arranged for garbage collection in Rome. Admittedly, not all his successors have lived up to his standards, but the particular practical Roman genius, comfortable with the exercise of power yet able to combine it with great sanctity, interested in the arts of civilization, gifted in ritual, has continued to distinguish the Roman Bishopric and the univeral Church it governs.

The Church has often found it difficult to resolve the conflict between the claims of Caesar and of God. She philosophically accepts that for fallen human nature this problem is insoluble. Her mistakes in the exercise of power make many of her children yearn for the imagined purity and simplicity of the pre-Constantinian Church. Power corrupts, they reason; therefore the unpowerful are incorrupt. Post-Vatican II liberals talk a good deal about the Constantinian Church, shackled to one corrupt state after another ever since. Even conservative Catholics feel depression about the heavy weight of pomp and bureaucracy bequeathed by the baroque era and admit to a wish that it would quietly melt away. Even Pope Paul, as jealous about the purity of Church doctrine as any pre-Constantinian Pontiff, recently remarked (hopefully, one felt) that he was prepared to leave the Vatican if Protestants found it too much of a stumbling block to unity, too symbolic of Rome's worldly power.

But then the Catholic comforts himself with the knowledge that the structure of the Church (as distinct from the trappings among which most popes and cardinals manage to lead holy, ascetic lives) has been an unequalled means of serving mankind. Liberals, too, recognize the usefulness of the power structure of the Church, which is why they want to get control of it. The vast educational system of the Church, taken over at all levels, can, they are sure, change the Catholic world-view in a generation. The perfected rapid trustworthy communications network can be used for propaganda purposes. Catholic Marxists (their term, not mine; I think the combination meaningless), installed in the Third World missions, supplied with unlimited funds from the huge rich post-

Vatican II foundations like the Canadian Catholic Organization for Development and Peace, can work unharrassed towards "social justice."

Liberals do not eschew power. Nor do they really, for all Rosemary Ruether's talk of "post-Constantinian messianism," want the Church to take only a prophetic role in the world's affairs. What they want is for the Church to intervene in causes *they* choose. It is a wrong use of power, for example, when the Church tries to exercise its influence in the abortion controversy. It is a right use to support the grape boycott. It would be hideously wrong to support a Catholic country like Portugal in any way. It would be gloriously right and messianic to join the World Council of Churches and send help to Frelimo.

If liberals do gain control of the Church's structures, and do bring about their anti-dogmatic revolution, thereby committing Catholicism to an opposite world view, Catholicism will have ended. Conservatives do not think that the Church structures are perfect or work perfectly. They accept the possibility that they have been too passive because of their pessimism about the prospects of social justice and that the liberal vision may be a useful corrective, prodding them along lines they should go. They also accept that the Church is in constant need of renewal. They are not against the renewal actually legislated by Vatican II. If, with the liberals holding the reins of interpretation and implementation, the prescriptions of Vatican II had indeed been carried out, if religious orders *had* become poorer and simpler, if the liturgy *had* been revitalized without a total break from the past, if the plan to give new responsibility to the laity had been at all respected by the clergy, if the churches were full, not empty, and the children singing in the church, not sneering at her, conservatives would rejoice and humbly submit to the new regime. Yet they cannot rejoice and they will not submit if renewal means disintegration, when liturgy and Catholic piety are in ruins, when members of religious orders lead affluent, upper-class lives, when the laity is abused or ignored.

The conservative realizes the need also for continuous personal renewal. In pre-Vatican II days there was enormous scope and motivation for personal renewal—Confession, fast days, a strict Lent and Advent, parish missions (periodic occasions for renewal, preached by visiting missionaries, the emphasis being on self-examination and repentance), retreats. When even these have disappeared, what hope is there for a mass renewal of the universal Church?

It is easy for a Catholic like me, who grew up in the Church when it was rich and orderly, to despair, to feel that recovery is impossible. One must remember that there were bad times before and the Church emerged from them strong and reformed. Perhaps this particular bad time seems the most dangerous and unpleasant because we have to live through it.

So what do you do when the ends of the world come upon you? Well, I don't know what the Cream of Antigonish is planning, but as for me and my house, we are going to rally round the Catholic Church and the moral order it stands for. We will do what St. Augustine did the last time civilization fell, and devote ourselves to preserving what we believe is true, because we see these truths as necessary not only for our own salvation but for the preservation of any moral and social order. This course of action will open us, as it did Augustine, to the temptations of unfairness, uncharity, and narrowness; polemics are polemical, whether Catholic or not.

We are conservatives; we are going to conserve. And it's uphill work, always against the *zeitgeist*. Sometimes even the stoutest conservative heart wearies. One's adversaries are so bright and confident, what they say sounds so persuasive. The conservative, in the small hours, will sometimes ask himself, "What if they're right?" and meditate upon the theme that the old order changeth, yielding place to new, from time to time, and perhaps this is one of the times. And the musing conservative will admit that he is temperamentally disposed to resist change, and left to himself, would never change anything at all. I am quite sure that if I had lived in the time of Christ, I would have rejected Him and gone on being an orthodox Jew. Unless, of course, He had stricken me with the hard stroke of Faith, as he did that most zealous of orthodox Jews, St. Paul. Which is why I have always considered myself lucky *not* to have lived at the time of Christ. And I have always felt the utmost sympathy for pagans like Quintus Aurelius Symmachus, who, after the gods of Rome were officially displaced by the Emperor, devoted his life and his fortune to keeping their altars warm.

Therefore, the Catholic conservative must be scrupulous that he is defending traditions not because they are *traditional* but because they are *true*. It is not the *Vatican* that is the important thing about the papacy; the Pope would be the infallible successor of Peter wherever he found himself, even as once at Avignon. (The conservative is likely, though, to insist that the Pope's leaving the Vatican would weaken the *idea* of infallibility.) But how can he be sure what is true? He can be sure if he is following the Church. He has entrusted his mind, will, and heart to the Church which has Christ's promise of inerrancy. This is no base bondage; its absence is not freedom. If he does not give "religious submission of his mind and will" to the Church, he knows they will be at the command of every prevailing hypothesis. They will not thereby be free to believe *nothing*, but, as Chesterton said, *everything*. The Act of Faith each Catholic learned as a child, after reciting the chief truths of faith, concluded in this manner: "I believe these and all the truths which the Holy Catholic Church teaches, because Thou hast revealed them, Who neither canst deceive nor be deceived."

I have come to think that the conservative has an unfair advantage over the liberal because with the gift of faith he was given the gift of a conservative temperament which makes it easier for him to accept a dogmatic religion. This very temperament, oddly enough, sometimes produces an impassioned liberal. For the conservative tendency is to stick tenaciously to what one was taught. Newman noted this rather ruefully when he was musing over the "inconsistency" of the Catholic Lacordaire's being a liberal, while he, Newman, still a Protestant, was an "anti-liberal."

> We were both of us such good conservatives, as to take up with what we happened to find established in our

respective countries, at the time we came into active life. Toryism was the creed of Oxford; he inherited, and made the best of, the French Revolution.[2]

It was, therefore, Lacordaire's basic conservatism that enabled him, though bitterly disappointed, to submit when the Church condemned his liberal activities. Also, it is often obedience to what they were taught in liberalized post-Vatican high schools and seminaries, rather than malicious infidelity, which has produced the present crop of young liberal priests.

The conservative in his charity should take into account the inborn temperament that inclines the liberal against the dogmatic in religion. Conservatives tend to consider all liberals infidels engaged in a conspiracy to destroy the faith of everyone else. There are probably, among those who are presently attacking Catholic dogmatism, men angry at the wasted years they served a faith they have now lost and resentful at the faith of others, but these are surely a minority. Conservatives should accept that the liberal fired up with a new idea, or bent on making a "progressive" change, genuinely believes, *at the moment*, that the new idea is true, and the change for the better. They should not be surprised, either, when they find, not too much later, that the liberal no longer believes what the conservatives took such pains to refute. Liberalism does not so much repudiate its errors as move on past them. So though, of course, it has to be done, it is something of a waste of time to combat furiously each new liberal enthusiasm as it is sent onstage.

The conservative mission must be chiefly to defend the great truths and cultivate them. The conservative is going to have to get used to defending them against many of his priests. For the sake of his blood pressure, he must accept that he is out of power, that the newest military technology is on the other side. Therefore, his form of warfare must be the guerrilla skirmish that makes the government remember him and what he stands for. Even though he loses all the battles, he must not lose heart and he must not surrender. He must stay alive.

Herewith some suggestions for the embattled conservative Catholic. Pray a lot. That goes without saying. Pray twice as much as you have been praying. Do it when you can in the Presence of the Blessed Sacrament. Every Catholic Church in which the Blessed Sacrament is reserved should be open in the daylight hours. If yours is not, ask your pastor why. He will say it is because of the growing occurrence of theft and vandalism. Offer to organize a roster of people to hold Perpetual Adoration during the daytime. Ask for a regular collection to pay a watchman. If the priest still refuses to keep the church open, make a large sign reading: "Father ——— has locked up the church." Sit in front of his house holding it.

What is most frequently stolen from churches is the sound system, a recent aquisition in most Catholic churches, since the nature of the liturgical changes seems to depend on the congregation's being able to hear every syllable. If it disappears from your church, thank God, and do not let your pastor replace it.

Tackle the priest after Mass every time he makes a change in the liturgy. If he says the change is authorized, ask him to show you the authorization. Even if you loathe the new liturgy, you have, I think, a duty to insist that it be respected.

The precept that binds a Catholic to contribute to the support of the Church and her clergy does not specify *which* clergyman. If the presence on CCODP (the Candian Catholic Organization for Development and Peace) payroll of so many "animateurs" and "Latin American leadership training centres" alarms you, send your contribution directly to a missionary priest or nun; most Catholics have a relative in the missions; ask round. At least the priest or nun will pray for you which is something you can bet your last CCODP dollar no animateur will do. If the Catholic Church joins the World Council of Churches, never again put a cent in the collection plate. If it comes to that, support your priest directly; personally help pay his grocery and gas bills.

Keep an eagle eye on the religious education given your children in Catholic schools. I do not see any reason why a Catholic school which disregards parents' wishes in the issues of religious and sex education deserves the allegiance of Catholics. Acquire the *Penny Catechism*[3] and teach your children at least the grammar of Catholicism at home. If your teenager will not be studying *Humanae Vitae* and the *Credo of the People of God* and the *Dogmatic Constitution on the Church* in your local Catholic high school, send him to the public secondary school. Turn up at adult education sessions and give the liberal priest and his Dutch catechism a workout. Have him read that section of the Vatican II documents that he claims supports what he is saying. Do not accuse people of heresy—just ask them politely to support their remarks from official Church teaching.

Read Catholic newspapers; write to and for them.

If by some liberal slip-up you get appointed to a parish council, liturgical team, or catechism committee, stick it out. Do not resign when the error is discovered. You can at least abate liberal change-worship a little, even if you cannot restore your parish-Mass-school to pristine orthodoxy.

If you have a good priest, as so many of us, thank God, still do, support him. Parish priests tend to be more conservative than liberal and to be less prone than religious priests to destructive enthusiasms. The typical parish priest is still a man of solid undemonstrative piety, who lives in a working-class style, plays a little golf and a little poker, has a large supportive circle of clerical friends and is healthily celibate, and holds a just, if skeptical appreciation of his parishioners' merits. Your priest may seem to you a trifle unenergetic; if he is not suffering an identity crisis, forgive him anything. Count your blessings.

The parish priest is likely to prefer the vernacular Mass, but he probably has not set his face against the Latin for ideological reasons. He is obedient, and if the bishops make a move to reinstate Latin, he will comply.

I have thus far in this chapter been discussing the spiritual side of the Church and how to defend it. But the lay Catholic, not having been called to the contemplative life in a monastery, has to try to involve himself in a Christ-like manner in the active apostolate in the world. What is the Catholic's duty towards the society he lives in? I have here to narrow my discussion to the duty of the Catholic in free, democratic, Western society. (The duty of the Christian under persecution is to suffer. Probably one's duty is clearer then. Religion thrives under persecution, yet reaches fewer people and holds only the strongest. Solzhenitsyn and Tolstoy came to feel that under a tyranny only the imprisoned are free.) Here we have at least the illusion that individual and collective action might press a government to act more justly.

Since, until quite recently, most Catholics in this country were working class, therefore relatively poor, uneducated, and bound to one place, the parish was the most important social structure in the Catholic's world, and it was natural that any good works they aimed at society would be directed through parish organizations. Before Vatican II, most Catholics belonged to some parish organization—the Knights of Columbus, the Catholic Women's League, the St. Vincent de Paul Society, the Holy Name Society, or one of dozens more. The "spirit of Vatican II" was very scornful of these organizations, largely because they were working class, but also because they were spending too much of their energy on fund-raising.

I heard one of the young priests I mentioned earlier go on at withering length about a Catholic Women's League meeting he had attended at which a great deal of time had been devoted to the discussion of who should get a presentation gold pin. Yet he and his associates devoted the first few planning sessions of their adult education program to a discussion of how to raise funds for his salary. Nor did he scorn the services of the Catholic Women's League in running a dance to produce said funds. There is good fund-raising and bad fund-raising. For a liberal cause (i.e., the grape boycott) by chic means (i.e., "starvation luncheons," visiting lecturers, teach-ins), fund-raising by Catholic ladies is still most acceptable.

Many of the Catholic societies have perished since Vatican II and those that are left are declining. This does not mean that the Catholics who belonged to them have found new outlets for social concern. On the contrary. Since few liberal causes appeal to them (they cannot see the theological difference between the UFW and the Teamsters), they have turned in upon their own concerns. That is a great pity. Because the Catholic in a pre-Vatican parish *was* world-minded. Every Catholic from the youngest schoolchild was involved with the foreign missions, which were the only way of reaching the destitute in Africa, China and countless obscure places. Every classroom, and most homes, had a "mite box," into which, like the poor widow in the Gospel, the Catholic put his little gift to his poorer brother. (When I was a child, I asked my mother, if I could save up five dollars to "buy" a black baby. "Yes," said my mother, "but don't bring it home." I must own a piece of everyone in the Congo called Mary, Patrick, Matthew, etc.) Crude? Perhaps. Useful? Certainly. Also uncorrupt. After the Second World War, when UNRRA was trying to reach the starving, it turned over its supplies to missionaries to distribute. It is interesting that the only post-Vatican II Catholic charitable organization to catch the popular imagination and flourish is the Co-Workers of Mother Teresa, laity who serve the poorest of the poor and lonely in their own parishes and send funds also directly to Mother Teresa. It is interesting, too, that the government of officially Hindu India distributes a great deal of its poor relief through her order.

Catholics are at a moment of decision (one prays it is not a continuing moment of uncertainty) about the nature, purpose and direction of their social involvement. They hear constantly that their pre-Vatican efforts were useless in the advancement of "social justice," that their piety has not been a help but a hindrance to the world. This is the constant theme of Canada's *Peritus par excellence*, Gregory Baum. He is always criticizing the Church for "its relative absence in social action"[4] and comparing it unfavourably with other churches.

> In Methodism and Anglicanism there has always been a strong minority of people concerned about social justice. The Roman Catholic Church, on the other hand, has a traditional piety which is narrowly individualistic. In our prayers and spirituality there has been no room for the concerns of society.[5]

This statement is not true. It is indefensible. The Church has not only always taught and practised the corporal works of mercy, she has from the beginning engaged herself with social concerns. She put down the blood feud among the barbarians thus preserving their society, even though those same barbarians were trying to destroy her material structures. She stopped duelling and trial by combat and forbade slavery. She came in the person of priests and nuns with immigrants and refugees, got them their first jobs, put their children into school, dealt with the new bureaucracy for them. Single-handedly she coped with the social problem of leprosy. Surely society is better for her large confident presence in her hospitals, schools, asylums, homes for the aged. Whenever she has intervened politically, whether against communism or divorce, she was combating what she saw as serious social dangers. That statement of Baum's is stupid, unhistorical and mischievous. And it is threatening to become accepted wisdom.

Baum's remarks were made in an interview concerning the formation of a Toronto organization called Catholics for Social Change of which he is a leading member. It has come into being because of the Church's "indifference" on certain matters—the lead poisoning debate, housing, the plight of Chilean refugees, the concerns of citizens' action groups, the fate of political prisoners in South Vietnam. In these causes, Catholics for Social Change "found more support from Anglicans and Protestants than from Catholics 'at any level.' "[6] (If they are really interested in collecting some Catholic support, CSC strategists might in the future disguise their leftist bias and include political prisoners in *North* Vietnam or the Ukraine.)

The Church on earth, in spite of its conviction and efforts, does not do enough for society, nor will it ever, because of the weak humanity of its members. Nevertheless, it must always try harder to intensify its efforts. But would it satisfy its critics if it pressed every one of its members into its traditional works of mercy? Are Mother Teresa and Jean Vanier engaged in the proper sort of apostolate? No, to both questions. Mother Teresa and Vanier are directly in the Catholic tradition of social works and that, according to its critics, has had a long trial and has not succeeded. In spite of all the sanctity of St. Vincent de Paul, St. Peter Claver, Father Damien, and Mother Teresa, there are still lepers in the gutters, black men in subjection, and babies in the dustbins of the world.

What is needed now, say Baum and the like-minded, is a change of consciousness, a different world view, a new direction for our efforts. A different concept of sin, of society, of humanity. "The task of the church equipped with the Gospel is to raise the consciousness of the community," said Baum at an ecumenical conference on the Survival of Canada and the Christian Church at St. Michael's College, Toronto, in 1973. That is, the consciousness of sin as "social," not "individual," not an evil confessed by a man in the confessional, but existing in the corporate institutions of a society, in the Church, the professions, the businesses. It is this "social" sin that causes war, genocide, advertising, foreign ownership, industrialization, land speculation.[7] It was this sense of social sin which the Canadian bishops should have stressed in their 1974 letter on the formation of conscience. Instead, this was "too individualistic. The Bishops seem to recommend a conformist conscience when what we need is a restless, creative conscience."[8]

If this sounds to the conservative Catholic very like a Marxist view of society, that's because it is. For it is well to be clear about what sort of social change Baum and Catholics for Social Change want to bring about. They want to replace this capitalist society by a Marxist one. Now there is no need for the Catholic to be committed to capitalism, any more than to feudalism, which are historical not theological developments. (Though it is generally done, it is even a mistake to identify the Catholic with the conservative in politics. In this country, they vote liberal or Social Credit, rather than Tory; in the United States, Democratic rather than Republican. There was a large reluctant shift to the Republican party in 1972 by Catholics because of the Democratic McGovern's stand on certain moral issues. Still, one of the leading conservative writers in the United States, James Hitchcock, supported McGovern. One of the few genuine populists in Canada, Joseph Borowski, ex-NDP Member of Parliament in Manitoba, is also one of the most conservative Catholics. Likewise, a large part of rural Quebec is radical on the right.)

The great Christian writer, C.S. Lewis said that if there existed an ideal Christian society, its economic life would be very socialistic and its morality very conservative. And Lord Longford, leader of the Catholic opposition in England to the abortion bill, wrote in his autobiography that he had been led to the Labour Party by the Gospels.

The new Catholic left, in Toronto or South America, differs from Lewis and Longford and Borowski not in economic policy but in world view. It is committed to the transformation of society by revolution. The Marxist view of the irresistible evolutionary process of humanity has been opportunely bolstered for the Catholic left by Teilhard de Chardin's "evolutionary Cosmos" process theology.[9] Neither Marxism nor Teilhardianism has room for the concept of original sin and the fall of man, therefore no need for a belief in individual redemption.[10] Both are deterministic and progressive, both hold that change is always for the better and man and society perfectible. To this world view, the traditional Christian, like Lewis, or any conservative Catholic, is in total opposition. This is why Baum and his Catholics for Social Change get no support from Catholics "at any level." For most Catholics still do hold the traditional world view. Mother Teresa is going to go on with glorious optimism teaching the street people of Calcutta how to limit their families by "reverential" means, those which the Church approves, and will not take up arms against the Congress Party or the multinationals. And most Catholics will go on admiring her and disliking Baum. Unless, of course, they can be converted, which process, as Rosemary Ruether noted, is comfortably under way. That is why, as a first step, the story of the Fall has disappeared from the catechism. And why "Teilhard de Chardin" Masses are so popular in university circles. And why every adult education seminar discusses "process theology." It is why liberal liturgical reformers arbitrarily translated "the *sins* of the world" as "the *sin* of the world" in the Mass.

It is really a sign of extraordinary religious sophistication on the part of very ordinary Catholics that they instinctively reject most liberal causes. They see past *what* the liberals are backing to *why* they are so doing. When, since Vatican II, they have taken up some social issue, like abortion, it is invariably one of which left liberals disapprove. Rosemary Ruether and

Mary Daly are pro-abortion. Baum, as he wrote recently in *Commonweal*, is "emotionally" against abortion (and who gives a damn about a theologian's emotions?) but swayed by the "witness" of liberal Protestants he admires.

So, inexorably set against the liberal concept of "social change" and, though sometimes mistakenly, against liberal causes, how does the Catholic address himself to helping society? The corporal works of mercy are still the same—feed the hungry, clothe the naked, shelter the homeless, visit the sick and the imprisoned, with the same consolation: "As long as you did it to one of these least, my little ones, you did it unto Me." Individuals, and existing Catholic societies, should consider fresh ways of doing the old works.

The virtual collapse of episcopal leadership and the disappearance of religious orders has given the laity unexpected scope for social action. Perhaps Vatican II's promised "age of the laity" is really coming to pass, though certainly not as intended. And the laity has, rather surprisingly for those who accept the view of laymen as downtrodden sheep, moved into the vacuum with cheerful purposefulness. The best recent example of this is the fight to prevent abortion on demand. As I have noted, the laity was for a long time on its own in this area. It reacted in an impeccably Roman Catholic way. It set up a Right to Life movement with two sides: one, for educational and political activities, the second, founded by Catholic convert Louise Summerhill, a practical caring organization called Birthright. Conservative Catholics might join either or both.

The Right to Life movement is mainly Catholic, though there are many Protestants, some Jews, and even a few agnostics. It has so far managed to avoid sectarianism. On the contrary, it has engendered a truly respectful and realistic ecumenical spirit.

Since this is a country where, to stay in power, politicians must sometimes defer to public opinion, the educational arm of the pro-life movement marches, lobbies, and collects signatures. Catholics are not easily moved to activities like these, but so deep in their being is imbedded the idea that an immortal soul exists from the first moment of conception, so steeped is the Catholic imagination in the exquisite stories and pictures of the Annunciation, Visitation and Nativity, that the Catholic marching on Parliament for the sake of the unborn considers himself, in a very real manner, to be taking part in a religious procession. (Not surprisingly, in a huge march on the Hill in November 1973, the Blue Army of Mary turned up, complete with banner.)

The Catholic engaged in political action today expects little from it. Gone are the days of John Courtney Murray and his theories of "civility" and compromise, his teaching that there is no final incompatibility between Catholicism and the American system (he might have said the "democratic" system of most of the Western World), and that Catholics need not try to make their government reflect Catholic truths. Catholics, who, accepting "pluralism," accepted divorce and the legalized sale of birth control devices, cannot stretch their civility to cover abortion on demand and legalized pornography. Some few can, of course. Jesuit Father Robert Drinan, Democratic Congressman from Massachusetts, and Sister Mary Anne Guthrie, candidate for the Democratic nomination in Tennessee, hold that abortion is a moral problem peculiar to Catholics and not a question of legislative action. Jesuit Father Richard McCormick has recently embraced the quality of life approach to euthanasia. Canadian Jesuit Father John Pungente, from his position as chairman of Manitoba's Film Classification Board, was shocked when police seized *Last Tango in Paris*. He had wanted to give it an "adult parental guidance" rating. All these priests, however, are Jesuits, members of a religious order that has gone off its collective head.

The ordinary Catholic realizes that there is little hope of accommodation with the values of liberal democracy in the 1970s. He finds that he is living in the post-Christian era, and that he is being shut out of the political sphere, as in pre-Constantinian days. Today, as then, public morality is decaying, public entertainment is murderous and pornographic, and government is dedicated to implementing an anti-Christian world view. Thus, the Catholics (and like-minded Jews and Protestants) engaged in collecting signatures for a petition to

Parliament beseeching it to legislate to protect human life from conception to natural death, though they hope to double their original estimate, also accept, quite without anger, that it will eventually make no difference, that a society bent on its own destruction cannot be turned away from it by the polite adherence of Christians (and Jews) to democratic rules. On this point, conservative and radical (not liberal) Catholics meet.

More and more Catholics are, like the Jehovah's Witnesses, opting out of the democratic process, not voting, not trying to influence MPs. They have come to regard their society not as pluralistic but as pagan, and to reconsider the terms of their allegiance to it. A bitter quarrel has arisen in the United States among conservative Catholics about Catholic involvement in the present sort of government. One school of thought, that of John Courtney Murray and *National Review*, is still optimistic about the possibility of being both loyal Americans and good Catholics. The other, represented by *Triumph* magazine (edited by Brent Bozell, convert and brother-in-law of *National Review's* editor William Buckley) and the *Christian Commonwealth Society*, believes that the present state is anti-Christian and has forfeited the loyalty and obedience of Catholic Americans. Catholics must now work towards its replacement by a Catholic political order. One has to be very optimistic to agree with either.

To stand publicly for Christian values, against pornography, for the value of human life, is, even now in Canada and America, to be labelled a bigot, a reactionary, or a Bircher. Joseph Borowski, protesting the obscenity of *Last Tango*, was called by the Toronto *Star* "the Archie Bunker of the Manitoba legislature," and when he resigned from the Cabinet because of his anti-abortion stand, the *Globe* congratulated Manitoba for being free henceforth from "yahoo politics." One recalls, too, the ridicule heaped upon Lord Longford ("Lord Porn") and on Malcolm Muggeridge. It is not hard to envisage a time when, as before Constantine, to be a Christian will be considered seditious and deserving of death. After all, programs that were considered crimes against civilization when Nazi Germany carried them out are now becoming perfectly acceptable social engineering tools —sterilization of the "unfit" and of the chronically poor (as recently in Alabama), abortion of the unborn whom tests suggest may be retarded, experimentation on live aborted babies—and the element of coercion has already entered into their use. When a nation which has lately been marching under the banner "In God We Trust" provides public money for laboratory experimentation on live young human beings, Christians may wonder what is their duty toward it, and whether they should lend countenance to its politics by sharing in its power structure.

There is, nonetheless, one further course I would suggest, whether the Catholic is warring on the theological or political front. Set up a conservative organization or join Catholics United for the Faith (even though, as the *Western Catholic Reporter* sniffed, "it is one American import we can do without"). This both cheers one up, or gives one a shoulder to cry on, and provides a visible conservative presence in the liberal wastes. The liberals are masters at this game. To rephrase Ruether, you don't have to leave the Church to agree with the Pope—set up a discussion group. Have a Forum (as CUF does). Bring in your own *peritus*.

Gregory Baum, speaking to the Newman Society at London University, England, in April 1974, dividing the Church into *them* (the parishes) and *us* (the universities, catechetical institutes, etc.), advised the Catholic intelligentsia to set up a group and make militant noises through it. A group of twelve persons, he said, were enough to form a front with a name like "Catholics for Social Change" (that's right, *our* "Catholics for Social Change"). The name gets known, you are reported in the media (they are, indeed) and you take up occasional newsworthy causes—he mentioned the case of a squatter in an abandoned house. That's all it takes, besides a little patience.[11] That's advice from a master, and conservative Catholics ought to take it under consideration.

The Catholic, no matter how bad things get, ought to consider himself fortunate to belong to the Church and pray for the grace of final perseverance. Even now, when so many of her members are doing their best to discredit her, she is more than ever worthy of Catholic allegiance, and the respect and gratitude of society. For she stands for everything we in the West call civilization; indeed, she might be said to have invented it. The world's most beautiful music was written to be sung at her Masses; the most beautiful pictures were painted to illuminate her Hours. She alone can make the Word flesh, can make of history a seamless garment, can resist the spell of contemporaneity. The promise of Christ to her is still true—she still holds the Keys of the Kingdom. The words of Pius XI of her are still valid: she is still "standing erect in the midst of the moral ruin which surrounds her." This is why she must continue as a visible sign in society.

Catholics who believe in her must not leave her, no matter to what degree of rage and despair they are reduced by the antics of her priests. The disorder is going to get worse throughout our lifetime; that doesn't matter. The gates of hell will not prevail. Descendants of ours as far removed in time from us as we are from Augustine will, if the ends of the world have not by then truly come, practise a Catholicism that would startle neither Augustine nor us, could we observe it.

Several years ago, in a storm of fury over what was happening I decided to leave the Church. I told my decision to a Catholic friend, a belligerent conservative of long standing. He was horror struck: "Never!" he roared. "Never! Don't let the bastards drive you out of the Church!" Not a pious sentiment, but it will do as a slogan for my own private Pilgrimage of Grace. Perhaps I shall have it embroidered in gold on one of those modish new banners, and carry it about to Catholic gatherings. Maybe they'll let me hang it with those other improving sentiments in St. Michael's, to cheer up the stranded conservative.

Courage, friends. What is needed now is a little dash, a little panache in the service of the King and the Kingdom. Let us keep ourselves warm at the Tabernacle. Let us go into battle "with a stirrup cup each to the Lily of Ladies who love us, Mary Immaculate!"

Where Peter is, there is the Church, And don't let the bastards drive you out of it.

NOTES

Chapter 1

1 "Continuing Reform After Vatican II," *The Month*, March 1973.
2 The quotation from Cardinal Newman throughout this chapter are from *Apologia Pro Vita Sua* and *Note A* to the same, *On Liberalism*.
3 William F. Buckley, *Up From Liberalism*. The comment pertains to political conservatism but is as true of religious conservatism.
4 An even riper example: Rosemary Ruether again, in an interview on CBC Radio, agreed with host Peter Gzowski's label of "obscene" for those football players who committed the shocking act of praying before and after their games. When Gzowski, pursuing the subject of worthy prayer, asked her what was the difference between the way she and the Berrigans prayed and the way football players and others prayed, she answered, modestly, that she thought it was the difference between truth and falsehood. There it is in a nutshell—the nature of truth revealed by a Catholic lady radical on a talk show.
5 This is a perfect example of Modernist reasoning. Modernism is so insidious because it keeps the formula of the teaching but empties it of its traditional meaning. It seeks to "demythologize" the Scripture, to explain in natural terms the miraculous. The Protestant theologian Rudolf Bultmann, the leading proponent of this type of exegesis, is the particular hero of liberal Catholic scriptural scholars.
6 Newman, "On Consulting the Faithful in Matters of Doctrine."

Chapter 2

1 Quoted by "Xavier Rynne," *Vatican Council* II (New York, 1968).
2 "Christ, the one Mediator, established and continually sustains here on earth His holy Church, the community of faith, hope and charity, as an entity with visible delineation through which He communicated truth and grace to all. But, the society structured with hierarchical organs and the Mystical Body of Christ, are not to be considered as two realities, nor are the visible assembly and the spiritual community, nor the earthly Church and the Church enriched with heavenly things; rather they form one complex reality which coalesces from a

divine and a human element. For this reason, by no weak analogy, it is compared to the mystery of the incarnate word. As the assumed nature inseparably united to Him, serves the divine Word as a living organ of salvation, so, in a similar way, does the visible social structure of the Church serve the Spirit of Christ, who vivifies it, in the building up of the body. This is the one Church of Christ which in the Creed is professed as one, holy, catholic, and apostolic, which our Saviour, after His Resurrection, commissioned Peter to shepherd, and him and the other apostles to extend and direct with authority, which He erected for all ages as "the pillar and mainstay of the truth. This Church constituted and organized in the world as a society, subsists in the Catholic Church, which is governed by the successor of Peter and by the Bishops in communion with him, although many elements of sanctification and of truth are found outside the visible structure. These elements, as gifts belonging to the Church of Christ, are forces impelling toward Catholic unity."

3   Interview published in *Christian Order*, December 1973.
4   If you are not a Catholic and you want to know what the Catholic Church officially believes and teaches in 1974, read the *Credo of the People of God*; you will find it in Appendix A of this book. If you are a Catholic, reduced by your priest to that state of panic where you hear yourself saying: "I don't know what to believe anymore," try the *Credo*. And teach it to your children, for it is very unlikely that they will get it from their Catholic school.
5   Rosemary Ruether, "Continuing Reform After Vatican II."
6   As witnessed by the spectacle of Princeton, and of the Canadian universities Brock, Trent, and Toronto, where demonstrating students prevented the proponents of racial inequality theories from speaking. The SDS leader who led the Toronto riot said in a hearing on the matter that error had no right to be heard.
7   Albania recently shot a priest for baptizing a baby; in China saying Mass brings a life sentence; Mao and Hoxha are acting logically, for Catholicism and Marxism stand for exactly opposite world views, and the existence of either threatens the other.
8   Even for hard-nosed conservative Catholics like me, who make it a rule to believe two impossible things before breakfast, Loreto is fairly far down the list of pieties. The story is that after the fall of the Latin Kingdom of Jerusalem in 1291, Mary's house was miraculously transported by angels to Fiume, Italy, to preserve it from desecration. Since it was not properly venerated there, it was relocated three more times (by angels) ending up at Loreto, in the Marches of the Adriatic. This devotion appealed to medieval and baroque extravagance, and was declared authentic by Pope Julius II, in 1507. There is a Feast Day Mass for December 1. Many popes gave treasures to the shrine, including Pope John, whose gift of a ring, golden chalice and monstrance was part of the haul gained by robbers in January 1974,

when the shrine was looted. Our Lady of Loreto is the patron saint of airmen.
9 Reported in a letter to *America*, April 15, 1972, by Rev. Joseph W. Oppitz, C.S.R.
10 My convert husband once wrote the Pope, to my absolute astonishment. Just the sort of thing a Protestant *would* do, we told him. I shouldn't think anyone outside Canada even read his letter, for he got an answer from a Secretariat in Ottawa, conveying the papal blessing. It was nice to have, but we would have liked to give our blessing to him.

Chapter 6

1 Moderator McClure's objection to the Omnibus Bill was limited to the section that permitted lotteries. A typical manifestation of Manichaeism in the United Church.
2 The two best studies are: *Retreat From Faith*, by Professor James Daly and others from the St. Athanasius Society, Box 6245, Station F, Hamilton, Ontario, L9C583; and, *Remarks on the Canadian Catechism*, by the Rev. Aloysius M. Ambrozic, a professor of New Testament exegesis at the Toronto School of Theology. Published by Mission Press and distributed by the Catholic Truth Society, 67 Bond Street, Toronto, Ontario, M5B 1X4.
3 Individual bishops gave interviews. A Toronto newspaper quoted Bishop Emmett Carter thus: "The Bishop of London said that Pope Paul's controversial birth control encyclical does not, in his opinion, constitute an outright ban on the use of the pills which regulate birth." The Bishop said he had been misquoted. The *Catholic Register* asked him how. It reported that: "The Bishop agreed that he said he interpreted a section of the encyclical as allowing the use of pills to regularize fertile and infertile periods but questioned the wording which accompanied the development of his thought."
4 I have used the account by the *Western Catholic Reporter* for October 3, 1968, because it is the fullest and most revealing account of the Winnipeg meeting and the way post-Conciliar Catholic business is done.
5 The Winnipeg *periti* were: Jesuit moral theologian Father Edward Sheridan; Father Ora McManus, chairman of the Western Canadian Conference of Priests; Father Andre Naud, President of the Canadian Institute of Theology; Father Charles St. Onge, director of the French section of the Canadian Catholic Conference's family life bureau; and Bernard Daly, director of the English section of the same bureau. If it seems to be stacking the deck to appoint as consultors on a statement on *Humanae Vitae* the same men— Naud, St. Onge, Daly, McManus—who had led public dissent against it, one must

remember that that is the way the Holy Spirit reaches "progressive Bishops" in these renewed post-Vatican II days.

Chapter 7

1 *Globe and Mail,* August 7, 1968
2 *Gaudium et Spes,* the Council document on the church in the modern world, says: "But in their manner of acting, spouses should be aware that they cannot proceed arbitrarily, but must always be governed according to a conscience dutifully conformed to the divine law itself, and should be submissive toward the Church's teaching office, which authentically interprets that law in the light of the Gospel". And later: "Sons of the Church may not undertake methods of birth control which are found blameworthy by the teaching authority of the Church in its unfolding of the divine law." This latter sentence was one of the passages subjected to Papal amendment. Pope Paul wanted it to read: ". . . *have been or will be* found blameworthy . . ." The Bishops stuck out for: ". . . *are* found blameworthy . . ." which, until 1968, they thought was open-ended.
3 Recently, a Canadian Government report on our efforts in this direction in Libya noted sadly that though Libyan Moslems had quickly learned the natural family planning methods taught by Canadian teams, they had used their knowledge to *increase* the number of their children. Very funny.
4 *Gaudium et Spes,* 50.
5 Recently, summer 1974, Xerox Corporation agreed to withdraw the booklet from distribution after the newly formed Catholic League for Religious and Civil Rights threatened legal action.

Chapter 8

1 At least one hierarchy, the French, disregarded the Pope's revision of the General Introduction. The official "Nouvel Missel des dimanches" both in its 1969 and 1973 editions, has this description of the Mass—"*il s'agit simplement de faire memoire de l'unique sacrifice déjá accompli.*" The refusal of the French bishops to change this has caused charges that Masses in France celebrated according to this avowed intention are not valid. Likewise, the Canadian hierarchy has authorized as its only Catechism, the Paulist Press *Come to the Father* series whose teaching on the Mass carefully avoids traditional Catholic teaching on Sacrifice, transubstantiation, and the Real Presence. Its eight years of catechesis, though ambiguous to the point where St. Thomas Aquinas himself would find himself at a loss to sum up what the post-Vatican II Catholic Church believes and teaches about the Mass, is definite about the memorial meal aspect which is so central to Protestant theology on the Eucharist. The Grade V program

Building the New Earth puts it this way on the Parents' Page (119): "Does the fact that the Mass is now celebrated in English help us to understand better that the Mass is a meal, "in memory of the Lord," an act of thanksgiving for his death and resurrection?" In an earlier book (I, P.121) the catechism states firmly: "We avoid stressing the miraculous side of the consecration of the bread and wine . . ." The French and Canadian catechists have been selective about what they took from the *Constitution on the Sacred Liturgy*, and might never have heard of the Council of Trent, the *Credo of the People of God* or *Mysterium Fidei*.

2 William Buckley, *Cruising Speed*.
3 He gave an unintentionally comic Donner and Blitzen list of them: "Neither Kuss nor Schelkle nor Schlier nor Schnackenburg nor Vogtle. . . ."
4 J.D. Crichton, *The Church's Worship: Considerations of the Liturgical Constitution* (New York: Sheed & Ward, 1964).
5 Louis Bouyer, *The Liturgy Revived: A Commentary on the Constitution* (Notre Dame, Indiana: University of Notre Dame Press, 1964).
6 I. Stuber and Claud Nelson, *Implementing Vatican II in Your Community* (New York: Association Press, 1967).
7 Quoted by "Xavier Rynne," *Vatican Council II* (New York: 1968). This account of the Council, containing material from his earlier books on each session gives one a new insight into the word "triumphalist." It's fun to read, though, if you simply transpose the good guys and the bad guys.
8 I want to say at this point that I firmly believe that the New Mass is *valid*. I absolutely reject "the Great Sacrilege" thesis. I am not about to say that a Mass promulgated by a Pope and approved by the world's bishops is invalid. I quite see, though, why the shock has driven some Catholics into repudiating it. I think that the New Mass is weaker doctrinally than the old, shows a hesitancy and confusion utterly foreign to the nature of the Tridentine Mass, and is incomparably less beautiful and devotional. I think that its weaknesses have prevented it from taking hold, and I think it cannot stand.
9 Louis Bouyer, *The Decomposition of Catholicism* (London: Sands and Co., 1969).

Chapter 9

1 *National Catholic Reporter*, November 16, 1973.
2 If you have to look it up, it's Luke 18:10-14.
3 Kevin and Dorothy Ranaghan, *Catholic Pentecostalism*.
4 Charles Lam Markmann, *The Buckleys* (New York: William Morrow and Co., 1973).
5 A mass discovered by Flacius Illyricus, a historian and Reformer, and published in 1557. He mistakenly believed it to date from the end of

the sixth century and thus to be older than the "Romish Mass," but it was actually a much later Mass, full of all sorts of medieval liturgical abuses.

6   Jungmann says: "If Mass were only a service of instruction or a Communion celebration, the position [facing the people] would be more natural. But it is different if the Mass is an immolation and homage to God. If today the altar *versus populum* is frequently chosen, this is the result of other considerations that came into play . . . as a reaction to earlier conditions." In the primitive Church, Mass was said versus populum: "only when there was some special reason for it, as, for example, if the altar was linked to a martyr's grave . . . the side facing it had to be open to give them access to the grave."

7   Archbishop Hayes of Halifax severely scolded the group who wanted a Latin Mass. He himself meets every week with a pentecostalist prayer group, and presumably has moved with them beyond Latin.

Chapter 11

1   Lines he wrote for Goldsmith's *The Traveller*.
2   Newman. *Note A* to *The Apologia, op. cit.*
3   Reissued in a revised edition in 1971 by the bishops of England and Wales and available from the Catholic Truth Society, 201 Victoria Street, London, SW1, England.
4   Toronto *Star*, June 21, 1974. "Catholic says his church trails in social concern."
5   *Ibid.*
6   *Ibid.*
7   "Marxism point to the sins of society, priest says". Toronto *Globe and Mail*, Feb. 3, 1973. The *Globe*, originally founded to combat Catholicism in Ontario, nobly carries on. Actually, it and the huge Toronto *Star* seem to feel that a week's news is not rounded without a piece on Baum and a shot of his mild mug.
8   *Star* interview, *op. cit.*
9   For a superb explication of Teilhard de Chardin's "theology fiction," and the Council's rejection of it, see Jacques Maritain, *The Peasant of the Garonne*.
10 Cf. the *Canadian Catechism: Come to the Father*, compulsory since 1966 in every Catholic grade school in Canada. The charming picture story of the Creation has lots of butterflies and giraffes, but something is missing. No Adam, no Eve, no Eden, no apple, no serpent, no banishment. Hence, in the later books, no need to talk about the Sacrifice of the Atonement, no Catholic teaching on the Mass. No Catholicism.
11 As reported in *Christian Order*, July, 1974. "Dr. Baum Comes to Town."

APPENDIX A

THE 'CREDO' OF THE PEOPLE OF GOD

proclaimed by His Holiness Pope Paul VI

With this solemn liturgy we end the celebration of the nineteenth centenary of the martyrdom of the holy apostles Peter and Paul, and thus close the Year of Faith. We dedicated it to the commemoration of the holy apostles in order that we might give witness to our steadfast will to be faithful to the deposit of the faith[1] which they transmitted to us, and that we might strengthen our desire to live by it in the historical circumstances in which the Church finds herself in her pilgrimage in the midst of the world.

We feel it our duty to give public thanks to all who responded to our invitation by bestowing on the Year of Faith a splendid completeness through the deepening of their personal adhesion to the word of God, through the renewal in various communities of the profession of faith, and through the testimony of a Christian life. To our brothers in the episcopate especially, and to all the faithful of the holy Catholic Church, we express our appreciation and we grant our blessing.

A Mandate

Likewise, we deem that we must fulfill the mandate entrusted by Christ to Peter, whose successor we are, the last in merit; namely, to confirm our brothers in the faith.[2] With the awareness, certainly, of our human weakness, yet with all the strength impressed on our spirit by such a command, we shall accordingly make a profession of faith, pronounce a creed which, without being strictly speaking a dogmatic definition, repeats in substance, with some developments called for by the spiritual condition of our time, the creed of Nicea, the creed of the immortal tradition of the holy Church of God.

In making this profession, we are aware of the disquiet which agitates certain modern quarters with regard to the faith. They do not escape the influence of a world being profoundly changed, in which so many certainties are being disputed or discussed. We see even Catholics allowing themselves to be seized by a kind of passion for change and novelty. The Church, most assuredly, has always the duty to carry on the effort to study more deeply and to present, in a manner ever better adapted to successive generations, the unfathomable mysteries of God, rich for all in fruits of salvation. But at the same time the greatest care must be taken, while fulfilling the indispensable duty of research, to do no injury to the teachings of Christian doctrine. For that would be to give rise, as is unfortunately seen in these days to disturbance and perplexity in many faithful souls.

Await Word

It is important in this respect to recall that, beyond scientifically verified phenomena, the intellect which God has given us reaches *that which is*, and not merely the subjective expression of the structures and development of consciousness; and, on the other hand, that the task of interpretation—of hermeneutics—is to try to understand and extricate, while respecting the word expressed, the sense conveyed by a text, and not to recreate in some fashion, this sense in accordance with arbitrary hypotheses.

But above all, we place our unshakable confidence in the Holy Spirit, the soul of the Church, and in theological faith upon which rests the life of the Mystical Body. We know that souls await the word of the Vicar of Christ, and we respond to that expectation with the instructions which we regularly give. But today we are given an opportunity to make a more solemn utterance.

On this day which is chosen to close the Year of Faith, on this feast of the blessed apostles Peter and Paul, we have wished to offer to the living God the homage of a profession of faith. And as once at Caesarea Philippi the apostle Peter spoke on behalf of the twelve to make a true confession, beyond human opinions, of Christ as Son of the living God, so today his humble successor, pastor of the Universal Church, raises his voice to give, on behalf of all the People of God, a firm witness to the divine Truth entrusted to the Church to be announced to all nations.

We have wished our profession of faith to be to a high degree complete and explicit, in order that it may respond in a fitting way to the need of light felt by so many faithful souls, and by all those in the world, to whatever spiritual family they belong, who are in search of the Truth.

To the glory of God most holy and of our Lord Jesus Christ, trusting in the aid of the Blessed Virgin Mary and of the holy apostles Peter and Paul, for the profit and edification of the Church, in the name of all the pastors and all the faithful, we now pronounce this profession of faith, in full spiritual communion with you all, beloved brothers and sons.

PROFESSION OF FAITH

We believe in one only God, Father, Son and Holy Spirit, creator of things visible such as this world in which our transient life passes, of things invisible such as the pure spirits which are also called angels,' and creator in each man of his spiritual and immortal soul.

We believe that this only God is absolutely one in His infinitely holy essence as also in all His perfections, in His omnipotence, His infinite knowledge, His providence, His will and His love. He is *He who is*, as He revealed to Moses;[1] and He is *love*, as the apostle John teaches us;[5] so that these two names, being and love, express ineffably the same divine reality of Him who has wished to make Himself known to us, and who, "dwelling in light inaccessible,"[6] is in Himself above every name, above every thing and above every created intellect. God alone can give us right and full knowledge of this reality by revealing Himself as Father, Son and Holy Spirit, in whose eternal life we are by grace called to share, here below in the obscurity of faith and after death in eternal light. The mutual bonds which eternally constitute the Three Persons, who are each one and the same divine being, are the blessed inmost life of God thrice holy, infinitely beyond all that we can conceive in human measure.[7] We give thanks, however, to the divine goodness that very many believers can testify with us before men to the unity of God, even though they know not the mystery of the most holy Trinity.

The Father

We believe then in the Father who eternally begets the Son; in the Son, the Word of God, who is eternally begotten; in the Holy Spirit, the uncreated Person who proceeds from the Father and the Son as their eternal love. Thus in the Three Divine Persons, *coaeternae sibi et coaequales*,[8] the life and beatitude of God perfectly one superabound and are consummated in the supreme excellence and glory proper to uncreated being, and always "there should be venerated unity in the Trinity and Trinity in the unity."[9]

The Son

We believe in our Lord Jesus Christ, who is the Son of God. He is the Eternal Word, born of the Father before time began, and one in substance with the Father, homoousios to Patri,[10] and through Him all things were made. He was incarnate of the Virgin Mary by the power of the Holy Spirit, and was made man: equal therefore to the Father according to His divinity, and inferior to the Father according to His humanity;[11] and Himself one, not by some impossible confusion of His natures, but by the unity of His person.[12]

He dwelt among us, full of grace and truth. He proclaimed and established the Kingdom of God and made us know in Himself the Father. He gave us His new commandment to love one another as He loved us. He taught us the way of the beatitudes of the Gospel: poverty in spirit, meekness, suffering borne with patience, thirst after justice, mercy, purity of heart, will for peace, persecution suffered for justice sake. Under Pontius Pilate He suffered—the Lamb of God bearing on Himself the sins of the world, and He died for us on the cross, saving us by His redeeming blood. He was buried, and, of His own power, rose on the third day, raising us by His resurrection to that sharing in the divine life which is the life of grace. He ascended to heaven, and He will come again, this time in glory, to judge the living and the dead: each according to his merits—those who have responded to the love and piety of God going to eternal life, those who have refused them to the end going to the fire that is not extinguished.

And His Kingdom will have no end.

The Holy Spirit

We believe in the Holy Spirit, who is Lord, and Giver of life, who is adored and glorified together with the Father and the Son. He spoke to us by the prophets. He was sent by Christ after His resurrection and His ascension to the Father; He illuminates, vivifies, protects and guides the Church; He purifies the Church's members if they do not shun His grace. His action, which penetrates to the inmost of the soul, enables man to respond to the call of Jesus: Be perfect as your Heavenly Father is perfect (Mt. 5:48).

We believe that Mary is the Mother, who remained ever a Virgin, of the Incarnate Word, our God and savior Jesus Christ,[13] and that by reason of this singular election, she was, in consideration of the merits of her Son, redeemed in a more eminent manner,[14] preserved from all stain of original sin[15] and filled with the gift of grace more than all other creatures.[16]

Joined by a close and indissoluble bond to the Mysteries of the incarnation and Redemption,[17] the Blessed Virgin, the Immaculate, was at the end of her earthly life raised body and soul to heavenly glory[18] and likened to her risen Son in anticipation of the future lot of all the just; and we believe that the Blessed Mother of God, the New Eve, Mother of the Church,[19] continues in heaven her maternal role with regard to Christ's members, co-operating with the birth and growth of divine life in the souls of the redeemed.[20]

Original Offense

We believe that in Adam all have sinned, which means that the original offense committed by him caused human nature, common to all men, to fall to a state in which it bears the consequences of that offense, and which is not the state in which it was at first in our first parents—established as they were in holiness and justice, and in which man knew neither evil nor death. It is human nature so fallen, stripped of the grace that clothed it, injured in its own natural powers and subjected to the dominion of death, that is transmitted to all men, and it is in this sense that every man is born in sin. We therefore hold, with the Council of Trent, that original sin, is transmitted with human nature, "not by imitation, but by propagation" and that it is thus "proper to everyone."[21]

Reborn of the Holy Spirit

We believe that our Lord Jesus Christ, by the sacrifice of the cross redeemed us from original sin and all the personal sins committed by each one of us, so that, in accordance with the word of the apostle, "where sin abounded, grace did more abound."[22]

We believe in one Baptism instituted by our Lord Jesus Christ for the remission of sins. Baptism should be administered even to little children who have not yet been able to be guilty of any personal sin, in order that, though born deprived of supernatural grace, they may be reborn "of water and the Holy Spirit" to the divine life in Christ Jesus.[23]

Baptism

We believe in one, holy, catholic, and apostolic Church, built by Jesus Christ on that rock which is Peter. She is the Mystical Body of Christ; at the same time a visible society instituted with hierarchical organs, and a spiritual community; the Church on earth, the pilgrim People of God here below, and the Church filled with heavenly blessings; the germ and the first fruits of the Kingdom of God, through which the work and the sufferings of Redemption are continued throughout human history, and which looks for its perfect accomplishment beyond time in glory.[24] In the course of time, the Lord Jesus forms His Church by means of the sacraments emanating from His plenitude.[25] By these she makes her members participants in the Mystery of the Death and Resurrection of Christ, in the grace of the Holy Spirit who gives her life and movement[26] She is therefore holy, though she has sinners in her bosom, because she herself has no other life but that of grace: it is by living by her life that her members are sanctified; it is by removing themselves from her life that they fall into sins and disorders that prevent the radiation of her sanctity. This is why she suffers and does penance for these offences, of which she has the power to heal her children through the blood of Christ and the gift of the Holy Spirit.

The Word

Heiress of the divine promises and daughter of Abraham according to the Spirit, through that Israel whose scriptures she lovingly guards, and whose patriarchs and prophets she venerates; founded upon the apostles and handing on from century to century their ever-living word and their powers as pastors in the successor of Peter and the bishops in communion with him; perpetually assisted by the Holy Spirit, she has the charge of guarding, teaching, explaining and spreading the Truth which God revealed in a then veiled manner by the prophets, and fully by the Lord Jesus. We believe all that is contained in the word of God written or handed down, and that the Church proposes for belief as divinely revealed, whether by a solemn judgment or by the ordinary and universal magisterium.[27] We believe in the infallibility enjoyed by the successor of Peter when he teaches ex cathedra as pastor and teacher of all the faithful,[28] and which is assured also to the episcopal body when it exercises with him the supreme magisterium.[29]

We believe that the Church founded by Jesus Christ and for which He prayed is indefectibly one in faith, worship and the bond of hierarchical communion. In the bosom of this Church, the rich variety of liturgical rites and the legitimate diversity of theological and spirtual heritages and special disciplines, far from injuring her unity, makes it more manifest.[30]

One Shepherd

Recognizing also the existence, outside the organism of the Church of Christ, of numerous elements of truth and sanctification which belong to her as her own and tend to Catholic unity,[31] and believing in the action of the Holy Spirit who stirs up in the heart of the disciples of Christ love of this unity,[32] we entertain the hope that the Christians who are not yet in the full communion of the one only Church will one day be reunited in one flock with one only shepherd.

We believe that the Church is necessary for salvation, because Christ, who is the sole mediator and way of salvation, renders Himself present for us in His body which is the Church.[33] But the divine design of salvation embraces all men; and those who without fault on their part do not know the Gospel of Christ and His Church, but seek God sincerely, and under the influence of grace endeavor to do His will as recognized through the promptings of their conscience, they, in a number known only to God, can obtain salvation.[34]

Sacrifice of Calvary

We believe that the Mass, celebrated by the priest representing the person of Christ by virtue of the power received through the Sacrament of Orders, and offered by him in the name of Christ and the members of His Mystical Body, is the sacrifice of Calvary rendered sacramentally present on our altars. We believe that as the bread and wine consecrated by the Lord at the Last Supper were changed into His body and His blood which were to be offered for us on the cross, likewise the bread and wine consecrated by the priest are changed into the body and blood of Christ enthroned gloriously in heaven, and we believe that the mysterious presence of the Lord, under what continues to appear to our senses as before, is a true, real and substantial presence.[35]

Transubstantiation

Christ cannot be thus present in this sacrament except by the change into His body of the reality itself of the bread and the change into His blood of the reality itself of the wine, leaving unchanged only the properties of the bread and wine which our senses perceive. This mysterious change is very appropriately called by the Church *transubstantiation*. Every theological explanation which seeks some understanding of this mystery must, in order to be in accord with Catholic faith, maintain that in the reality itself, independently of our mind, the bread and wine have ceased to exist after the Consecration, so that it is the adorable body and blood of the Lord Jesus that from then on are really before us under the sacramental species of bread and wine,[36] as the Lord willed it, in order to give Himself to us as food and to associate us with the unity of His Mystical Body.[37]

The unique and indivisible existence of the Lord glorious in heaven is not multiplied, but is rendered present by the sacrament in the many places on earth where Mass is celebrated. And this existence remains present, after the sacrifice, in the Blessed Sacrament which is, in the tabernacle, the living heart of each of our churches. And it is our very sweet duty to honor and adore in the blessed Host which our eyes see, the Incarnate Word whom they cannot see, and who, without leaving heaven, is made present before us.

Temporal Concern

We confess that the Kingdom of God begun here below in the Church of Christ is not of this world whose form is passing, and that its proper growth cannot be confounded with the progress of civilization, of science or of human technology, but that it consists in an ever more profound knowledge of the unfathomable riches of Christ, an ever stronger hope in eternal blessings, an ever more ardent response to the love of God, and an ever more generous bestowal of grace and holiness among men. But it is this same love which induces the Church to concern herself constantly about the true temporal welfare of men. Without ceasing to recall to her children that they have not here a lasting dwelling, she also urges them to contribute, each according to his vocation and his means, to the welfare of their earthly city, to promote justice, peace and brotherhood among men, to give their aid freely to their brothers, especially to the poorest and most unfortunate. The deep solicitude of the Church, the Spouse of Christ, for the needs of men, for their joys and hopes, their griefs and efforts, is therefore nothing other than her great desire to be present to them, in order to illuminate them with the light of Christ and to gather them all in Him, their only Savior. This solicitude can never mean that the Church conform herself to the things of this world, or that she lessen the ardor of her expectation of her Lord and of the eternal Kingdom.

We believe in the life eternal. We believe that the souls of all those who die in the grace of Christ—whether they must still be purified in purgatory, or whether from the moment they leave their bodies Jesus takes them to paradise as He did for the Good Thief—are the People of God in the eternity beyond death, which will be finally conquered on the day of the Resurrection when these souls will be reunited with their bodies.

Prospect of Resurrection

We believe that the multitude of those gathered around Jesus and Mary in paradise forms the Church of Heaven, where in eternal beatitude they see

God as He is,[15] and where they also, in different degrees, are associated with the holy angels in the divine rule exercised by Christ in glory, interceding for us and helping our weakness by their brotherly care.[19]

We believe in the communion of all the faithful of Christ, those who are pilgrims on earth, the dead who are attaining their purification, and the blessed in heaven, all together forming one Church; and we believe that in this communion the merciful love of God and His saints is ever listening to our prayers, as Jesus told us: Ask and you will receive.[10] Thus it is with faith and in hope that we look forward to the resurrection of the dead, and the life of the world to come.

Blessed be God Thrice Holy. Amen.

1. Cf. 1Tim. 6:20.
2. Cf. Lk. 22:32.
3. Cf. Dz-Sch. 3002.
4. Cf. Ex. 3:14.
5. Cf. 1 Jn. 4:8.
6. Cf. 1 Tim. 6:16.
7. Cf. Dz.-Sch. 804.
8. Cf. Dz-Sch. 75.
9. Cf. *Ibid.*
10. Cf. Dz.-Sch. 150.
11. Cf. Dz.-Sch. 76.
12. Cf. *Ibid.*
13. Cf. Dz.-Sch. 251-252.
14. Cf. Lumen Gentium, 53.
15. Cf. Dz.-Sch. 2803.
16. Cf. Lumen Gentium, 53.
17. Cf. Lumen Gentium, 53, 58, 61.
18. Cf. Dz-Sch. 3903.
19. Cf. Lumen Gentium, 53, 56, 61, 63; Cf. Paul VI, Alloc, for the Closing of the Third Session of the Second Vatican Council: AAS LVI (1964) 1016; Cf. Exhort. Apost. Signum Magnum, Introd.
20. Cf. Lumen Gentium, 62; cf. Paul VI, Exhort. Apost. Signum Magnum, p. 1, n. 1.
21. Cf. Dz-Sch. 1513.
22. Cf. Rom 5:20.
23. Cf. Dz-Sch. 1514.
24. Cf. Lumen Gentium, 8, 5.
25. Cf. Lumen Gentium, 7, 11.
26. Cf. Sacrosanctum Concilium, 5, 6; cf. Lumen Gentium, 7, 12, 50.
27. Cf. Dz-Sch. 3011.
28. Cf. Dz-Sch. 3074.
29. Cf. Lumen Gentium, 25.
30. Cf. Lumen Gentium, 23; cf. Orientalium Ecclesiarum 2,3, 5,6.
31. Cf. Lumen Gentium, 8.
32. Cf. Lumen Gentium, 15.

33. Cf. Lumen Gentium, 14.
34. Cf. Lumen Gentium, 16.
35. Cf. Dz-Sch. 1651.
36. Cf. Dz-Sch. 1642, 1651-1654; Paul VI, Enc. Mysterium Fidei.
37. Cf. S. Th., III, 73, 3.
38. Cf. I Jn. 3:2; Dz-Sch. 1000.
39. Cf. Lumen Gentium, 49.
40. Cf. Lk. 10:9-10; Jn. 16-24.

APPENDIX B

EXCERPT FROM *CHRISTIAN ORDER*

This material is quoted from *Christian Order, February 1974*, from the article "The Old Mass" by Father Paul Crane, S.J.

> The faked translation concerns the opening sentence of the conclusion to Pope Paul's Apostolic Constitution, Missale Romanum, which introduced the New Mass. The Latin original runs as follows:
>
>> "Ad extremum, ex iis quae hactenus do novo Missali Romano exposuimus, quiddam nunc congere et efficere placet."
>
> The official English (ICEL) translation of this sentence reads:
>
>> "In conclusion we wish to give *the strict force of law* to all that we have set forth concerning the new Roman Missal."
>
> The official French translation is the same:
>
>> "Our terminer Nous voulons donner *force de loi*. . . ."
>
> And also the Italian:
>
>> "Infine, vogliano dare forza di legge. . . ."

Crane gives the Catholic Truth Society's official translation of the sentence from the Apostolic Constitution:

> "In conclusion, we wish to lay stress on one particular thought arising from the various things we have been explaining about the New Roman Missal."

Crane adds:

> The translators appear to have added a sentence paragraph, not in the Latin of the Apostolic Constitution and immediately preceding its last

paragraph in translation. This sentence-paragraph in all three translations, but not in the original Latin, orders the regulations to the Apostolic Constitution to come into effect on November 30th of that year the First Sunday of Advent, 1969. Here is the English of the interpolation:

> "We command that the regulations of this Constitution shall come into force on November this year, the First Sunday of Advent.

In the Catholic Truth Society's translation, there is no mention of the date when the new Ordo was to come into compulsory use.

DATE DUE